D0991546

335.437
P942c

Capitalism, Consumption and Needs

Edmond Preteceille and Jean-Pierre Terrail

Translated by Sarah Matthews

Basil Blackwell

TABOR COLLEGE LIBRARY

HILLSBORO, KANSAS 67063

890966

English translation © Basil Blackwell Publisher Limited 1985

Chapters one to three first published in French as
Besoins et mode de production:
Du capitalisme en crise au socialisme
© 1977, Editions sociales, Paris

Fourth chapter © Edmond Preteceille 1985

English translation first published 1985

Basil Blackwell Publisher Ltd
108 Cowley Road, Oxford OX4 1JF, UK

Basil Blackwell Inc.
432 Park Avenue South, Suite 1505,
New York, NY 10016, USA

All rights reserved. Except for the quotation of short passages for the purposes of criticism and review, no part of this publication may be reproduced, stored in a retrieval system, or transmitted, in any form or by any means, electronic, mechanical, photocopying, recording or otherwise, without the prior permission of the publisher.

Except in the United States of America, this book is sold subject to the condition that it shall not, by way of trade or otherwise, be lent, re-sold, hired out, or otherwise circulated without the publisher's prior consent in any form of binding or cover other than that in which it is published and without a similar condition including this condition being imposed on the subsequent purchaser.

British Library Cataloguing in Publication Data

Preteceille, Edmond
    Capitalism, consumption and needs.
    1. Capitalism
    I. Title   II. Terrail, Jean-Pierre
    III. Besoins et mode de production. *English*
    330.12'2   HB501
    ISBN 0-631-12461-6

Library of Congress Cataloging in Publication Data

Preteceille, Edmond.
    Capitalism, consumption, and needs.

    Rev. translation of: Besoins et mode de production
    by M. Décaillot, E. Preteceille, J.-P. Terrail.
    Includes index.
    1. Consumption (Economics) 2. Marxian
    economics. I. Terrail, Jean-Pierre. II. Décaillot,
    Maurice. Besoins et mode de production. III. Title.
    HB801.P742 1984   335.43'7   84-12481
    ISBN 0-631-12461-6

Typeset by Freeman Graphic, Tonbridge, Kent
Printed in Great Britain by The Pitman Press Ltd, Bath

Contents

Introduction

The question of needs is at the heart of social conflict. It is a current issue — is one for or against austerity? — and is central to the debate over the present crisis, its nature and its outcome. Is the crisis our fate, the inevitable price of progress, a result of the exhaustion of resources, to be met with sacrifices and restrictions? Or is it the effect of capitalist relations of production, the result of the unfettered accumulation of profit, and does it therefore call for a new mode of production that links control of their work by the workers to the increased satisfaction of the needs they have developed?

Is the question of needs a valid or a false theoretical problem? Is it a decisive and complex concept in the articulation of economic, political and ideological questions, or is it the old idealist *ignis fatuus*, the unhealthy vestiges of humanism which still linger on in Marxism? Or is it the normalisation, channelling and suppression of desires by technocracy?

Essential social needs remain unsatisfied today. Yet it is not long since we were told that the question was out of date. Perhaps in the nineteenth century Marx might have had a point, but growth, opening the way to abundance, had swept all that aside. During the fifties and sixties efficiency of the 'production machine' of the major capitalist countries, the new methods of forecasting and regulation available to the state and the development of the welfare state all seemed to prove that this was true. Social democracy, following its own line of loyalty to capitalism, sought only to improve state intervention so as to ensure a more just distribution of the benefits of growth. In this context, apologias for and critiques of the consumer society grew up side by side. And then came the crisis, shaking the whole edifice.

By emphasising in the harshest way that capitalist countries are no more sheltered now from economic disruption, unemployment and mass poverty than before, the present crisis calls for profound ideological readjustments. When it is a question of making the people concerned accept a standstill in production, mass lay-offs, the decline of entire regions and a reduction in buying-power, the argument that the system's capacity to satisfy social needs is indefinite appears to have been overtaken by events. When it is a question of redirecting mass consumption by putting pressures on its cost, so as to make the entire state machine available to help prop up the international structuring of capital, then what is urgently needed is the agonising reappraisal of the dominant ideology of the preceding decade.

The first U-turn came at the beginning of the seventies, with the wave of more or less concerted 'environmentalist' policies, in response to the first, though muffled, effects of the crisis. One can see here in outline the devaluation of the idea of progress and the opposition of the 'quality of life' to the old pair, growth and needs. Then, as the crisis worsened, the workers' persistent difficulty in understanding just how growing insecurity of employment, combined with austerity, was going to enhance the quality of life led to a change in emphasis, and the accent was placed on defensive solidarity. Faced with the energy crisis, an increase in international competition, the ambitions of the Third World and the growth in unemployment, it was a question of maintaining the profits on which jobs depended, cutting down on social costs and wages, rationalising and restructuring businesses, and giving priority to exports. As for consumption and needs, not a word was said.

The considerable scope of the means mobilised to diffuse the ideologies of crisis, together with the active participation of social democracy in the policy of austerity, helped to undermine popular struggles. But the workers' resistance to a decline in their living standards, though varying from country to country, never ceased. On the contrary, new demands appeared for improving conditions of work, the emancipation of women, national independence, the quality of the environment and of consumption, and so on. The reality of entirely unsatisfied desires cut through denials and repression; where needs are concerned, it is not so easy to turn the page.

What then is the relationship between social struggles and the global economic situation? Are they to be seen as rearguard actions, putting a brake on essential structural changes and so holding back the true solutions? This is the dominant view. Or are they demands which should be met to a reasonable degree so as to set consumption going again and get out of the crisis of overproduction? That is the answer, more Keynesian than Marxist, of a reformist left which recognises the persistence of struggles and the failure of policies of austerity, and aims to reconcile increased public intervention to sustain investment in production along its present lines with the compensations of a more extensive social policy. But is this reconciliation possible if one continues to regard the capitalist logic of investment and utilisation of labour as essential, and market relations as the dominant form of circulation?

And what if these unsatisfied needs, far from being only a regrettable consequence or a sign of failure, were themselves one of the elements which constitute the crisis? The question may appear surprising because it runs counter to present-day common sense, but it is nonetheless worth looking at. It implies a theoretical analysis, over and above the contingencies of the moment, of the very concept of needs. The identification of needs as a psychological or cultural phenomenon, whose expression is confined to the market for consumer goods and whose satisfaction can be correlated with the quantity of goods acquired, produces a particular kind of response, which legitimises austerity. This separation between production and needs, between the 'economic' and the 'social', is the assumption that must be questioned first of all.

Marx opposed this conception of a dichotomy, and laid down the framework for an analysis of needs as the articulation between production and reproduction. But it is true that this theory is not elaborated to the same degree as the rest of his work, especially the analysis of the movement of capital. Nor should it be expected to be able to provide an account of the present state of the consumption process.

The development of capitalist societies has done more than confirm the socio-historical nature of needs. It has also highlighted the contradictions and structural limitations inherent in a purely capitalist mode of satisfying needs. The increasing control by the state in developed capitalist countries over a significant extent of the provision for those needs, in areas such as health and education, and, by that token, the state's considerable influence on the definition of needs, is evidence of a qualitative change in the relationship of our societies to the needs of their members. Cannot this recognition – however partial, fluctuating and fraught – be seen as the manifestation of a profound demand for the satisfaction and expansion of needs, a demand rooted as much in the movement of production as of consumption? Perhaps the crisis can also be seen as the incapacity of one mode of production, of one particular social system, to respond to that demand . . .

The liberal approach to these problems remains strictly formalistic, but Marxist writings may also be accused of a certain delay in dealing with the issue. The classic debates on pauperisation in the workers' movement have not always contributed to an advance in concrete knowledge, any more than the more or less Marxist theses of the embourgeoisement of the working classes through excessive market consumption, or its normalisation through the state machinery for collective consumption.

A proper insistence on the determining character of the social relations of production has overshadowed not only the necessary analysis of the specific structure of modes of consumption, but also an analysis of the relations between the two spheres, which has been reduced to a single, mechanistic determination. Today, the crisis and the social movements that have developed within it emphasise these deficiencies, and demand a new theoretical effort to go beyond such over-simplifications. It is necessary to develop an analysis embracing all the practices of reproduction, an analysis that will go beyond a quantitative description of consumption and the schematic opposition between the market or the individual and the socialised or the collective. This analysis would bring out not only the deficiencies and inequalities but also the economic, ideological and political consequences of the modes through which capitalism and the state organise consumption, and it would emphasise popular struggles and methods of resistance and innovation. Such an analysis must be based on an examination of the needs which both reflect and shape this resistance; needs which are not just items in a catalogue to be established in the future, steps already built in the staircase of history, but the articulation of several social dynamics that require clarification: the employment of living labour, the social conditions of consumption, and political practices ranging from the methods used by the state to the most diverse social struggles.

This last point is another important aspect of the ideological implications of the concept of needs, for it occupies a strategic place in teleological conceptions of history. Even within the bounds of Marxism, which is not immune on this score, this view, in its humanist guise, can serve as the point of departure towards idealism, leading the social movement towards utopia or reform.

This is to say no more than that the problem is highly complex, and that all its aspects cannot be dealt with thoroughly here. This would not in any event be possible in a strictly theoretical work, for it would be necessary to draw not only on philosophy but also on history, political economy, sociology – in short, the whole range of concrete analyses of the social process. And political practice, too, has a contribution to make. The elements which we put forward here are a contribution to the debate in all its forms: there are theoretical propositions, research hypotheses, established results and political investigations.

The first chapter is devoted to an examination of the main lines of argument in some of the most significant non-Marxist works, to bring out both their contribution and their limitations as well as attempting to clarify the appropriate conditions for a materialist approach.

It is to an analysis of the specific dimensions of such an approach that the second chapter is addressed, with an investigation of the validity of the concept of needs in the field of historical materialism and an attempt to specify its content in the context of the general development of the contradictions of capital.

The contemporary development of needs, in the context of state monopoly capitalism and its crisis, is discussed more systematically in the third chapter. The analysis of the modes of consumption is the particular focus here, above all in relation to collective consumption and the effects of state intervention.

Finally, the fourth chapter stresses the relationship between the development of needs and political policies and social struggles. Approaching the analysis of the crisis from this point of view it attempts to highlight the content, conditions and possibilities for change in the needs which operate in this context, and the perspectives for social change which are opened up by the growing divergence of needs from the domination of capital.

1

Commodity fetishism and the ideal of needs

The development of state monopoly capitalism, and particularly its present crisis, has necessarily brought the question of social needs, their nature and their theoretical status, to the forefront of every ideological confrontation between classes. This trend is all the stronger because the increasing economic role of the state and the growing hold of large-scale capital on sectors such as distribution, urban development, leisure and so forth, have fostered the development of social conflict outside the work place, in the sphere of consumption.

The concept of need is inherent in the vulgar realism of bourgeois ideology, and was a central element in its confrontation first with feudal spirituality and later with materialist dialectics. From Locke to the theoreticians of the affluent society, it is always by reference to the obvious nature of needs, taken to be the very essence of human existence, that justifications of the individual's right to appropriate – and thus to alienate through sale – his own person and goods, are explained; indeed, the whole structure of economic liberalism is work out *from this premise*. The free expression of the needs of the free worker in the market-place, in the sphere of consumption – this bourgeois vision of the highest degree of freedom depends on a close link between needs and consumption.

In this sense, the appearance of consumption as a theme in the mainstream of debate does not date from the 'consumer society'. The very concept of consumption as a particular moment in social life came into being at almost the same time as political economy: as early as 1695 Boisguillebert attributed the impoverishment of France to a decline in consumption. The representation of consumption as a specific autonomous practice gained precision with the historical development of capitalism. In the late eighteenth century the precursors of the utilitarianism, notably Condillac, introduced the figure of the 'consumer', an abstract being endowed with 'needs', capable of assessing the utility of the goods offered him in the market. A century later, this theme was sytematised by the founders of the neo-classical school. Jevons (1871) worked out the principles of the behaviour of the rational consumer. In a liberal economy, the rational consumer exercises freedom of choice to maximise his 'utility' and, according to Walras's theory of general equilibrium, organises the economic system in line with the hierarchy of needs. Capitalism is thus presented as a perfectly democratic society, where economic activity is entirely governed by the 'sovereign consumer'.

The appearance and elaboration of the theme of consumption in bourgeois thinking reflects the birth and growth, under the development of capital, of a specific mode of consumption, *market* consumption. With the breakdown of feudalism, the process of primitive accumulation separated the producer from both the means of consumption and the means of production. By destroying the traditional unity between the worker and the instruments of his work, capital separated production and consumption: the production of the free worker, that is, of a market in labour-power, also entailed the creation of a market for means of production and a market for means of consumption. The resulting autonomy of the spheres of production and consumption altered their relations. In precapitalist societies, production is essentially the production of use-values: it is limited by the extent of existing consumption. The appearance of the value-form did not of itself radically alter this relationship; the small producer and vendor did produce *goods for sale,* but only for a local market with whose capacity he was thoroughly familiar. Moreover, the aim of his activity remained the obtaining of use-values so that he could reproduce that activity again on the same scale. But the irruption of the logic of capital freed production from the predetermined limits of consumption. The process of capitalist production, in which the production of value is an end in itself, shatters the unity of production and consumption. This rupture, which is at once spatial, temporal and logical, makes the value-form possible, but not inevitable: the value-form develops with the consolidation of capital, the expansion of markets, and the mass production of goods.

Bourgeois theories of consumption present a very one-sided view of these processes. In such theories, the rupture between production and consumption is seen as the radical externalisation of these moments in social practice. The logic of consumption appears as the primary, determining, autonomous moment, while productive labour is reduced to a simple instrument for provisioning the market, owing its autonomy to its necessary skill. This sort of conception of the relation between production and consumption, in which the radical difference between production for value and production for use-value has been entirely obliterated, makes it possible, since liberal society does not recognise the producers' labour except in relation to the consumers' satisfaction, to subordinate the demands of the first to the interests of the second. The fallacious confrontation of 'producer' and 'consumer' is reinforced in the dominant theme in liberal thought, which compresses the expression of needs to the sphere of consumption: could workers refuse to pay the price of satisfying needs which they would feel (only) as consumers?

The implicit identification of all consumption with market consumption, the reductionist view of social needs that assumes they are no more than the relation of the individual to a series of consumer choices, the instrumental conception of a process of production which does not give rise to any form of antagonism between classes: all these are so many reefs on which the reformist defences of capitalism have come to grief. From the beginning of this century, when the economist Charles Gide proposed setting up a consumer morality in response to the workers' demands for emancipation, to the philosopher Herbert Marcuse's denying the absolution of revolution to the working class under developed capitalism on the grounds of its excessive consumption, needs have never been seen in relation to the sphere of production, and the mode of consumption has always been regarded as the touchstone of social conflicts. The importance of a real change of ground in the scientific approach to the question of needs is demonstrated by the work of the sociologist Jean Baudrillard.[1] While claiming to denounce the bourgeois conception in the most radical way, Baudrillard takes this conception to its logical limits and ends by concluding that 'needs' are immanent in capitalist society. But this is no more than the final outcome of the twofold naturalist reduction of all consumption to market consumption, and of social needs to the sphere of consumption.

It is true that the idealist conception of needs has only been able to persist by undergoing a transformation. The development of objective social knowledge since the end of the nineteenth century has made it progressively more difficult to treat the individual as no more than the repository of needs that can be explained in terms of human nature, or to account for the arbitrary play of desires in anything other than historical terms. Twentieth-century academic sociology, whether functionalist or structuralist, has taken up the critique of this subjectivist/essentialist arrangement, substituting culture for nature and the social group for the

---

[1] J. Baudrillard, *Le système des objets* (Paris, Gallimard; 1968); *La société de consommation* (SGPP, 1970); *Pour une critique de l'économie politique du signe* (Gallimard, 1972); *Le miroir de la production* (Castermann, 1973); and in translation, *For a Critique of the Political Economy of the Sign* (Telos, 1983); *Mirror of Production* (Telos, 1983).

individual. Nonetheless, the fact that the very concept of 'need' should today be called into question by currents of thought outside Marxism – either implicitly, as in sociological inquiries into cultural practices which deny themselves the very use of the term (for instance, the works of Pierre Bourdieu) or explicitly, by theoreticians who reduce the idea of social needs to an ideological outcome of market relations – bears witness to the present crisis in the dominant ideology.

This development calls for an explanation of the status of needs within scientific materialism and suggests the limitation of the idealist approach, thus calling into question its own capacity to represent or produce anything other than a symptom of those limits.

Marx's analysis distinguished the scientific characteristics of the capitalist mode of production by examining the *value-form,* revealing the essential contradiction of private production, and exposing the historical limits of capitalism.

He wrote of our society that 'the commodity form has become the generalised form of the product of labour'[2] and is so familiar as to appear to be 'an over-riding' law of nature'.[3] Yet this 'commodity fetishism', which at first sight seems a careless mistake, is fraught with consequences. The commodity form does not arise spontaneously: it is only under historically determined social conditions that the products of labour and labour-power are exchanged as commodities. To take this for granted, to treat the commodity as a *natural* form, and not as a social form of the things produced, makes it impossible to see behind the relation of commodity and object the relations between men and private production, or to recognise behind capital as object, a social relation of exploitation.

Commodity and capital fetishism, which see in the spheres of production and circulation only natural relations between things, necessarily bring about a distortion, since they block out of the *social* relation of production. They conceive of the social and the economic as belonging to different spheres, opposed to one another as culture is opposed to nature, or necessity to chance; or, to use the terms employed by Weber, to whom this distinction owes its most celebrated formulation, as opposed as the 'purposive rational action' of the economic agents that combine the factors of production with maximum efficiency in order to obtain a specific result at least cost, and the 'affective', 'traditional' or 'value-rational' actions of the agents that, insofar as they are subject to needs, act in a manner that is always tainted with irrationality on account of their unconditional attachment to values that are independent of the means at their disposal.

[2] Karl Marx, *Capital* (Lawrence & Wishart, 1954), Vol. I, Part I, Chapter I, Section 3.
[3] Ibid., Section 4, p. 75.

The characterisation of the economic as the sphere of instrumental rationality necessarily excludes needs, which this interpretation locates in the first stages of a rational activity that aims at their specific satisfaction. To the materialist approach, which does not start from man and his needs, 'but from production at a definite stage of social development',[4] there is thus opposed an *idealism of needs,* the logical complement to commodity fetishism and capital.

In this chapter we will attempt to demonstrate the main lines of argument that consistently emerge from an examination of non-Marxist literature, whether economic or sociological. We hope to show that there are several ways of repressing the question of the relationship between needs and production, and of separating the relations between production and the practice of consumption.

At the first level, which could be termed the substantialism of needs, the satisfaction of needs functions as a systematic explanatory principle. This problematic sees the social in terms of a model of ends and means (needs and the means by which they are satisfied), and develops an *instrumental* concept of economic and social activity. In the final analysis, it functions on two distinct levels: that of political economy and that of sociology. In discourses which are separate but complementary, complementary but separate, contemporary political economy and most sociology agree in recognising a common justification for their being discrete academic disciplines: the separation, indeed the opposition, of the economic and the social.

It may be argued that given these assumptions any treatment of the question of needs is bound to contain contradictions since it involves both bourgeois political economy (which sees itself as concerned with the rational *response* to needs).[5] The two disciplines are based on the assumption of the separate nature of their interests – in one case economic, in the other social – and they come together only to affirm their heterogeneity.

However, the psychologism of needs and the image of the consumer society are the common response of bourgeois economic theory and idealist sociology to the problem they have set themselves, and the structure and internal coherence of this response is our first line of inquiry here.

---

[4] Karl Marx, *Grundrisse,* trans. Martin Nicolaus (Allen Lane, 1973), Introduction, p. 85.

[5] Talcott Parsons, the American sociologist and disciple of Weber, was referring to the need to combine these two approaches when he described consumption, the site of the expression of needs as a 'frontier process', marking the area where the economic and the social came together. It was in an attempt to meet this need that Parsons formulated his 'general theory of action' to ensure the coexistence of sociology and economic theory. See Talcott Parsons and N.J. Smelser, *Economy and Society* (Routledge, 1956).

The literature of economics and sociology nonetheless includes various approaches which attempt, one way or another, to avoid the tautologies contained in theories of the consumer society. Thus, among classical economists, productive labour is not reduced to a relation purely expressive, in the sphere of instrumentality, of needs, but possesses a specific logic that produces its effects in the spheres of circulation and consumption (the determination of value through labour) and on society as a whole (the generation of social classes and their antagonism). From an entirely different point of view, trends in contemporary sociology seek to avoid the substantialism of needs by developing a differentialist approach to patterns of consumption (for example, Veblen and Goblot), an attempt which in its most developed forms (Bourdieu, for instance) seeks to eliminate any vestige of the psychology of motivations, and goes as far as to question the historicity of the form of need-as-object itself (Baudrillard). The limitations of these different attempts derive from the fact that the classical economists do not take the analysis of the logic of social relations of production to its conclusion, while the differentialist sociologists are content to postulate the fundamentally determining character of these relations without dealing with the concrete effects of their operation. Their thinking is thus of interest as much because of their actual contributions to the theory of needs (at least so far as the sociologists are concerned) as because of their difficulties: these give a negative illustration of the effectiveness of relations of production, which remain eternally absent. It is significant that the same 'oversights' produce identical effects in the classical economics of Ricardo and the modernist sociology of Baudrillard.

THE IMAGE OF THE CONSUMER SOCIETY

The instrumentalisation of economic and social life, which is the necessary corollary to a blocking out of the social relations of production, posits need as the original impetus behind human action, and thus lays the foundation for the image of the consumer society. In this sense, the image does not appear solely as the special theme of contemporary 'sociology' or 'social economics', but as the very structure of a particular approach to economic and social life, an approach as old as political economy and sociology themselves.

To refer exchange value to use-value, and circulation to consumption: this is the only way to reconcile the need to find an external basis for the closed system of equivalences defined by the first stage of vulgar economics (mercantilism) with the apologetic imperative which assumes that the 'intimate aspects' of bourgeois society have not been thoroughly exposed. However, attempts by the utilitarians and, subsequently, the neo-classicists to adopt this standpoint and base value in need or, more generally, to posit economic constants as 'dependent on the human consciousness' (Pigou, *Economics of Welfare*) meet the same insurmountable difficulty: the appreciation of the utility of a good cannot be reduced solely to the need/object relation, but must assume a confrontation between several goods and their market price. Thus marginalism – even in its most recent form of a theory of general equilibrium – cannot claim to constitute a true theory of value and price, but is at the most simply an empirical description of exchange. The 'theory' of utility-value is in this sense entirely superfluous . . . but one can easily understand its necessity: it underwrites the fiction, implicit in all neo-classical analysis, of the instrumentality of economic activity, and establishes the image of the consumer society – the market-place and production at the service of man (the 'sovereign consumer') and his needs.

Keynes, using the concept of 'effective demand' to focus interest on the relations between income and demand, marked the transition from speculative to empirical marginalism, and opened the way to the upsurge of empirical research into consumer behaviour which has been so important in contemporary bourgeois economics.

The assertion of the principle of use-value has become somewhat blurred, without the essence of the neo-classical problematic being in any way affected. For Keynes, consumption remains 'the only aim and the unique object of any economic theory'; if income should somehow manage to insinuate itself between need and commodity, it must in the final analysis be the individual consciousness, in the form of the propensity to consume, that regulates the relation between income and demand.

The conjuncture of the 1930s (overproduction and unemployment) revealed the abstraction of the neo-classical theory of the consumer as irrelevant. Keynes was confronted with a double imperative: to take a more concrete view of the disturbances in the functioning of the system, and specifically to account for the deficiency of demand, but without calling into question the logic of capitalist exploitation. Post-Keynesian authors (Friedmann, Duesenberry, Katona et al) have taken a further step in this direction and have attempted to clarify the psycho-sociological 'motivation' which leads consumers to translate their income into effective demand, particularly in terms of their social 'reference' groups. Any questioning of the relationship between these groups and production relations, and any doubt of the dogma of the sovereignty of the consumer is assiduously avoided: there is no possibility here of revising the postulate which defines economic activity as a means of satisfying needs that are engendered outside it.

The challenge by the neo-liberal John Kenneth Galbraith to the belief that during the era of monopolies the consumer could effectively remain king of the market economy, created something of a stir during the 1960s. This author, to whom we owe the concept of a consumer (or affluent) society, is the star economist of the American Democratic Party. His criticism of the neo-classical position remained purely empirical (the power of the large conglomerates today enables them to have a significant influence on demand: this is the 'reverse lead'), and never developed into a different theoretical conception of the relationship between relations of production and needs. Thus, while appearing to challenge it, Galbraith effectively reinforced the ideological impact of an instrumental conception of economics: putting the emphasis on the 'conditioning' of the consumer by the monopolies does not in any way contribute towards creating a theory of needs. The idea of the consumer society is not new: it was already implicit in the blocking out of production relations, that is, in all forms of discussion in vulgar economics, which restricts itself to system-atising the appearances of bourgeois society.

Political economy is happy to refer all questions of the aims of economic activity to sociology. How does sociology stand, then? Admittedly, it opposes to the subjectivist individualism of vulgar economics the image of the collective subject: sociological relativism cannot work without the socialisation of the subject. But it can manage just as well as economics without any mention of a theory of the subject and his needs. Thus the classical culturo-functionalist approach, making equal concessions to an instrumentalist interpretation of culture, offers only pseudo-answers to the problem of a truly sociological treatment of needs. The obvious impossibility of giving a purely physiological content to social needs, the 'goals' of culture,[6] leads to the celebrated distinction between primary and secondary (cultural or social) needs, a vast tautology analogous to the 'vicious circle' of prices and demand in vulgar economics. 'Need shapes cultural reaction but this reaction, in its turn, shapes the need,' wrote Linton. This is to abandon the problematic of ends and means by declaring that the means are contained in the ends. Anthropology and sociology, by refusing to take history into account, make it impossible for themselves to offer any solution to the problem: since 'primary' needs are initially the same everywhere, why is the 'cultural reaction' that shapes the 'secondary' needs, and alters the 'primary' needs, always different, and how has it evolved? They are thus reduced, so far as localising the ultimate aims of social activity is concerned, to oscillating between a more or less

---

[6] Culture here is 'the work of man, the *means* of attaining his goals', in the terms used by Malinowski (*A Scientific Theory of Culture*, Oxford University Press, 1960, p. 150). (This work is easy to criticise, but the theoretical 'naivete' of the author emphasises rather than distorts that quality.)

naïve physiologism (from Malinowski to Lévi-Strauss's 'objective structures of the psyche and the brain') and the tautologies of the 'maintenance of structural permanence' (Radcliffe-Brown and structuralism), taking in on the way the historicising constructs of the kind of sociological functionalism cobbled together by people like Merton.

The notion of *aspirations,* according to its promoters, aims to smooth over the problems of functionalism[7] by making it possible to consider the truly social content and the historical development of needs. Thus, for Chombart de Lauwe, 'in terms of needs which are linked to impulses deriving from the individual himself . . . aspiration must depend on historical and social conditions, since it is linked to desire and value.'[8] The accent here is on the connection between needs and general social development. Chombart de Lauwe does not put forward any theory of the form this connection might take, except to assert that it operates through the medium of aspirations; that is to say, it involves the effects of economic and social development on the individual consciousness. But nothing is said about the way that development shapes ideas, nor about the conditions under which aspirations appear as needs. To state a connection is not to set out a theory of determination: the reasoning remains purely formal, explaining everything, and thus explaining very little. The theory of 'aspirations' does not really go beyond the substantialist and subjectivist conception which sees need as the initial impulse behind social activity.

In the final analysis, one can distinguish, in both vulgar economics and functionalist sociology, two main constants of the psycho-sociology of needs. The first is that need is conceived of as a *lack,* a deficiency, a void, in terms of the origin of individual action and of social practice alike. This belief closely reinforces the way the notion works in terms of practical ideologies, where it makes it possible to explain any action (any social fact) by referring it back to the individual as an attribute.

One can find in Sartre a learned philosophical version of this model: by presenting itself 'as a definitive absence within the organism', need constitutes the initial impetus of history: for it 'institutes the first contradiction' which praxis will surpass and negate. Praxis is thus 'born of need': 'An organic function, need and praxis are strictly linked in a dialectical order.'[9]

The second belief is that the interplay of the individual and society (as external subjects interacting with each other) makes it possible to account for the social nature of needs, which are still conceived of as immanent in

---

[7] *Cf.* P.H. Chombart de Lauwe, *Pour une sociologie des aspirations* (Gonthier, 1969), p. 12.
[8] Ibid., p. 18.
[9] J.-P. Sartre, *A Critique of Dialectical Reason,* trans. A.S. Smith (New Left Books, 1976).

the body or psyche of the individual. A few pages of Durkheim's *Suicide* offer an excellent example of the form which a substantialism of needs can take in sociological discussion, as well as its possible ideologico-political reactionary applications.[10] Human needs, according to Durkheim, can be distinguished from animal instincts by their unlimited nature. This is not without inconveniences, for 'inextinguishable thirst is constantly renewed torture . . . satisfaction received only stimulates instead of filling need.' It is thus necessary that a limit should be placed on the needs of the individual, a limit which must be placed 'by some force exterior to him': men 'must receive it from an authority which they respect, to which they yield spontaneously. Society alone can play this moderating role.' The limits 'beyond which the passions must not go' are clearly specified for each social category, and every individual, as a function of his position in society, respects these limits, for 'at least if he respects regulations and is docile to collective authority, that is, if he has a wholesome moral constitution, he feels it is not well to ask more.'

Thus from any perspective, the image of the consumer society appears, in the final analysis, to be rent by division and by the opposition between needs and the means of satisfying them (whether because of economics, culture, praxis, society, or whatever).

It is this dichotomy between the economic and the social, between needs and the means of satisfying them, that makes it an inherent impossibility for the conceptual framework of the image of the consumer society to address the question of needs outside the sphere of consumption and the market-place, that is, in terms of production.

These dead-ends are so many invitations to abandon the problematic of ends and means, and approach the subject from another direction. There have been a variety of non-Marxist approaches, both economic and sociological; here we will briefly attempt to show the limitations imposed on any move to break away from the substantialism of needs if it ignores or only partially recognises the logic of the process of social production in terms of the forces and relations of production.

PRODUCTION AND CONSUMPTION

The various approaches may be identified by the way they treat the problem of the relations between production, consumption and needs, since the clarification of the mechanisms by which production can succeed in matching needs is the central question for any economic theory.

[10] Emile Durkheim, *Suicide: A Study in Sociology* (Routledge & Kegan Paul, 1966), pp. 247–50.

For neo-classical apologists, of course, the most pressing requirement is to show that in the kingdom of free enterprise these mechanisms are at their best, assuring to each the maximum satisfaction. The demonstration of the 'sovereignty of the consumer' and the way in which it operates was still fairly abstract in Walras (1873), since he had not taken into account the distribution of incomes, and hence the difference between need and effective demand. The reasons for this omission are clear enough. On the one hand, income enters into the relationship which marginalism asserts to be an immediate one, that between need and demand and, in consequence, price. On the other hand, to recognise that demand is relative to the distribution of income means admitting that it stands in some sort of relation to production, and thus calls into question the principle of the externality of production and consumption, or production and needs, ends and means.

Pareto began by posing the question of the simultaneous satisfaction of different consumers and thus of total social welfare. But his argument reveals the same limitation: the optimum, defined by the equalisation of marginal utilities to prices by two exchangers, is relative to a given structure of the income distribution. This was not to be taken into account in marginalist analyses until Pigou (1920): a significant half-century after the elaboration of Walras's theory of general equilibrium.

Introducing the structure of the income distribution does not of itself resolve the question of welfare, since this concept, of course, was bound to be introduced in the only way compatible with the logic of the neo-classical argument: by postulating the independence of this distribution to the structures of production. Hence all the difficulties encountered by theories of welfare economics from Pigou to the present day.

According to these theories, the conditions for establishing the economic optimum within society concern consumption – the equalisation of marginal utilities to prices for each consumer – as much as they concern production – the choice of the most efficient methods of production in terms of resources. This assumes that the relations of the substitution of factors are identical between all branches and the most efficient allocation of each factor between branches, which assumes the equalisation of marginal productivity within each branch.[11] Now the condition of consumption, in terms of the Paretian optimum, assures the maximum satisfaction of consumers only within a given structure of incomes. In the same way, the real choice of the most efficient method of production depends on the quantities to be reproduced, and thus on

---

[11] For a discussion of these questions, see Maurice Dobb, *Welfare Economics and the Economics of Socialism* (Cambridge University Press, 1969).

demand and therefore on the structure of incomes. Finally, the optimisation of the allocation of a factor assumes a knowledge of the price of the final products, and thus a structure of demand governing these prices, and therefore a given income structure. It thus appears illusory to seek to define the conditions of an optimum independently of the distribution of incomes. But on the other hand, could one start from a definition of the ideal distribution so as to achieve that optimum by manipulating the other variables? If one assumes that the ideal structure of incomes is achieved in t_0 and that an improvement in production is sought on this basis, it follows that changes in the quantities and prices of products, together with any ensuing shift of the labour force, will inevitably entail a change in the structure of real incomes.[12] If one assumes that the ideal disposition would be attained in t_1, taking account of actual prices, through changes in the plan of production, this then assumes a change in the structure of prices, just as the distribution of incomes obtaining in t_1 would have quite another significance, and so on.

Whichever way one looks at it, then, it appears impossible to pose the problem by considering the structure of incomes and demand on the one hand, and that of production on the other, as facts external to each other, to be adjusted through a series of separate variations. To analyse the satisfaction of needs in a framework of social utility, assumes a given consideration of the distribution of incomes, and therefore disregards the way in which this distribution is determined by production, both directly – through the levels of skill of the labour-power employed – and indirectly, through the price structure.

This appears to us the most important lesson to be learned from the difficulties encountered by neo-classical analyses in their attempts to prove that the market economy ensures the 'best' satisfaction of needs: the equalisation of production and consumption is carried out through a *process of development* of which production, the distribution of income, and the fixing of prices through the free inter-play of supply and demand are only *specific moments*.

But this, in fact, alters the direction from which these questions of economic theory are approached. For to grasp the mechanism of equalisation one no longer starts from a micro-economic theory of individual consumption, from an assumption of the individual's needs and a hierarchy of needs, but from an appreciation of the logic of the global process of *production and the reproduction of capital*. The question then becomes: what type of adjustment between needs and production ensures the exercise of the law of value?

---

[12] The same distribution of monetary incomes represents a different structure of real income if the structure of prices is different.

Certain classic Marxist texts and historic debates throw light on the way this question can be posed and resolved.

Marx elucidated, through a logico-historical analysis of the transformation of values into prices of production,[13] a mechanism which is valid for fully developed capitalism. Starting from an ideal situation in which production and needs are universally in balance (petty commodity production), the investment of capital in branches with a low organic composition initiates a considerable displacement of productive forces, both material and human. But if one abstracts the quantitative development of production, the appearance of the market would be considerably altered at the (ideal) end of this process of equalising profit rates. The adjustment of production to needs is now established on quite a different level: from the moment that values are transferred to production costs, the effective demand for some goods is increased, while for others it is diminished. This makes it possible for Marx to assert, in contrast to vulgar economics, that in the final instance production rules both supply and demand. The displacement of productive forces is in fact subject to the quest for maximum profit, which is itself governed by: (1) the technical and organic composition of the capital to be invested; (2) the effective demand, determined by distribution and thus by production relations.

Of course, effective demand differs from socially effective need. But by playing on the first, production in its ceaseless movement more or less satisfies the second, incorporates it in the reproduction of labour power or excludes it, and thus plays a role which should not be overlooked in the formation and development of socially effective need.

A materialist approach to the problem of needs thus not only requires that the order of determination between production and consumption established by vulgar economics be reversed, but also demands the rejection of *any autonomisation of the spheres of consumption and need in relation to the universal development of capital*. It was an acute awareness of this problematic that prompted, and makes it possible to understand, Lenin's remarks on economic theory, where he specified, at each stage of the development of the mode of production, the localisation of the principal contradictions.

Capitalism develops through a succession of specifically economic crises, whereas crises of underproduction in pre-capitalist formations had extra-economic causes (natural disasters, wars etc). Their interpretation poses a problem: underconsumption or overproduction? For Sismondi and, later, for the Russian Populists, the first possibility appears the right

[13] Marx, *Capital*, Vol. I, Part II, Chapter IX.

one. At the moment that it brings about significant increases in the productivity of labour, the growth of capital lowers the income of the mass of producers, who are transformed into wage earners and unemployed. 'The narrow capacity for absorption of the human stomach' makes it impossible for the increase in production to be absorbed by the minority of enriched capitalists; there remain the external markets, in which increasingly fierce competition puts a brake on growth and provokes periodic crisis.

This interpretation ultimately makes consumption, which limits production, the dominant instance in the hierarchy of economic activities. Carefully following Marx, Lenin took pains to refute this view and underline the historically progressive role of capitalism. Lenin stressed, firstly, that since a large share of the annual product is not distributed in incomes but is consumed productively, the expansion of final consumption does not immediately limit the development of the internal market. Secondly, that the expansion of the capitalism at the expense of precapitalist methods of production leads to an expansion, not a contraction, of the internal market. Capital produces at one and the same time the commodities, the needs for these commodities, and the incomes that make it possible to acquire them. Thirdly, that the necessity of external markets for capital is not a question of the *realisation* of value, but is linked to capitalist conditions of *production*: natural expansiveness and the unequal development of different branches of capitalist production.[14]

These remarks all derive from a single principle: that it is mistaken to regard the relation between capitalist production and its market (consumption) as being a relation of external pressures which may or may not be in accord, depending on circumstances. In fact, the crises of capitalism manifest a contradiction between production and consumption, and the real causes must be sought in the *internal* contradiction inherent in the production process itself; and Lenin stresses that the principal contradiction opposes productive forces and relations of production, not production and consumption.

Lenin's dictum that the question of realisation cannot be separated from the question of production, that 'if production relations remain unexplained . . . all argument about consumption and distribution turn into banalities or innocent, romantic wishes'[15] has not always been understood – even by Marxists.

For instance, Rosa Luxemburg criticised Marx's scheme of expanded reproduction (described in *Capital,* Volume II, Chapter XXI) on the

[14] V.I. Lenin, *Collected Works* (Moscow, Foreign Language Publishing House, 1960–70).
[15] Ibid., Vol. II, p. 202.

grounds that it made it possible to conceive of the harmonious and unlimited development of capitalism. This criticism makes no sense unless it is linked to the Populist view that it is at the level of the laws of realisation that the need for external outlets becomes imperative, and that this can provide an explanation of crises.[16] These constructs cannot be made to do more than they are capable of. Only by taking into account the logic of the entire process of capitalist *production* (which Marx only tackles in Volume III of *Capital*) and its internal contradictions is it possible to understand not only the possibility but the necessity of unequal development in the different sectors of production, of overaccumulation of capital and overproduction of commodities – in short, the difficulties in the sphere of realisation itself. Moreover, the failure to recognise that the contradiction between production and consumption has a source outside itself – and its corollary, the reduction of the logic of capitalist development to the need for external outlets – led Rosa Luxemburg to overlook the new character of *capitalist* production at the imperialist stage. Hence she fails to grasp the specific nature of international relations at this stage (the export of *capital,* the *political* oppression of the colonies etc.).

Some contemporary works on capitalism demonstrate a similar failing. Baran and Sweezy's *Monopoly Capital*[17] is particularly significant: the relegation of the material characteristics of the labour process to an aside makes it impossible to analyse such contradictory forms as value/use-value, production relations/productive forces, which are typical of the monopolist stage; within the framework of an analysis of the 'giant firm', production relations themselves are reduced to inter-individual relations; this necessarily excludes the possibility of situating the principal contra-dictions of monopoly capitalism at the level of the process of production. It is scarcely surprising that for Baran and Sweezy these contradictions, which take the form of the impossibility of absorbing the monopolist surplus, are limited to the sphere of realisation.

CLASS DIFFERENCES AND RELATIONS OF PRODUCTION

One of the most significant attempts by sociologists to escape from an elementary substantialism of needs is represented by what might be called the 'differentialist' movement. Here, the need to which all others can be referred is no longer that of reproduction in terms of the nature of individuals or structures, but need for a symbolic manifestation of the

[16] Rosa Luxemburg, *The Accumulation of Capital* (Routledge and Kegan Paul, 1951).
[17] P.A. Baran and P.M. Sweezy, *Monopoly Capital: An Essay on the American Economic and Social Order* (Monthly Review Press, 1966).

individual's position in society: social status, class membership and so on.

Consumption thus becomes the production and, in most cases, the reproduction of differences. The claim of differentialist sociology to hold an independent view of consumption behaviour at least assumes a link with production relations, and thus merits closer examination.

The psychologism of differentiation: Veblen and Goblot

Moralists and caricaturists have not had to wait for the advent of modern sociology to demonstrate the ostentatious character of consumption and the discriminatory way in which it functions. The sociological movement which elevated these observations into a systematic analysis of social consumption is based on two important works: Veblen's *Theory of the Leisure Class* (1899)[18] and, perhaps less well known, Goblot's *La barrière et le niveau* (1925).[19] Veblen wrote:

> The desire of everyone is to excel everyone else in the accumulation of goods. If, as is sometimes assumed, the incentive to accumulation were the want of subsistence or of physical comfort, then the aggregate economic wants of a community might conceivably be satisfied at some point in advance of industrial efficiency; but since the struggle is substantially a race for reputability on the basis of an invidious comparison, no approach to a definitive attainment is possible.

This treats the social in terms of ends and means, and the crucial end here – systematic differentiation – does not depend on any socio-historical determination: 'The dominant incentive was from the outset the invidious distinction attaching to wealth.'[20]

The substitution of the 'man of distinction' for *homo œconomicus* does not alter the principle of analysis: as with the neo-classical economists, production has no logic of its own except to fuel consumption.

Certain categories of consumer objects are particularly well adapted to their function of conferring distinction: such as clothing (Veblen) or house-furnishing (Goblot). Consumption not only makes it possible to distinguish oneself from others, but also provides one with an identity. Goblot notes that any group that attributes social superiority to itself conceals any individual inequalities so as to emphasise its collective superiority; conformity is thus the indispensable complement to distinction.

---

[18] Thorstein Veblen, *The Theory of the Leisure Class* (Allen & Unwin, 1924).
[19] E. Goblot, *La barrière et le niveau* (Presses Universitaires de France, 1967).
[20] Veblen, *The Theory of the Leisure Class*, pp. 32 and 26.

The phenomenon of fashion is a supreme example of this contradiction. Fashion follows a logic of moral depreciation [*divulgation*]. Once it has become widespread, it has to be changed: it is at once a (moving) barrier and a level: 'It does not distinguish individuals, but whole classes.'[21]

Used in this way, the principle of differentiation loses some of its psychologism and makes it possible to grasp a real dimension of consumption behaviour. That it should still be far from giving a full picture is demonstrated by the following example. The upper classes both have below them classes from which they need to distinguish themselves, and also possess adequate distinctive material with which to do so. One can argue that for members of the upper classes the principle of differentiation functions as it should ('What distinguishes the bourgeois is distinction,' wrote Goblot). But the position of the working classes is different in both respects. Veblen asserts that no social class 'denies itself some kind of conspicuous consumption'. He is nonetheless forced to admit that popular consumption is principally a function of the 'spirit of conformity'. But conformity to what? In the absence of any reference to production, the answer implicit here is the satisfaction of organic needs. Now it is in relation to popular consumption that the consumption of the upper classes determines itself: could it be that underlying the differentialist approach there is yet again a substantialism of needs?

Symbolic relations and production relations: Halbwachs and Bourdieu

The works of Halbwachs and of Bourdieu and his team can be related to the differentialist movement, and are among the most fruitful treatments of patterns of consumption.

We owe to Halbwachs two studies of popular consumption. The first work, *La classe ouvrière et les niveaux de vie* (1912) is a study of the effects of income level and family size on the organisation of the family budget and demonstrates the homogeneity of working-class patterns of consumption; the regularity of these patterns makes it necessary to consider the concrete *social* reality of a 'scale of values and a hierarchy of needs'. The second study, *L'évolution des besoins dans les classes ouvrières* (1933) shows that available statistics make it possible to introduce a new variable, class membership (manual worker, white-collar worker, executive), and to demonstrate that people with *similar incomes* have different patterns of consumption (white-collar workers spend more on housing and less on food than manual workers, executives spend more on clothing than white collar workers).

Thus 'the conditions of social life' explain the essential modes through

---

[21] Goblot, *La barrière et le niveau*, p. 49.

which the family budget is organised; these cannot be understood unless they are located within the totality of family and social practices. Needs derive from a 'social feeling' of what should be consumed, in relation to the dominant representation of the group. This 'social sentiment' has two points of reference: family and class. There are, writes Halbwachs, 'close links between family feelings and class feelings'. By emphasising the family as the unit of consumption, but with class determining family practice in the final analysis, he avoids what could otherwise have been a substantialism simply enlarged from the individual to the family.

Class membership thus acts on consumption in an indirect way through family practices, but it also has a direct effect: a given type of *occupational practice*, in a manner corresponding to social relations outside work and outside the home, determines certain patterns of consumption. Its action finally makes itself felt through the *symbolic dimension* of consumption: to consume is to conform to certain class habits and thus to convey an accurate idea of one's class status.

Thus, according to Halbwachs, consumption is governed by a twofold logic: that of *work* and the conditions and constraints it imposes on social life; and that of the symbolic relations of distinction and identification between classes.

That a relation has been established between work and consumption, a rare occurrence in sociological writing, is worthy of note and merits further discussion. The logic of work is not the logic of production: Halbwachs does not refer to a place in the production process, but exclusively to the 'work situation', a place within the work process.

Thus, according to Halbwachs, modern industrial workers are in the course of their work isolated from the materials of production: they come into contact with them only through an intermediary. It is this shared feeling of isolation that provides the basis of class consciousness and makes it possible to understand the specific nature of social relationships, both familial and extra-familial, outside work, and, equally, makes it possible to understand patterns of consumption. But that the industrial enterprise should be at once the site of exploitation, of a direct confrontation between labour and capital, and thus, *for that very reason,* the most favoured site for the trade union and political organisation of the working class, is something Halbwachs overlooks: for him, production is all but a matter of social relations. Social classes are *defined by the forms of work and their place in the work process, but have only symbolic interrelations.* The slide towards an idealist approach, towards a 'psychology' of social classes, thus becomes inevitable.[22]

[22] M. Halbwachs, *The Psychology of Social Class*, trans. Claire Delaveney (Heinemann, 1958).

This silence on relations of production denies the possibility of any historical theory of class and class relations or any historical theory of social needs: that is undoubtedly the reason why Halbwachs, despite his considerable contribution, does not achieve a decisive break with the abstract, sociologising approach to needs, the approach in which, as in Durkheim, everything is played out in terms of individual/society relations. For him, actual needs proceed by a sort of 'social derivation' from 'primitive' needs: the distance between them becomes greater and greater the further one gets from the working class – which is close to the 'organic appetites' – and the closer one comes to the 'upper classes' in which social life is 'more intense'. 'Society' thus 'gradually' empties 'our needs of all their primitive organic content', tending to 'impose its own mark on individual needs'.[23]

Bourdieu takes up Halbwachs's distinction between the orders of determinants of consumption behaviour and then systemises it by distinguishing between 'attributes of situation' and 'attributes of position' in class behaviour:

> Each social class owes to the fact that it occupies a historically defined position in the social structure, and that it is affected by the relations which link it to the other sections which go to make up the structure, *attributes of position,* which are relatively independent of intrinsic proprieties (i.e. *attributes of situation* such as certain kinds of occupational practice or material conditions of existence).[24]

Whereas Halbwachs placed the main emphasis on attributes of situation, Bourdieu sees attributes of position as of prime importance. Differences of situation, and above all of position, are on a symbolic level the object of a systematic expression which 'transmutes differences of fact into significant distinctions'.[25] The symbolic order thus takes the form of a system. It possesses a certain autonomy and has its own logic, drawing distinctions in terms of status groups rather than classes which, as in Goblot, define themselves less by the possession of wealth than by how they utilise it.

The factors contributing to this significant distinction are extremely diverse: 'One must include in the symbolic of class position not only expressive acts, that is, acts specifically and intentionally aimed at expressing social position, but also the entirety of social acts which,

[23] M. Halbwachs, *La classe ouvrière et les niveaux de vie* (Alcan, 1912), pp. 411–13, 440 and 432.
[24] P. Bourdieu, 'Conditions de classe et positions de classe', *Archives européennes de sociologie,* No. 2, 1966, p. 201.
[25] Ibid., p. 214.

without one either knowing or desiring it, express or betray, in the eyes of others and especially of strangers to the group, one's position in society.'

From this perspective, it cannot be true that 'actions most directly oriented towards economic ends are totally devoid of symbolic function. This is particularly true, obviously, of acts of consumption which, as Veblen has shown, always express, if only in a secondary manner, the social position of those practising them in that they are characteristic of a given status group.'

Hence, *cultural* consumption activities, whose economic cost does not immediately represent their most decisive dimension (listening to music, visiting museums, attending lectures, the cinema, watching television etc.) constitute a particularly effective means of expressing class position. This cannot be accounted for by a psychology of motivations, which Bourdieu vigorously attacks, because it has condemned itself 'to restricting itself to psychological functions as they are lived, that is to say, to "satisfactions" and "reasons", instead of seeking out the social functions which the "reasons" serve to conceal, and whose fulfilment moreover achieves directly experienced "satisfactions".'

Bourdieu's approach displaces the source of needs by referring them to a symbolic logic which brings together social classes and is distinct from individual consciousness: from this point of view, cultural consumption and activities bear a 'class ethos' – a system of norms and values belonging to each class – and which only an analysis of class relations can make comprehensible.[26]

As a major attempt to break away from the substantialist conception of need as a lack, this approach emphasises the specificity of a *mode of consumption* whose relations do not necessarily correlate perfectly with the corresponding relations of production and distribution. It is in this area that, while appreciating the full extent of Bourdieu's contribution, one can also perceive its limitations.

First of all, his approach reveals the difficulty that is to be found in all 'differentialists'. The play of 'significant distinctions' to a large extent excludes the working classes, since it 'organises itself objectively with regard to them, except as a foil or, more precisely, as nature,' as Bourdieu himself says.[27] In dealing with working-class patterns of consumption this approach cannot avoid placing the emphasis on their material living conditions, that is, on their situation and class position (and on their 'natural' needs?). But this raises a fundamental problem, and one which

---

[26] Bourdieu and his team have applied this problematic in their particularly illuminating studies of the consumption of photography (*Un art moyen*, Editions de minuit, 1965) and of visits to museums (*L'Amour de l'art*, Editions de minuit, 1966).

[27] Bourdieu, 'Conditions de classe et positions de classe'.

Bourdieu avoids: the problem of *the relation between class situation and class position*. This is due to the ambiguity of the concept of 'class position'. Bourdieu accepts the materialist thesis of the primacy of production relations over symbolic relations, and even asserts the necessity of 'establishing how the structure of economic relations can, by determining the social conditions and positions of social subjects, also determine the structure of symbolic relations, which develop according to a logic which cannot be reduced to that of economic relations.' By begging the question at this point, however, he postulates that a study of the determined (symbolic relations) can be carried on independently of the determinant (production relations). This is not fortuitous. It is the unacknowledged reflection of the attribution of a real autonomy to symbolic relations that implicitly underlies his argument.

Class position is first presented to us as being, like class situation, constitutive of the socio-economic order: it is the situation/position complex which expresses ideological/symbolic relations.[28] But it becomes apparent that Bourdieu is ready to dispense with the economic as soon as it is no longer a question of situation but of position: differences of situation are unquestionably engendered within the economic, but relations of position take place elsewhere. As in Halbwachs, the system of class position and opposition is real only in the sphere of ideological/symbolic relations and consumption relations. The oppositions are never located at any other level than class ethos and styles of living. Since Bourdieu accords a determining role to 'class position', the distinction he establishes elsewhere between class and group status also remains hypothetical. Relations of production and the class struggle disappear, and it is significant that when it comes to defining classes Bourdieu refers at times to the socio-occupational category – but only as indicating a particular condition (job, skill, form of payment) and not a position in economic relations through which this condition has been produced – and at times to a relation to culture, treating the 'upper classes' as 'the cultivated classes'.

This silence on relations of production necessarily affects the study of the mode of consumption, even if that study is confined to cultural consumption. One has only to recall that the question of consumption poses itself in the wider framework of the reproduction of labour-power, which refers directly to the conditions of the production process, to be convinced that the opposite is true. The functioning of the educational system, an important mediator in cultural behaviour (as Bourdieu himself admits) must be linked to relations of production, just as the 'social

[28] Ibid., p. 212.

mobility' of classes which, according to him, is a constituent element in 'class position', must be directly linked to changes in the production process.

USE-VALUE AND EXCHANGE VALUE

Before discussing some of the propositions put forward by Baudrillard, whose most recent work attempts to take the differentialist approach to consumption to its logical conclusion, it may be helpful to look briefly at some aspects of the relation of Ricardo to Marx.

If Marx considered Ricardo the greatest bourgeois economist, 'the economist of production *par excellence*', it is because, unlike Adam Smith, he did not consider production to be limited by needs, but perceived that it generated the impetus for its own development; in asserting the absolute priority of labour values, Ricardo clearly brings out the opposition between profit and wages, capital and labour. And yet – due to the irreducible limitation of his class point of view – he persists in conceiving 'wage labour and capital as the natural law and not as a historically determined form of society' (Marx). Ricardo was consequently no more capable than his predecessors of resolving the interrelation of production and needs.

Ricardo's assumption that capitalist relations of production were universal throughout history made it impossible for him to analyse the value-form.[29] The discussion of the value-form demonstrates that two commodities do not become equivalent either as use-values or as samples of the same substance – labour except under specific circumstances, when there is an identity between use-value and value, and thus between concrete labour and abstract labour, the value appearing in exchange as use-value and in abstract labour as concrete labour. An analysis of the form of the exchange relation is thus indispensable to a theory of commodities, to the extent that this alone can reveal the essential contradictions of their nature. If one considers a commodity as a yolking-together of opposites – value and use-value – it is then possible to analyse the capitalist process of production as a process that both produces use-value and increases capital. This clarifies the contradiction between productive forces and relations of production and makes it possible to

[29] 'He begins with the determination of the magnitude of value . . . by labour time but . . .*does not examine* the form, . . . the *nature* of this labour ' Karl Marx, *Theories of Surplus Labour* (Lawrence & Wishart, 1968), Chapter X, p. 164 *et passim*. [Marx's criticisms of Ricardo's failure to understand together the quantitative and qualitative aspects of value and the labour which produces it are contained in Section 2 of this chapter. *Trans.*]

conceive of the development of bourgeois society, in the final analysis, as a succession of concrete forms of the contradiction between value and use-value and between abstract labour and concrete labour, a contradiction that demands a historical resolution.

Ricardo analyses only the substance of value: for him, exchange value is nothing but the simple *sign* which denotes use-value in the sphere of circulation; he considers it 'simply as a transient form, as a purely formal element in bourgeois production'.[30] By ignoring the contradictory content of commodities, he ignores the contradictory character of the capitalist process of *production,* and thus misunderstands the contradictions of *circulation.* Market exchange, for him, was essentially the exchange of product for product, and money was reduced to the function of a means of circulation, the materialisation of the sign-value.[31]

There is thus no possibility of accounting for the crises in the capitalist system that accompany any interruption in circulation. Whereas, to quote Marx,

> *The most abstract form of the crisis* (and therefore the formal possibility of crisis) *is thus the metamorphosis of the commodity itself*; the contradiction of exchange-value and use-value, and furthermore of money and commodity, comprised within the unity of the commodity, exists in metamorphosis only as an involved movement. . . .
>
> The possibility of crisis therefore lies solely in the separation of sale from purchase. It is only in the form of a commodity that the commodity has to pass through this difficulty here.[32]

If the commodity form is not analysed, this difficulty cannot be properly grasped: the exchange of product for product excludes the impossibility of realising its value. Capitalism, according to Ricardo, cannot experience any real overproduction of capital or commodity, since no contradiction between production and consumption is possible. Capital, the method of accumulation and indefinite development of forces of production, could not be limited except by needs. But, as Ricardo himself shows, needs are themselves indefinite.

Ricardo, commented Marx, forgot only one thing: that 'there is an absolute difference between the overproduction of goods and the over-production of commodities'. The latter are produced by the employment of wage labour, and wages make possible the satisfaction of only those

[30] Ibid.

[31] David Ricardo, 'On the Principles of Political Economy and Taxation' in *The Works and Correspondence of David Ricardo*, ed. P. Sraffa and M.M. Dobb (Cambridge University Press, 1951), Vol. I, Chapter VII, p. 146.

[32] Marx, *Theories of Surplus Value*, Part II, Chapter XVII, pp. 509 and 508.

needs necessary to the reproduction of labour power, and not needs in themselves. That is why 'production is limited by the profit of the capitalists and not by the needs of the producers';[33] and crises reveal these limits.

Thus Ricardo, who here shows a marked superiority to Sismondi, has 'grasped the positive essence of capital . . . correctly': but not 'its specific restrictedness'.[34]

Now the simultaneous apprehension of both the universality and the limit of capital assumes that *production and needs are not treated separately*: it is precisely because he was not able to analyse these internal contradictions of production that Ricardo failed to grasp the contradictions between consumption and production.

He had a conception of class *opposition* but, failing to understand the contradictions of capital which call for its historical passage, he over-looked class *struggle,* which at one and the same time expresses the contradictions of the mode of production, constitutes an active condition of its development, and heralds its dissolution.

The same causes produce the same result in the work of Baudrillard, the sociologist of consumption par excellence. Starting from a pre-Marxist analysis of commodities, he fundamentally ignores the contradictions inherent in the capitalist mode of production and the class struggle, and what he proposes turns out to be no more than a rehashing of the image of the consumer society.[35]

Consumption, according to Baudrillard, constitutes a practice specifi-cally linked to the historical growth and development of industrial mass production. The rationale of the relation of the consumer to 'the object of consumption' cannot be grasped except through the relation of the (structured) system of consumers (class relations) to the (structured) system of objects. The object is not consumed in its materiality, but in its difference: it is in becoming a *sign* (of the class difference) that it becomes a consumer object. 'Consumption, insofar as it has a meaning, consists in the active and systematic manipulation of signs.'[36]

Today the consumption of signs does not only involve the elite (*cf* Veblen) but all social classes. Through the network of value-signs, the dominant classes control the code, which represents 'a structure of power and control more subtle and more totalitarian than that of exploitation'[37] (in the Marxist sense of the term).

[33] Ibid., Chapter XVII.
[34] Marx, *Grundrisse,* p. 410.
[35] At least Ricardo tackled the question from the right direction, that is to say, in terms of production.
[36] *Le système des objets,* p. 276.
[37] *Pour une critique de l'économie politique du signe.*

The emergence and the generalisation of the 'object-form' in which, Baudrillard explains, use-value, exchange value and sign-value converge, calls for the development of a new theory, the 'political economy of the sign'. This theory calls into question, firstly, the vulgar economy of consumption, that is, the substantialism of needs which sees consumption through a subject/object relation commonly apprehended as 'need'; secondly, the differentialist approach in its most psychological aspects (Veblen); and, finally, Marxist theory itself. For Baudrillard, use-value would not, as in Marxist theory, be the natural form of the commodity, but 'its practical guarantee, a rationalisation pure and simple' of the sign exchange-value: in other words, a *social form* in which the objects are objectivised during the bourgeois era, and which appears at the same time as 'the deprived individual defined in terms of his needs'. Marx's analysis of commodities is also subjected to the logic of a signifier (exchange value) which is to produce 'the evidence of the "reality" of the signified and the referrent' (use-value and needs).[38] The political economy of the sign, as a critique of the use-value form, goes further than Marx by asserting that 'far from designating something beyond political economy, use-value is nothing but the horizon of exchange-value'. The production of use-value and the satisfaction of needs do not constitute origins and horizons operating outside the market society, but make up its specific ideology; what market exchange has abolished, and what should entail its own abolition, is *symbolic exchange,* a totalising relation in which the object is not autonomisable as such and codifiable as a sign, but is indissolubly linked to the concrete relation in which the exchange operates, in a fundamentally *ambivalent* manner: 'a medium of relation and of distance, the gift is always both love and aggression . . . the total manifestation of a concrete relation of desire.'[39] From this point of view socialism can offer no real solution: prisoners of the productivist ethic, embroiled in the trap of use-value and needs, its apologists could not help contributing to the reinforcement of the 'code'.

As an empirical validation of this logical, original and seductive construction, Baudrillard proposes his study of 'the system of objects' and their differential manipulation by consumers. The real sociographical dimension of this work helps to reinforce the element of truth present in the differentialist argument: but it does not in our view demonstrate, any more than the remarks of Veblen, Goblot and the rest, the capacity of this argument to exhaust the meaning of patterns of consumption and bring them together in a general theory.

The key to Baudrillard's theoretical argument lies in the treatment of

[38] *Le miroir de la production,* p. 18.
[39] *Pour une critique de l'économie politique du signe,* pp. 62–63.

use-value as a specific social form of market production. However, his criticism of Marx on this point derives from a fundamental misunderstanding of the Marxist theory of commodities. The absence of the concept of value, and the systematic referral of use-value to exchange-value and not to value, are indications of this misunderstanding, and indicate an approach to commodities whose logic is analogous to that of the classical economists. Seeing in the relation of use-value to exchange-value the relation of signified to signifier, Baudrillard is content merely to place them in juxtaposition, in the same way as he juxtaposes 'the logic of utility' and 'the logic of equivalence'.

For Marx, in fact, exchange-value (or value-form) is the relation between two commodities, and his analysis makes it possible to grasp the secret, the contradictory essence of the commodity as the union of two hostile poles, *value* and use-value.[40] The relation of value to use-value, far from constituting a juxtaposition of forms, defines the internal contradiction 'immanent to the nature of the commodity'. Revealed by the deciphering of the social form (exchange-value)[41] which enables it to 'move' in the sphere of circulation, this contradiction pre-exists the entry of the product into circulation: to demonstrate its nature is thus to analyse the particular (abstract/concrete) character of the private labour of the commodity producer, and is thus an analysis of the *historically determined contradictory nature of the process of market production,* which until Marx's time had been hidden by commodity fetishism.

It is clear that the capacity to transcend the classical theory of labour-value through an analysis of the value-form played an absolutely decisive role in the way Marx changed the basis of economic theory.

But Baudrillard's thinking is rooted in an age before this great step forward. By reducing the theory of value to a logic of equivalence, by lending to Marx the Ricardian concept of exchange-value as the 'simple formal mediation of commodities', he fails to grasp the latter as the union of opposites. It is thus impossible for him to discern, behind the appearance of circulation, the contradictions between the mode of production and the logic of the essential relations this engenders. For this reason, in the final analysis, his criticism of 'the fetishism of use-value' demonstrates the same limitations as commodity fetishism.[42]

[40] 'When, at the beginning of this chapter, we said, in common parlance, that a commodity is both a use-value and an exchange value, we were, accurately speaking, wrong. A commodity is a use-value or object of utility, and a value.' Marx, *Capital,* Vol. I, Part I, Chapter I, Section 3, p. 30.

[41] Exchange value in this sense in Marxism is not, as Baudrillard would have it, the social form of use-value, but the movement of the contradiction between value and use-value in circulation.

[42] As Patrice Grevet, whose work provides a complementary critique of the modernist subjectivist approach to needs (see *Besoins populaires et financement public.* Editions sociales, 1976), remarks, Baudrillard also misunderstands the Marxist concept of use-value: this is, strictly speaking, a social form, being the element of a social heritage outside the individual, and whose existence specifies human sociality as against animality.

This also explains why the 'political economy of the sign', over and above any exercises in style, very soon brings us back on to familiar ground. The perpetuation of the developed market society assumes the sale of an increasing number and variety of commodities: the growing importance of 'consumption', both as practice and ideology, thus becomes increasingly indispensable to it. Under these conditions, the masters of the system are led into an ever stricter control and programming of consumption. In a society in which, and here Baudrillard turns to Galbraith, 'the control of demand becomes an element of strategy'; the monopoly of the 'code' (of the system of signs regulating consumption), which corresponds to the monopoly of the means of production, becomes the most pressing requirement. It effectively confers the control of needs, and these then appear as a true productive force: 'Demand, that is to say, needs, correspond more and more to a simulated model. These new productive forces do not present any challenge to the system: they are an anticipated response, the system even controls their emergence itself.'[43] Any wage demand thus favours the system and contributes to its permanence. In short, production is geared to meet needs, which are the motor of the system and so on. This has a classic air: an attempt to shift Marx to the left, and we are back with Galbraith and the rest who sing the praises of the consumer society.

The banality of these conclusions derives from a misunderstanding of dialectics (lucky 'system', which, having mastered the 'code', has disposed of all its contradictions and is not 'presented with any challenges . . .') but is also related to a fundamentally idealist epistemology (dressed up in the highly fashionable form of the terrorism of the signifier).

Although taken from Hegelian philosophy, the concept of *form* has played, since Marx, a central role in the materialist theory of ideologies, designating the totality formed by a category of practice and its ideal equivalent. As a practical category, the form partakes of the 'apparent movement', and an essential element in scientific endeavour consists in clarifying, over and above the form, the process which produced it and which itself partakes of the 'real movement'. The theory of real movement (the social process of capitalist production, for instance) thus makes it possible to grasp in the reality of their determinations the practices of apparent movement (circulation, exchange, individual consumption) as corresponding practical ideologies (the illusions of competition, the ideologies of market consumption and, in particular, the substantialism of needs).

Now Baudrillard may well emphasise that the 'same logic' runs

[43] Baudrillard, *Le miroir de la production*, p. 106.

through 'material production (the system and production relations) and the production of signs (culture etc.)', but his denial of any 'separation between the sign and the world' is, in fact, a submission of the world to the 'sign': of the referent to the signified, and of the signified to the signifier. This reduction of the real to the signifier – and of ideology to the sign – makes it impossible to conceive of the production of the sign, and its logic. Hence, if Baudrillard goes on to assert a certain reality, the practical dimension of the sign must partake *exclusively* of the apparent movement: there can be no question of deducing from the form (say, the market form) the real movement (the contradiction between value and use-value), which is its essential characteristic; there is a phenomeno-logical confusion of the real and apparent movement which negates any sort of scientific inquiry. Thus Baudrillard ensnares himself in a trap: an idealist criticism of ideologies is impossible. His criticism of the 'use-value form' enables him to describe as ideological the image of the 'individual defined by his needs', and denounce the substantialism of needs as being a specific relation of the market ideology. But by reducing the 'world' to the 'effect of reality' of the sign, that is to say, by reducing the real movement to the apparent movement, he denies himself the means to create what would at once be an alternative theory of needs and a theory of both the contradictory historical determinations of market consumption and its necessary representations. Thus, in the final analysis, his description of the real necessarily shares the same structure as the market ideologies of consumption he is at such pains to criticise.

The materialist critique of value-form reveals first of all the necessity of commodity fetishism insofar as it proceeds from this form itself (obscuring the logic of production and its relations, with the ensuing referral of the apparent movement of circulation to the sphere of needs and consump-tion, a reference which constitutes the structure of the image of the consumer society). But also, and above all, it takes account of the real movement which produces this form and underlies fetishism: the contra-diction between value and use-value, the attribution of use-value to capital and its productive process, and so on. The critique of the market ideologies of consumption takes this as its foundation, and on the strength of this sees itself as opening up new theoretical territory in which to postulate (and help resolve) the problem of needs.

Let us make the point again: opening up this territory does not consist in throwing use-value 'out of the field of the market economy' (Baudril-lard's reading of Marx) but, on the contrary, in conferring on it 'a role which is of a different importance from that accorded to it in traditional (political) economy.'[44] The 'logic of utility' and the 'logic of equivalence'

---

[44] Marx, *Capital,* Vol. II.

(and also of non-equivalence, of exploitation, which he appears to overlook) are not, as Baudrillard supposes, superimposed in an expressive relation. The logic of the real unity, the mode of production, derives at one and the same time, and in a *contradictory manner,* from both. Only by grasping the dialectical unity of value and use-value, of relations of production and productive forces, is it possible to break away from the schema of the consumer society; this involves setting out the contradictions between production and consumption – that is, the dependence of consumption on production and the impossibility of capitalist production satisfying needs – and thus restoring the question of needs to the context of the class struggle.

DESIRES AND NEEDS

Before asking ourselves more precisely what a materialist approach to needs might be, a few critical remarks on the confusion between needs and desires may be helpful. Although there is no question of our reducing desire to a need, as the theory of the unconscious invites us to do, to identify needs with desires does not in our view constitute anything more than the beginning of a solution.

Today the problem of the theoretical conception of needs has taken on a major importance in the politico-ideological confrontation over the nature of the crisis and its outcome. The reception of Baudrillard's work in a series of recent publications, themselves subscribing to the new ideological configuration which is a necessary element in reformism in France at the time of the open crisis in monopoly state capitalism, bears witness to this. This movement, heralded by a reiteration of certain of the themes of the Frankfurt School and a return in force of Freudian (anti-)Marxism, appears, under cover of a critique of the economism inherent in Marxism, to aim at the liquidation of materialism.

Among these works, Marc Guillaume's *Le Capital et son double*[45] may serve as an example, both because of its theoretical references (to the convergence of technocratic reformism – Attali, Rocard – and left-wing idealism) and because of the way in which Guillaume endorses the most significant characteristics of the ideology of our time. It presents itself as a 'cadres' version of Baudrillard's thesis, and is an attempt, through relying on the crucial force of desire in the human species,[46] to extend his approach to an analysis of the state, of collective facilities and so on. Marxism, according to the author, can be seen to be out of date, as

[45] Marc Guillaume, *Le Capital et son double* (PUF, 1975).
[46] G. Deleuze et F. Guattari, *L'Anti-Oedipe* (Editions de minuit, 1972).

providing no explanation of the reproduction of social relations within the consumer society today. How, for example, asks Guillaume, can one continue to explain the expansion of the demand for goods in terms of 'needs' when the objects produced are, for the most part, superfluous rather than necessary? One must recognise the eclipse of the utility function before the sign function, and be prepared to pass from 'the order of need to the order of desire', which 'contradicts the principle of a primarily economic explanation of the reproduction of social relations'.

We will confine ourselves here to a few observations.[47]

Firstly, by not referring to patterns of consumption except in terms of social, semiotic and ideological relations external to the sphere of production, Guillaume's work places itself squarely in the line of works we have already examined. The author indeed attempts to lend Baudrillard's approach a bit more flexibility by evoking an imaginary moment of consumption in its relation to use. But he does not break out of the 'enclosed territory of private consumption',[48] in which all the mechanisms appear beautifully oiled; the omnipresence of desire ensures the strict functionality of the sign, which guarantees the efficacy of the publicity campaign, which stimulates demand, which reproduces the social relations and so on. One might ask the author whether it is not an essential characteristic of bourgeois ideology, in all its historical versions, to mask the contradictions inherent in the regime and simultaneously deny its necessary historicity?

Secondly, however much Guillaume may cover himself,[49] this is in fact a fundamentally *psychological* interpretation of the social. As for substituting the machine of desires for *homo œconomicus*: this only has to be thought to be achieved. No further complicated theories are needed to understand social practices: 'The activity itself is its own end since if we undertake it, it is because we wish it.' Thus the state may be referred to as 'the desire for a state', consumption as 'the desire for signs' and so on. But there is one small difficulty: the continuance of capitalism can always be explained by the permanence of the desire for it, but in order to account for the 'symbolic destructuring' carried out by capital, which provokes a displacement of the site invested by that desire (from pre-capitalist personal relations to the contemporary world of objects and 'abstract' institutions), one must take into account a socio-historical development which desire does not explain. A second question for the author is related

---

[47] For a systematic treatment see G. Kebabdjian, 'Réformisme et idéalisme dans le socialisme utopique renaissant', *Economie et Politique*, No. 258, 1976.
[48] Guillaume, *Le Capital et son double*, p. 37.
[49] Ibid., p. 14.
[50] Ibid., pp. 40, 48, 152.

as much to the criticism of idealism as of economism: is it not precisely the characteristic of idealist thinking to have recourse to history only long enough to explain a world which does not itself explain history?

Thirdly, no economic theory can leave aside the question of needs with impunity. By putting it to one side and substituting the question of desire, the author finds himself back, logically, on the other side, at the lowest level of the substantialist conception of needs: the only objective needs, for him, are related visibly to a historical physiological demand. This enables him to assert, in all political innocence, that developed capitalism has long since satisfied the 'fundamental needs'. . . .

Finally, what is one to think of this blossoming of 'theories' which, at the precise moment when capitalist *production* relations are undergoing a profound crisis, proclaim the negligible character of the role of the economic infrastructure in the reproduction and development of social relations?

2

The historical and social
nature of needs

The possibility of systematically applying the concept of 'need', and of raising to the level of a historical and social theory a notion so embedded in the language of daily life, appears to depend on two preconditions.

First of all, a scientific treatment of 'needs' must be capable of developing a critique of the subjectivist/idealist use of this term. Both in its academic version and in the language of daily life, 'need' refers to the need of the individual being, just as an attribute is referred to the substance. But materialism also demands the rejection of a cultural concept which, while it refuses to accept the empiricism that sees all needs as proceeding from the subject as their ultimate source and thus emphasises their historical and social relativity, nonetheless ignores their relations to the sphere of material production, its social relations and its contradictions.

Given these premises, the question may then be put in these terms: is there a place for a 'Marxist theory of needs' and if so, where? The problem is given greater importance by the numerous references to the subject in Marx's own works and other Marxist 'classics', but these tend to be incidental, more or less allusive remarks rather than a formal definition or an explicit theory of human needs. Thus in order to isolate the necessary lines of thought, one must begin by returning to the principles of the materialist theory of history.

PRODUCTION, REPRODUCTION AND NEEDS

Let us go straight to the heart of the matter: the relations between man and nature, the specific logic which lends meaning to history. These relations are to be perceived as labour, in terms of the social distribution of labour time, and the distribution of the members of society among different areas of production; the logic of the relations should be grasped through the particular mode of this distribution.

> Every child [wrote Marx] knows that a country which ceased to work, I will not say for a year, but for a few weeks, would die. Every child knows too that the mass of products corresponding to the different needs require different and quantitatively determined masses of the total labour of society. That this necessity of distributing social labour in definite proportions cannot be done away with by the *particular form* of social production, but can only change the *form it assumes,* is self evident. No natural laws can be done away with. What can change, in changing historical circumstances, is the *form* in which these laws operate.[1]

Thus any human society, which has to consume in order to survive, and produce in order to consume, having a certain quantity of labour-power at its disposal, distributes a more or less significant part of the social labour time available amongst the different kinds of labour process, in order to satisfy the corresponding needs.[2]

The adjustment of production to needs is ensured by a certain *economy* of the social labour time available. Here, since it is a question of *natural* necessity, we are dealing with the most general, most abstract characteristic of any social formation. It is this 'determination of time', wrote Marx, 'to which, in the final analysis, every economy can be reduced.'[3] Every concrete social formation is characterised by a particular mode of this determination of time or, in other words, by the specific manner in which the correspondence of production and needs is ensured: thus by a *socially* determined model of the exercise of natural law, a specific logic of distribution of social labour over time. The materialist theory of social formations consists primarily and fundamentally in a simultaneous analysis of this logic and of the concrete forms in which it is realised within a particular historical context.[4]

In so defining economic activity as the mode of adjusting production and needs we are confronted by a crucial problem. We have already said that it would be impossible to base a scientific approach to social and historical life on an instrumental conception of production, which would then be reduced to a means of satisfying needs. To conceive of needs as

[1] Karl Marx, *Letters to Dr Kugelmann* (Martin Lawrence, n.d.), 11 July 1868. [Marx's italics.]
[2] 'To examine production divorced from this distribution which is a constituent part of it, is obviously idle abstraction.' Karl Marx, *A Contribution to the Critique of Political Economy* (Lawrence & Wishart, 1971), p. 202.
[3] Ibid.
[4] Marx's *Capital,* completely centred on the analysis of the *law of value,* the capitalist *mode* of applying natural law, thus provides the theoretical tools essential to any analysis of bourgeois society.

independent of production is to accord them a logical primacy and refer the history of human societies to the development of needs, culture, attitudes of mind, the human subject, or whatever: in each case to factors of which history takes no account, to facts outside history.

Now the only possibility of making history an object of scientific knowledge so that it does not, in consequence, 'have to be written according to a norm situated outside itself' – such as needs – is to base it on 'the development of the real process of production, and to do so by starting from the immediate production of material life'.[5]

It is then impossible to conceive of production as being independent of the needs which it is called upon to satisfy, any more than one can conceive of needs as independent of the production which satisfies them. We are led to conclude that the determination of needs, like their satisfaction, is only a moment in the same process of social production. This can only be understood in one way: the needs that production satisfies are the needs of production itself, the demands of its reproduction.

The needs of social production, that is to say, the conditions of the distribution of social labour time which regulate the process, can be understood at two levels. Firstly, there is the question of the imperatives that bear upon the immediate relation with nature, and thus with a given state of the development of the productive forces: the length of labour time required by each type of labour process, whether in terms of producing the means of consumption or the means of production, the labour time necessary for gaining skill by the appropriate human labour force. Secondly, there is the question of the constraints relative to the social organisation of production: the nature and quantity of the goods necessary to the functioning and reproduction of the essential social relations engendered in the process of production – the maintenance and reproduction of the producers as much as the non-producers (and thus, should the need arise, of the dominant class as such).

It is the *unity* of these two series of conditions, of the dimensions of social production (forces of production/relations of production), which the concept of the mode of production aims to grasp. Thus we arrive at the *first* result, that for historical materialism there are no 'social needs' which are not required and produced by the action and reproduction of the mode of production.

The thesis, briefly stated, is of course no more than the first stage of a scientific approach to needs which must at the same time take account of the real movement of their production, of the particular manner in which

[5] Karl Marx and Frederick Engels, *The German Ideology* (Lawrence & Wishart, 1974).

they are consciously apprehended, and of their individualisation.

It is nonetheless an essential stage, which precisely articulates needs with the general movement of society, and thus confers a concrete substance on the simple and much too vague assertion of the historical and social character of human needs; furthermore, by radically displacing the very terms in which the question is stated, this formulation renders meaningless the endless controversies about the distinction between 'natural' needs and needs 'created by society', between 'necessary' needs and 'superfluous' needs, and so on.

The thesis briefly outlined above also leads to a closer reading of Marx's thoughts, in the 1857 Introduction, on the relations between production and consumption:

> Consumption accomplishes the act of production only in completing the product as product by dissolving it, by consuming its independently material form, by raising the inclination developed in the first act of production, through the need for its repetition, to its finished form; it is thus not only the concluding act in which the product becomes product, but also that in which producer becomes producer. On the other side, production produces consumption by creating the specific manner of consumption; and further, by creating the stimulus of consumption, the ability to consume, as a need.[6]

How does this determination of needs operate? The need for an object, says Marx, 'is created by the perception of it', and he concludes, 'production . . . thus produces the object of consumption, the manner of consumption and the motive of consumption.'

This formulation is however highly abstract, and the location of the problem in terms of the opposition of subject and object remains ambiguous, tending to tautologies of the reciprocal action between the individual and society which can then be taken up by culturalist sociologising of every kind. And insofar as Marxist thinking on the question of needs has not gone beyond this, it can often appear somewhat schematic and psychologising. One must thus go further, and Marx, in the same text, indicates the direction to be taken: if consumption appears as a moment in the social process of production, it is because the individual consumes 'as a *productive* and self-reproducing individual'; it is because the agents of consumption are the agents of production, and their needs derive from the position they occupy in relations of production. This position is defined as much by their role in the process of the

---

[6] Karl Marx, *Grundrisse*, trans. with a Foreword by Martin Nicolaus (Allen Lane, 1973), pp. 92–3.

deployment of the material means of production as by their position in the social relations of production.

In the continuing course of its reproduction, the process of social production produces in effect not only material goods but also well-defined social agents, that is to say, historical forms of individuality made up of a whole body of inclinations and capacities, of 'instincts', of specific frameworks of behaviour which correlate with the demands of the mode of production, whose reproduction in turn has its own exigencies. By transforming nature, men produce themselves as producers and transform themselves: from this crucial thesis, which is fundamental to a materialist understanding of history, all the consequences which relate to a consideration of needs should be derived.

Thus it is impossible to treat the direct producers as abstract individuals who might, indeed, play an intimate part in a given culture outside the sphere of production, but from the point of view of production are nothing but so many elementary labour powers, whose only importance lies in their distribution between different branches of activity. The total number and the specific distribution of workers does indeed constitute an essential aspect of the functioning of a mode of production. It is equally true that the industrial revolution has *tended* to reduce a large part of concrete labour, whatever the activity, to simple, unskilled labour, the mere expenditure of labour force, to 'abstract' labour. But what appears at any given period to be elementary labour, requiring no particular skill, is nonetheless historically relative; as Marx said, 'simple average labour . . . varies in character in different countries and at different times.'[7] The qualities demanded of a simple worker in large-scale industry in the 1980s are not the same as they were in 1850. And all concrete labour in large-scale capitalist industry cannot be reduced to simple average labour.

Direct producers make up the living part of the productive forces; their historical individuality corresponds to a given state of those forces, and changes as they change. Productive activity is characterised as conscious activity, but an understanding of the modes of transforming nature and its results is born of practical experience, and widened by its reproduction. The workers' skill – that 'world of productive inclinations and instincts' (Marx), the scientific and technical knowledge whose transmission can, to some extent, be ensured outside the specific site of production – is at one and the same time a product and a demand of productive activity.[8]

---

[7] Karl Marx, *Capital* (Lawrence & Wishart, 1954), Vol. I, Part I, Chapter I, Section 2, p. 44.

[8] This can lead to a misunderstanding of the degree of autonomy that scientific work may acquire at a particular stage of social development, but this autonomy, as is well known, can only be relative.

The work process is the site where, through a specific development and organisation of the productive forces, presided over by a determined logic of the social relations of production, a practical appropriation of nature operates and particular modes of sociality, arising as much from the co-operation of the producers as from their final confrontation with class exploitation, come together. It is thus the site where representations of the world and society form and reform, and where social values and models for behaviour are developed – in short, those essential elements of a culture (social, class-based) which must profoundly affect the totality of non-productive practices, and which make a powerful contribution to shaping patterns of consumption and the needs which find expression in the social, political, ideological and symbolic forms of the relation of the social agents to nature and society. The presence of the cultural and the ideological at the very heart of the labour process, and its effects at the level of social relations outside production, constitute a substantial area of analysis which has been insufficiently explored by materialist research.[9]

Thus at different levels one can see that so far as direct producers are concerned, certain needs are objectively induced and required by the reproduction of the process of production. Firstly, there is the need for a given amount of labour power distributed in different proportions among different branches of activity, and hence a need for the reproduction of the labour power consumed in the previous process of production (whether it involves individual compensation for physiological wear or biological renewal of the social group). Secondly, there is the need for a skilled labour force commensurate with the demands for its distribution between the different labour processes and different positions. Thirdly, in class societies, it is necessary to ensure that the producers are inserted into the ideological relations which perpetuate, in different modalities (social/technical), existing relations of exploitation. And fourthly, there are the needs of social, political and family organisation, needs arising from the ideological and symbolic appropriation of the world and society, and the corresponding forms of material consumption, to the extent that these needs proceed, indirectly but necessarily, from the social mode of material production.

The contradictory nature of these demands is immediately evident: this

---

[9] This time-lag may be due in part to a mechanistic representation of the Marxist concepts of base and superstructure: turning the distinction in method into an actual separation will obviously exclude any consideration of the presence of ideology from questions of production – and will consequently exclude questions of production from ideology. However, the theoretical work on this subject by Lucien Sève in *Marxisme et théorie de la personalité* should be mentioned, together with such very different studies as Baudricourt's research on the ideology of pastoral societies (CERM) or Verret's examination of working-class culture (*La Pensée*, No. 163, 172). Similarly, there has been some contemporary historical research, such as Duby's work on the history of 'mentalities'.

contradiction is characteristic of all regimes of exploitation and, more or less openly depending on their stage of development, it provokes the practical confrontation of class interests. But for the sake of clarity, let us for the moment leave to one side this crucial dimension of the question of social needs.[10]

Since the constraints we have just listed are those of the very operation and reproduction of the mode of production, they impose themselves not only on the direct agents of production but also, to a great extent, on the dominant class itself. The prime need of this class is in fact to reproduce itself as a social agent defined by the mode of production, and thus to reproduce the objective and subjective conditions of its mode of exploitation.

There are no exploiters without the exploited, and without the exploited being capable of putting into practice the material means of exploitation: the reproduction of producers could not leave the dominant class untouched. This requirement has been unequally perceived and unequally satisfied, but its permanence throughout history makes it possible to interpret certain practices of the dominant classes. From the first characteristic forms of social differentiation, among primitive communities of settled farmers in particular, anthropologists have shown the control exerted by dominant individuals or groups through the workings of kinship relations; this control is exercised not only in terms of the distribution of the means of subsistence but also, and perhaps above all, through the distribution of individuals (women, slaves) among the kinship groups, and thus operates through the biological reproduction of the producers. In agrarian societies differentiated into classes, the mode of reproduction of the producers does not always necessarily depend on the immediate control of the dominant class (because of class endogamy, auto-consumption of village communities), but the dominant class is nevertheless closely involved in the human conditions of the production of wealth and the limits set to the degree of exploitation; this is demonstrated, for instance, by the care taken by both the ancient Greek and then the Roman state to ensure the provision of wheat to ill-favoured rural areas and small urban producers. In this respect, the development of capitalism and the individualisation of the forms of reproduction of the labour force, through the process of market consumption, do not modify the basic facts of the question. As Marx observed:

[10] A crucial dimension because if one misrepresents it – as we do deliberately in the following pages – one will inevitably be left with a functionalist conception of social needs. We tackle that question in the next section.

Within the limits of what is strictly necessary, the individual consumption of the working-class is, therefore, the reconversion of the means of subsistence given by capital in exchange for labour-power, into fresh labour-power at the disposal of capital for exploitation. It is the production and reproduction of that means of production so indispensable to the capitalist: the labourer himself. The individual consumption of the labourer, whether it proceed within the workshop or outside it, whether it be part of the process of production or not, forms therefore a factor of the production and reproduction of capital; just as cleaning machinery does, whether it be done while the machinery is working or while it is standing. The fact that the labourer consumes his means of subsistence for his own purposes, and not to please the capitalist, has no bearing on the matter. The consumption of food by a beast of burden is none the less a necessary factor in the process of production, because the beast enjoys what it eats.[11]

The traditional practices of De Wendel in the Fentsch valley in Lorraine or of Michelin in Clermont-Ferrand, among a good many others, are specific but significant examples of the interest capital has in controlling the conditions of the reproduction of labour-power; an interest which manifests itself here in a stringent hold on both material aspects (housing, distribution of consumer goods, transport) and ideological aspects (academic and religious organisations, press etc.). Such practices, which make it possible to establish isolated pockets of labour where competition works exclusively for the benefit of the employers and the control of reproduction operates through generations of workers, provide some proof that under a capitalist regime the 'private' and 'free' nature of consumption is relative.

Obviously, the dominant class is equally involved in the reproduction of the *material* conditions of the production process. There too it is a question of imperatives which may entail a limitation of the levels of exploitation (the village community, for example, has to have a surplus available so that it can be assured of seed for sowing; or the subsistence of the artisans necessary to the construction and maintenance of the tools of labour), and which may require direct intervention in the production process. The logic of the 'Asiatic' mode of production, where the organisation by the state-class of major works beyond the scope of the grassroots communities is a direct condition of agricultural production, provides a significant example. The age-old structural stability of 'classic' Asiatic formations (Mesopotamia, Egypt, China) may be attributed both to the universally autarchic character of the village community and to the indispensable intervention of the state as a necessary moment in the process of reproduction. The state, in fact, ensures the maintenance of the

[11] Marx, *Capital*, Vol. II, Part VII, Chapter XXIII, p. 572.

material conditions of production (irrigation, transport); it directs the organisation of production (fixing their calendar and some of their modalities);[12] it organises the operations of stocking and redistribution which in the long term guarantee a balance between production and consumption.[13] Under these conditions the intervention of the 'economic high command' ensured by the machinery of the state leads to a regression in the productive forces, a disorganisation and diminution of production, a turning-in upon themselves of the village communities, in short, the disappearance, in the end, of the taxable base without which no dominant class can establish lasting reign. That is why, as the history of ancient China in particular shows, barbarian invasions, like the tendency to develop private seigneurial relations of the feudal type, always ended in the installation of new imperial dynasties which reconstituted the bureaucratic state machine and regenerated the taxable base through a policy of major works[14] – thus demonstrating the truth that invaders cannot impose themselves as the dominant class except by taking over the objective needs of the reproduction of the mode of production.

In bourgeois society, in which the logic of capital imposes the systematic growth of the process of production, the reproduction of the conditions of production assumes that only a fraction of the surplus value should be devoted to investment. The needs of the capitalist, as social agent, are those of capital:

> So far, therefore, as his actions are a mere function of capital – endowed, as capital is, in his person, with consciousness and a will – his own private consumption is a robbery perpetrated on accumulation. . . . Along with this growth, there is at the same time developed in his breast, a Faustian conflict between the passion for accumulation, and the desire for enjoyment[15]

---

[12] 'Priests in the Sumerian temples could judge precisely how much grain was needed to sow a field of particular dimensions.' V. Gordon Childe, *The Dawn of European Civilisation* (Routledge & Kegan Paul, 1957).

[13] In China, 'it was the educated bureaucrats who took on all mediating and administrative functions: they looked after the calendar; they organised transport and exchange; they were in charge of the construction of roads, canals, ditches and dikes; they oversaw all public works, especially those aimed at tempering the harshness of nature, and preventing floods and droughts; they set up reserves in case of famine and encouraged every kind of irrigation. They were at one and the same time the architects, engineers, administrators and managers of society.' E. Balazs, *La bureaucratie céleste* (Gallimard, 1968), p. 36.

[14] Public ownership, in this way, contains the seeds of private ownership, generalised slavery being a considerable advance on feudal dependence. See F. Tokeï, *Sur le mode de production asiatique* (Budapest, 1966).

[15] Marx, *Capital*, Vol. I, Part VII, Chapter XXIV, Section 3, pp. 593–4.

The fraction of surplus of value which the capitalist as the agent of capital 'needs' to accumulate is to a great extent independent of the spontaneous 'inclination towards pleasure' of capitalists as private individuals: it depends primarily on previous accumulation, on the state of competition, on technological development etc. More precisely, this inclination towards pleasure is itself related to the process of production, it is a product of its development. Thus, during the transition from feudalism to capitalism, while capital needs to have a significant rate of accumulation in order to impose the superiority of its mode of production, it is the 'Protestant ethic', the spirit of Puritanism and of renunciation of worldly pleasures, which presides over its development, at a moment when the practices of conspicuous consumption among the feudal aristocracy are most blatant. But these very demands of capital have to undergo a change, as do the practices of its agents:

> At the historical dawn of capitalist production – and every capitalist upstart has personally to go through this historical stage – avarice, and desire to get rich, are the ruling passions. But the progress of capitalist production not only creates a world of delights; it lays open, in speculation and the credit system, a thousand sources of sudden enrichment. When a certain stage of development has been reached, a conventional prodigality, which is also an exhibition of wealth, and consequently a source of credit, becomes a business necessity to the 'unfortunate' capitalist. Luxury enters into capital's expenses of representation. [16]

If the reproduction of the human and material conditions of production is dependent on the needs of the dominant class, then *a fortiori* there follows the necessity for this reproduction to operate under the conditions of exploitation. This demand for the reproduction of the relations of production works both as the necessity for determined forms of social and material organisation of the process of production (making possible production and the skimming-off of over-production) and as the necessity for obtaining the consent of the producers to their own exploitation – a consent which assumes a repressive as well as an ideological intervention by the dominant class. This, of course, is a question of the 'enormous superstructure' and its central support, the organisation of the state. The political and juridical organisation of the dominant class in and by the state, the machinery of repression and hegemony – so many products of the antagonism inherent in a certain stage of social development,

---

[16] Ibid., p. 592. This development, at once an obligation imposed upon and an opportunity presented to the dominant class to actively appropriate increasing social wealth, will in its turn provide an important stimulus to the enrichment of the social heritage in both cultural and material terms.

representing the immediate needs of a dominant class which could not otherwise find a foundation for its domination and hegemony, the conditions *sine qua non* of the reproduction of exploitation. Every sector of social life is touched in one way or another by the hegemonic practices of the dominant class, from production to the family and consumption patterns (conspicuous consumption, for example, demonstrating the essential superiority of the haves, individualised consumption isolating the have-nots): practices which thus contribute to shaping the needs of the dominant class as much as those of the dominated classes.

This brief discussion of the most general aspects of the objective content of social needs should be sufficient to show the possibility of a materialist approach to needs, and demonstrate that such an approach involves mobilising the entire materialist theory of social and historical development. With this solid foundation, it is now possible to pursue the idea of the social determination of needs by posing the question of the process of their historical transformation.

SOCIAL CONTRADICTIONS AND THE HISTORICAL DEVELOPMENT OF NEEDS

In referring the real movement of needs to the constraints of the reproduction of the mode of production, one must avoid the trap of functionalist or structuralist sociologising, which ignores the fact that there can no scientific approach to society which is not at the same time a theory of history: that sociologising which, by advancing the principle of the 'maintenance of structural permanence' to explain social development, adopts the point of view of reproduction. [17] In so doing, it can at best describe the behaviour of social relations, but, like bourgeois political economy, it is unable to understand how they come about. [18] Here, the convenient methodological choice of the point of view of reproduction (justified because any production process, considered in its continuity, is a process of reproduction), joins with the negation of the very concept of production. *To start* from the principle of the reconstitution of the structure not only makes it impossible to explain the production of what is different, but also to conceive of the possible (re)production of what is identical. For Marxism, reproduction is only a moment in the theory of

[17] The central truth of each social fact being seen through its relations, its contribution to the permanence of the social structure, i.e. to the needs for the reproduction of the social system.

[18] In fact, bourgeois economists 'can certainly see how production operates *within* the capitalist relation, but cannot see how that *relation* itself is produced, nor that simultaneously there are produced within it the material conditions for its dissolution, which removes its *historical justification* as a *necessary form* in economic development and social wealth.' Marx, *Capital*, Vol. I, Chapter VI (unpublished); see also *La Pensée*, No. 156, 1971, p. 10.

the mode of production, and one must not neglect the fact that in this sense reproduction is always the *production* and *transformation* of use-values as well as social relations, and thus of needs.[19]

A materialist approach to social needs must thus refer them to the demands not only *required* but *produced* by the operation and reproduction of a mode of production. Only by locating the problem in this way is it possible to understand why, while the needs are always those of the reproduction of a determined mode of production, this mode of production can find itself unable to satisfy them; why, in other words, among the needs of the reproduction of a mode of production, there can come to maturity the need for its replacement by a higher economic and social order, and thus the need for its *non*-reproduction.

It is in fact the development of the internal contradictions of a mode of production, the historical ripening of the contradictory character of the demands of its reproduction, which explains that such a situation can come about. In a word: a given form of the organisation of social production reaches its historical limits when it can no longer respond to the constraints of the reproduction and development of the productive forces which have been created and grown up within it.

Any class society must reproduce both its productive forces and the social relation of exploitation which regulates their creation. This double constraint and its contradictory determinations preside over the historical development of social needs. It is thus impossible to consider the historicity of needs without referring them to the logic of the mode of production as a contradictory union between relations of production and productive forces, or to see them outside the context of the class struggle.

On precapitalist social formations

This formulation is not only true of capitalism. It is important to emphasise this point, because the illusion of the immanence of 'needs' and their historicity to bourgeois society often crops up. There is, of course, a crucial difference between capitalist accumulation, which is permanently widening the process of production and constantly transforming needs, and precapitalist forms of reproduction. The difference is between private production for value and the production assumed by a given social relation

---

[19] 'The act of reproduction itself changes not only the objective conditions – e.g. transforming village into town, the wilderness into agricultural clearings etc. – but the producers change with it, by the emergence of new qualities, by transforming and developing themselves in production, forming new powers and new conceptions, new modes of intercourse, new needs, and new speech.' Karl Marx, *Precapitalist economic formations*, trans. Jack Cohen, ed. and with introduction by E.J. Hobsbawn (Lawrence & Wishart, 1964), p. 93.

(of kinship, political etc.) whose aim is use-value, that is to say, 'the reproduction of the individual in certain definite relationships to this community',[20] and whose growth can be located in a different historical period. But to infer from this opposition a picture of precapitalist societies in which a form of production is perpetuated according to the mode of straightforward reproduction, which has no end but the satisfaction of predetermined needs – themselves outside any materialist determination – testifies to a fundamentally idealist attitude, which would at most recognise the primacy of the productive process only for the capitalist phase of social development. This attitude is far from innocent, since it leads, in the final analysis, to the identification of the logic of capital with that of socialist production, under the common designation of 'productivist systems', by arguing the persistence, under socialism, of a systematically enlarged mode of reproduction, and of market consumption. Such an approach necessarily neglects the vital difference between capitalist and socialist production, whose product might take on the value-form but which, once production is established (through democratic planning and involvement of the workers) achieves a mode of regulation which represents a radical break with the logic of capitalist accumulation.

This type of 'leftist' critique of capitalism, which can occur in many guises, and finds a not inconsiderable echo in the current crisis, reveals a form of petty bourgeois socialism which is incapable of referring the crisis to the concrete contradictions of capital, and is consequently unable to see true socialism as the practical movement towards a solution, the outcome and the way out of these contradictions; it thus finds in an idealisation of precapitalist social forms the models of the concrete social relations which socialism 'should' realise.

The challenging of bourgeois rationality, of a world taken over by the 'icy waters of egotistical calculation', does not date from 1968. As early as 1858, Marx was writing: 'thus the ancient conception, in which man always appears (in however narrowly national, religious or political a definition) as the aim of production, seems very much more exalted than the modern world, in which production is the aim of man and wealth the aim of production.' He noted in the first place that the disappearance of the limited form of *bourgeois* wealth made it possible to pursue another form of wealth, 'real wealth': the unrestricted development of the capacities and needs of the producers. We will return to this point. He also noted that the 'superiority' of the ancient world is satisfying only from a *'vulgar* and *mean'* point of view: for the man they were concerned

[20] Ibid., pp. 80–1.

with reproducing was himself a mean individual, with limited capacities and needs.[21]

Thus the greatness of bourgeois society lies in the way in which it brought about what was historically necessary for the transcendence of the limitations of precapitalist forms: by developing material and cultural wealth, it liberated – however grudgingly – the capacities and needs of producers and created the conditions of a superior economic and social order, whose aim is the production of real wealth.

The nature and extent of social needs derive in the final analysis from the state of social development: if needs are limited in primitive and peasant precapitalist societies, this is not due to some original 'natural' state which one could regain today by isolating oneself from the artificiality of modern life, but to the limited level of development and socialisation of the productive forces. These limitations do not prevent the productive forces from being involved in historical movement and revealing the inherent contradictions in the modes of production that produce them. It is in fact precisely the inability of these social formations to gain control of the emergence, rooted in the progress of their productive forces, of the contradictory needs of reproduction, that renders them historically finite.

Where the material means of production are most limited, in primitive communities without classes, the progress of productive forces takes a primarily demographic form, the normal effect of the reproduction of the process of production. The demographic order is never independent of social relations, but in these societies practices of demographic control should in principle make possible the limitation of that growth. Nevertheless, for a variety of reasons,[22] marked fluctuations in population are unavoidable. These fluctuations alter the state of needs and the way they relate to nature (the expansion of hunting territories, flocks, land clearance etc.), thus emphasising the risk of the exhaustion of resources linked to the normal functioning of a given mode of exploitation of land. The need can then arise, above a certain level of population, for a modification of this mode of exploitation and of the personal relations (of kinship, in particular) that govern it.

The demographic factor can also play a role, less noticeable and much more mediated but often decisive, in the history of the classes in precapitalist societies. The increase in the population of cities in ancient Greece and Rome thus constitutes a crucial moment in the process which changed the classical formations into slave societies, and in the end brought about their breakdown. Adherence to the community (citizen-

---

[21] Ibid., p. 84.
[22] See J.-P. Terrail, 'Population et mode de production', *La Pensée*, No. 179, 1975.

ship) is here defined by individual appropriation of land. The reproduction of the mode of production assumes the reproduction of each individual as a citizen, having access through that title to a certain area of cultivable land. Demographic growth, despite widespread restrictive practices, must thus sooner or later come up against the limits of the territory of the city. Fragmentation, emigration and colonisation, wars of conquest or defensive wars which bring back booty and labour, in turn stimulate the development of slavery, monetary exchange and mercantile capital.

One could also refer to the major population movement of the Middle Ages, which between the twelfth and fourteenth centuries profoundly changed Western Europe and contributed to setting up of the conditions for the general crisis of feudalism in the following century. This demographic growth is visible in a whole range of ecological and technological changes in the conditions of the work process, and is linked elsewhere to the evolution of the juridical status of the work force. This transformation – which makes possible the extension of serfdom and the substitution of the smaller family unit for the extended family and, as a consequence, a greater mobility of the producers – is a response by the dominant class to necessity, since the possibilities of profit from pillage were now restricted and in order to reproduce itself, it had to stimulate growth in labour productivity.[23] But the growth in population thus induced brought about new phenomena – a more extensive occupation of land, the development of communications and market circulation, urban growth, and, in the final analysis, the irrepressible development of mercantile capital – which challenged the reproduction of feudal relations.

The two historical processes described above show that the satisfaction of the needs of reproduction is the driving force for both the initial appearance and the subsequent development of new relations whose contradictory demands are increasingly difficult to contain within the limits of the existing social order. Let us return, for the sake of example, to classical society.

As we have seen, the transformation of city-states into city-empires was the result of the reproduction of the development of contradictions in classical society. Colonisation was a way of assigning territory to surplus citizens, as well as of ensuring the redistribution of resources among poor citizens who had not emigrated. It assumes the presence of a standing army, but this also represented a way of ensuring the subsistence of the least well-endowed citizens.

In the absence of noticeable increases in agricultural productivity, this process was in the long term inevitably brought up against its limits. The

[23] See G. Duby, *Guerriers et paysans* (Gallimard, 1973).

provisioning of the mother cities with food and the maintenance of the army were among the political leaders' chief priorities from an early stage, and in the course of time specific measures were needed. Thus in the fifth century BC, Athens began to favour foreign providers of wheat over her own merchants, and to control the trade in wheat scrupulously; while in Rome the same logic led to the provision of wheat for the city and the armies being progressively withdrawn from the free play of the market. These measures indicate the very real difficulties linked to the growth of both city and empire. In Rome, the imposition of a tax on the imperial territories emphasised the weight of the burden on the poorest sections of the population, particularly the small agricultural producer. The later empire saw the 'vicious circle' described by M. I. Finley: 'The army could not be enlarged beyond an adequate limit because the land could not stand further depletion of manpower; the situation on the land had deteriorated because taxes and liturgies were too high; burdens were too great chiefly because the military demands were increasing.'[24]

Roman society reached its historical limits because it could not take on the transformation of the methods, and thus of the relations of production, demanded by the reproduction of the human and material productive forces whose growth it had triggered.[25] Revolts of the oppressed (slaves, colonists, and those potential slaves, the 'barbarians') demonstrated the limits of the system, and the class struggle brought about its ruin.

Historical necessity, as we know, is only realised when men become its practical agents: the satisfaction of needs which a determined form of social production can no longer assume requires their intervention and their struggle. The way in which needs are 'taken in charge' by the class struggle nonetheless reveals profound differences according to the historical period, since until the eruption of the bourgeoisie at the heart of the social order, history does not recognise a properly and consciously revolutionary class and must await the advent of capitalism for the direct producers to be in a position to steer the social revolution. In this way, in bourgeois society the question of relations between reproduction, needs and the class struggle is posed in an entirely specific way.

Needs and the logic of capitalist development

The aim of capitalist production is the production of surplus value. The existence of a labour force on which it can draw at will makes it possible for capital to make systematic use of technical development and the

---

[24] Moses I. Finley, *The ancient economy* (Chatto & Windus, 1973), p. 176.
[25] See Charles Parain, 'De la société antique à la société féodale', *La Pensée*. No. 66, 1956.

expansion of the process of production to this end; competition and the quest for extra surplus value make this a permanent need. Indefinite accumulation is the law of capital, which would not be able to exist without constantly overturning its own material base.

However, capital does not develop its productive forces for their own sake but for profit: all development of material productive forces counts for nothing except as a means of exploitation of human productive forces, of devalorisation and reduction in skill of labour time, of the intensification and extension of labour.

The reproduction of the producers is thus subject to contradictory demands, which show the particular character of the creation of productive forces: they must in effect share in the development of the productive forces while at the same time producing surplus value, which hampers their own development. In reconstituting his labour-power in the sphere of consumption, the proletarian reproduces himself for himself, as productive individual, and as such as agent for the operation of capital: he cannot reproduce himself for himself except in reproducing himself for capital.

Capital cannot avoid developing the productive forces, but it can only develop them by hampering their own development because of its inability to satisfy the needs arising from that development. In the movement of its reproduction, capital thus produces the need of the producers to reproduce themselves not for capital, but for themselves in the logic of the development of productive forces freed from capitalist shackles. The abolition of capital, the most crucial need of the workers, thus appears to be inscribed in the very structure of its process. And by the same token, the workers' struggle for social emancipation appears, although this is not their final end, in the struggle for the reproduction of labour-power under capitalist conditions.

One can understand why the antagonism of capital and labour is never, as Engels put it, anything but the *manifestation* of the contradiction between the socialisation and development of productive forces and the maintenance of private production for profit. Whatever their immediate form, class struggles do not occur for fundamentally moral or ethical reasons, as a protest against alienation, as a confrontation between antagonistic conceptions of the world, or as the will to see the triumph of needs ideally defined: they express the contradictory demands of the process of reproduction of capitalist production.

The behaviour of the dominant class does not escape from these contradictory demands, since the immediate interests of capital impel the maximum extortion of surplus value – which implies devalorisation, over-exploitation, and the remuneration of the labour force below its value; for all that, it cannot dissociate itself from the conditions of reproduction of the source of its wealth. This situation generates contradictions within the very heart of the dominant class, which oppose the individual interest of each capitalist to those of capital as a whole, or of different fractions of capital to each other. In this latter case in particular, a question arises from the contradiction between the interests of investment capital in sectors competing for the reproduction of the labour force, and the interests of other sectors of the dominant class.

The interest of capital as a whole is that the market price of those goods which are absolutely indispensable to the reproduction of a labour force whose wages must be a proper reflection of the average, should be as low as possible. The appropriation of land, which enables agricultural production to escape the equalisation of profit taxes, and the incorporation of absolute ground-rent in the price of food products (and of agricultural raw materials), is an important obstacle to this. Thus the classic history of capitalism is marked by conflicts and compromises between land-owners and industrial capital on, for example, the question of free trade, with international trade playing a substantial role in fixing the domestic price of agricultural products.

It is not enough for capital to affect the cost of reproduction of the labour force: it must also impose *conditions* of reproduction suitable to the concrete modalities of the extortion of surplus value, thus making it possible to satisfy the demands for skill and shape the labour market by ensuring a balance of forces favourable to the employers and so on. The 'social policies' of the capitalist state play a crucial part in satisfying these demands, and it is around their determination that conflict between classes and sections of classes is played out, as in the case of housing policy, whose origins are analysed by Susanna Magri in the context of the 'housing crisis' at the end of the nineteenth and the beginning of the twentieth centuries.[26] At that time, in order to ensure its establishment in the Paris region, industrial capital had a need for pools of stabilised labour in which competition between workers would be significant. Workers in Paris had to be taken out of small-scale and craft production and put into large-scale industrial production. This required the setting up, in specific geographical areas, of housing estates which would ensure a minimal reconstitution of the labour force (health) and the family conditions for its regular renewal (housing) without at the same time being so costly as to stand in the way of the minimisation of industrial

[26] This research is worth attention; see in particular S. Magri, *Politique du logement et besoins en main-d'oeuvre* (CSU, 1972), and 'Besoins sociaux et politique du logement de l'Etat', *La Pensée*, No. 180, 1975.

wages. Now this necessary transformation of the mode of consumption, corresponding to the development of the production process, runs up against the demands made by the development of that section of capital involved in the production and circulation of housing as a commodity. It is in the specific context of that contradiction that one can site the intervention of public power, affecting both the characteristics of housing use and its exchange values – rents from 'social' housing incorporating the profits of the building industry and a proportion of the ground-rent but excluding the profit of circulation capital.

In a general way, state intervention and the setting up of 'public funds for private consumption' are shown to be historically necessary to cover what Patrice Grevet has called 'disjointed' needs which could not be covered through the wage form because they were too disparate (health needs), too difficult to break down, or too extensive (housing and education needs, for instance). [27]

However, the state is not simply an instrument in the hands of the dominant class, and it is impossible to reduce the significance of its intervention to the need to resolve the contradictions internal of that class to the common interest of capital. The contradictions between sections of capital, between those sections and capital as a whole, are always the specific effects of the primary contradiction between the development of the productive forces and relations of production: in other words, the conflicts which always appear to have as their background the antagonism between capital and labour. The whole history of capitalism bears this out: the workers never obtain the most minimal satisfaction of their demands without a bitter struggle. Thus their intervention constitutes an active element in the resolution of contradictions internal to the dominant class. In this way, the content of the social policies of the bourgeois state sanctions a given relation between the respective forces of capital and labour.

The needs expressed by the workers in their struggles are for the reproduction of their labour-power under the conditions of a given state of the production process. A critical re-examination of the reproduction and necessary development of labour-power can be conducted in terms of either the work process or the process of consumption. In the first case, struggles arise from the permanent tendency of capital to over-exploit the workers, and are aimed at the recognition of the value of labour-power (wages, skills) or at the necessity of its valorisation (professional organisation), and are opposed to its excessive abuse (length and intensity of work). Further on in the historical process, struggles concerning the mode

[27] See P. Grevet, *Besoins populaires et financement public* (Editions Sociales, 1976).

of consumption appear, and, as Magri has shown in the case of housing,[28] these involve the disparity between the conditions necessary for the reproduction of labour power in the sphere of consumption and the conditions of employment and of work imposed by capital.

These struggles constrain capital to ensure the reproduction and development of labour-power, but in so doing it is obliged to take upon itself the demands of the reproduction and development of its production process.

Marx's analysis (*Capital,* Volume 1, Sections 3 and 4) of the workers' struggles which accompanied the industrial revolution in Europe have illuminated this logic. The introduction of mechanisation made it possible for capital to break down the resistance of workers skilled in the old crafts, and to enforce the brutal submission of men, women and children to the rhythm of the machine and the 'barrack-room discipline' of large-scale industry. Capital was then 'in full flow': its appetite for overwork, its 'blind greed' were given free rein.

However, this was not without its contradictions. Since the immediate interest of each individual capitalist was to extort the maximum in overwork, capital 'had no care to the health or length of life of the worker, if not forced to it by society'. What happened in England during the nineteenth century shows 'with what speed capitalist production . . . attacks at its very roots the substance and strength of the people.'

To be sure, the rural exodus provided fresh supplies for the development of capitalist production, replacing those that had been used up. But there came a time when, because of the rapid extension of capitalist relations and the possibility of a feverish consumption of the worker's time, this source was no longer sufficient to make good the early exhaustion and wearing down of the industrial labour force: in the second third of the nineteenth century, the need to limit the working day became apparent to the English capitalist class – if not to each individual capitalist.

It is on the basis of this contradiction that the active resistance of the working class plays its part, a resistance which owes its own modality and potential to new forms of production. The submission of the worker to the machine as a 'hostile external force' represents the internalisation of industrial discipline and the concentration of the producers in large-scale production units: it is thus also a condition of the possibility of the collective organisation of workers for the defence of their class interests, and the satisfaction of their new needs.

The Factory Acts, the result of a half-century of struggle, by imposing limitations on the working day, health legislation and compulsory

---

[28]Magri, 'Besoins sociaux et politique du logement de l'Etat', *La Pensée*, pp. 102–3.

education, satisfied the minimal conditions for the reproduction of the working class. They made the development of capitalist production possible while at the same time imposing its acceleration: once extended across all sectors of production, the Factory Acts thus contributed to the rapid introduction of mechanisation, and gave impetus everywhere to the acceleration of technical developments and the intensification of labour, the conditions for the production of relative surplus value.

The gains made in the struggle to defend living and working conditions thus appear as a powerful factor in the development of the productive forces, facilitating a given form of exploitation, extending the domestic market and so on. Should one therefore infer that because they contribute to the (temporary?) resolution of the contradictions of capital, they consolidate its relations and reinforce its dominance?

These struggles make possible a revalorisation of living labour made necessary by the evolution of the work process. The satisfaction of the workers' needs in turn makes necessary, in the logic of exploitation, a renewed reinforcement of the dominance of dead labour, the setting up of new modalities for the extortion of surplus. It thus only constitutes a provisional solution which heralds, in other forms and on a larger scale, renewed manifestations of the contradiction between increasingly social-ised production and increasingly concentrated private ownership. The pursuit of accumulation involves, on the one hand, a raising of the organic composition of capital and a lowering of the profit rate, the increased waste of productive labour, and a greater overaccumulation of capital and overproduction of goods; and, on the other hand, the extension of exploitation to new social strata, who become aware that here lies the essential truth of their needs as the exploited.

The question of demands should thus be firmly sited within the contradictions of *capital*. The Factory Acts are significant in this regard. The limiting of the working day is necessary to preserve the working class, and thus to preserve capital; but for capital it represents the definitive impossibility of the production of absolute surplus value, and gives workers the renewed possibility of dedicating their free time to the satisfaction of their needs and in particular to preparing for their social emancipation.

In the same way, the declaration that primary education should be an obligatory condition of the employment of child labour was a response to the imperative demands of capital: the raising of the technical skills of the labour force was a vital necessity for 'modern industry' which 'imposes the necessity of recognising, as a fundamental law of production, variation of work' and 'compels society, under penalty of death to replace the detail-worker of today, crippled by life-long repetition of one and the same trivial operation, and thus reduced to a mere fragment of a man, by the fully developed individual, fit for a variety of labours'. But the devaluation of living labour, which is a demand of capitalist exploitation, tends at the same time to constantly reduce the great mass of workers to routine, boring, production-line work, needing no skill. On the basis of this contradictory tendency, which is inherent in the mode of capitalist production, and in the division between skilled and unskilled labour, the education of the workers takes on a contradictory character: it tends to increase the value of labour-power, and thus to reduce surplus value; it puts a brake on a reduction in skilled labour ('Ignorance is the mother of industry,' wrote Adam Smith); and by allowing the workers access to knowledge, however limited, it represents a considerable weapon in the struggle against capital: 'There is also no doubt that such revolutionary ferments, the final result of which is the abolition of the old division of labour, are diametrically opposed to the capitalistic form of production, and to the economic status of the labourer corresponding to that form.'[29]

The transformation of needs and the development of struggles for their satisfaction thus irresistibly take their place within the wider process of the reproduction of capitalist contradictions.

The ideological constitution of needs

So far we have been content to recall that social needs are, *essentially,* no more than the objective demands of the mode of production with regard to its agents.

The term 'needs' is usually reserved for the modalities of the individual's experience of these demands. Theoretical analysis, while refusing to make these modalities the site of their real movement, cannot be indifferent to the forms taken by the social and individual consciousness of needs, and the process through which they are constituted. Indeed, one of the main objects of theory is the study of the relationship of the phenomenal and real movement: in other words, the modes of the internalisation of the demands of production.

It is in this context that a specific discussion of needs, in fact, the very concept of needs, takes on its meaning. If, as has been said, the theory of needs calls on the whole corpus of the materialist theory of history, it nonetheless relates to a specific area, which other notions like 'class interests' do not exactly cover, to the extent that it demands consideration of the differentiated but articulated unity of practices determined by the

---

[29] Marx, *Capital,* Vol. II, Chapter XV, Section 9, pp. 487–8.

cycle of labour-power (production/consumption), of practical ideologies and the corresponding class struggles.

The mode of production determines certain forms of labour and the social relations of production and consumption: a body of social practices, in effect, from which spring a corresponding body of specific experiences and values, representations, and practical ideologies.

The anthropologist Marshall Sahlins provides an illustration which is particularly significant in terms of a materialist theory of needs.

Sahlins was concerned to demonstrate that the early period of hunting and gathering was not a time of anxious searching for daily subsistence but, paradoxically, the time of 'the first affluent society'. Such hunter and gatherer societies as survive, pushed back by colonisation to the most inhospitable areas, in fact devote only a small proportion of their potential labour time to obtaining foodstuffs (less than 50 per cent among the Australian aborigines or the Kalahari Bushmen; research into other communities of the same type, from Labrador to the Tierra del Fuego, confirms these results). What is more, a proportion of the effective labour time is spent on the acquisition, over and above what is necessary, of 'superfluous' foodstuffs particularly liked by the hunters. There is equally 'a sort of material affluence' in the sphere of non-alimentary goods due, according to Sahlins, to the abundance of raw materials, to the simplicity of manufacturing procedures, and to the communal ownership of tools and techniques.[30]

This abundance of foodstuffs and other goods is, of course, relative: it is linked to the limited nature of needs, to a particular mode of consumption, a mode which is itself part of a specific mode of social production. The hunting and gathering economy is stringently tied to the law of diminishing returns, and only the mobility of the communities enables them to escape its effects. The notorious 'prodigality' and 'lack of foresight' of the hunters is related to an imperative logic: the build-up of foodstores, which is incidentally much less profitable than the exploitation of new territory, would soon exhaust the resources of the area. The necessary mobility in turn imposes a severe limit of the quantity of goods that can be transported, and assumes that permanent goods and tools be kept to a minimum. This imperative is translated into the low value placed on material possessions whose social use does not correspond to the immediate reproduction needs of the producers.

The phenomenon of the internalisation of the imperatives of social life, which sees the demands of production as personal needs, is what interests us here. Marshall Sahlins rightly criticises the ethnocentrism of observers

[30] See Marshall Sahlins, *Stone Age Economics* (Tavistock Publications, 1974).

who interpret the low value placed on material goods – the acquisition of which nonetheles demands a real expenditure of energy – in terms of deprivation, negligence, lack of foresight, and the absence of a sense of ownership (one of them declared himself 'horrified at the indifference of these people'). 'It is wrong,' Sahlins claims, 'to say that in these peoples needs are *reduced,* that desires are *repressed,* or even that the notion of wealth is *limited.*' That attitude expresses a misunderstanding of the fact that needs are neither 'naturally limitless' nor simply a product of the perception of new goods and wealth; rather, they are the result of a process of internalisation of the needs of production.[31]

As Edmond Preteceille has suggested, the experience of a need thus appears as 'the subjective form of the objective determination of the social practices which structure the reproduction of the labour force.'[32] Under the conditions of capitalist society, characterised by the differentiation of social structures and class antagonism, the speed of historical changes, and the relative autonomisation of the sphere of consumption – which becomes a 'private matter' – the analysis of the ideological make-up of needs become a much more complex undertaking. It must take particular account of the effects of production practices on the forms of the consciousness of needs and on consumption practices; the effects of consumption practices on the forms of the consciousness of needs; and the effect of class struggles on both production and consumption practices, and the corresponding representations. Whether or not they principally take the form of political or ideological claims, social struggles are an essential factor in demonstrating the distortions between class situation and actual practice on the one hand, and the dominant ideology on the other – in a word, the objective demands of the mode of production.

Exploited labour, class struggles and needs

In the spheres of circulation and consumption, whose semblance has been represented by bourgeois ideology as an ultimate truth, wage-earners and employers appear as equally free and juridically equal subjects, exchanging equal value for equal value. But in the process of production, unequal exchange and a relationship of exploitation prevail. There the labour force

---

[31] Ethnographic studies show, in a manner which is highly significant in this context, that hunters and gatherers show an absence of desire, a total lack of interest, in objects which colonisation has brought within their reach but ownership of which would run counter to the demands of their mode of production. See Sahlins, *Stone Age Economics.*

[32] Edmond Preteceille, 'Besoins sociaux et socialisation de la consommation', *La pensée,* No. 180, 1975.

has value only as an exploitable object, while remaining at the same time the active element, the real subject.

This twofold contradiction characterises the practice and consciousness of the workers. The most complete dominion of the dominant ideology would not be able to remove exploitation: the permanence of the proletarian 'class instinct', even in its most dominated forms bears witness to these limits. (Did not the Luddites express a fetishism which identified capital and 'things'?) Similarly, the most confused consciousness of exploitation, the most elementary resistance to its effects, manifest in some or other demand for the valorisation of living labour, carry, perhaps without the workers themselves being aware of it, the demand for a different mode of development of the productive forces.

Nevertheless, it is a considerable step from class instinct to class consciousness, from spontaneous revolt to a struggle for the revolutionary transformation of society. Along that road, the reproduction of the production process, the formation and transformation of the workers through their participation in the setting up and development of the productive forces, and the experience of different aspects of exploitation, all play an essential part. It would be impossible to understand the transformation in women's consciousness in France today, or the way in which questions posed by the condition of women have come to a head, without taking into account the changes in the work women do (over the last hundred years, there has not been much change in the employment of women as a proportion of the total working population, but their rate of pay has gone up considerably); the demands on the development of women's personalities which these changes imply; and the significant degree of socialisation involved in their participation in the setting up of modern productive forces.

Thus work appears to be both an essential element in the formation and transformation of objective needs, as well as the indispensable pragmatic mediator of a conscious awareness of these needs.

However, as Jean-Louis Moynot has emphasised, one and the same class situation, one and the same aspect of exploited labour, would be lived differently by different individuals, according to the specific details of their own particular biographies, which are the product of a specific combination of social determinants.[33] The diversity of individual experiences tends to be broken down through the reproduction of the production process, which gives all workers the same class experience, but also tends to be reproduced through its development, which continually

[33] Jean-Louis Moynot, 'Determinations sociales et individuelles des besoins', *La Pensée*, No. 180, 1975.

adds new social strata to the working class (peasants and urbanised lower middle classes, immigrant workers, women etc.). Equally, the employers make use of these objective factors of differentiation (social and cultural background, nationality, skills, sex, age etc.) in their policy of dividing the workers, in their recruitment policies, in their use of technological progress and so forth.

One can thus see the crucial role of unifying class consciousness, which has fallen to class organisations and which they pursue by *indicating the objective content of needs* common to all workers, placing practical and theoretical class experience within the reach of each of its members, whatever their individual experience might be.

Class confrontations constitute a special moment in the process of developing a consciousness of the real social content of needs. It is therefore impossible to conceive of their relation in the form of a straightforward linear schema: need-struggle-satisfaction of need. Firstly, because they allow the integration of new needs into the social definition of the value of labour-power; class confrontations thus contribute, directly and indirectly, to the development of productive forces and their transformation, preparing the way for the subsequent appearance of new needs. Secondly, the role of class confrontations in the process of the internalisation of production needs sets up these (in a class society, contradictory) needs as the needs of the agents of production.

The formulation of demands by class organisations cannot *create* needs, but it plays an active and decisive role in making consciousness of their objective content possible, and giving workers access to a theoretical understanding of their class situation.

The objective demands of production do not necessarily find an exact expression in the forms of social consciousness: the fundamental need of the wage-earner to suppress capitalist exploitation can thus be experienced, at the most basic level of class consciousness, as simple exhaustion, as the need for rest linked to the constraints of exploited labour. It is in terms of the state of the class struggle, and class experience, that a given dimension of exploitation will find its expression as a demand: either as spontaneous revolt (machine breaking, slowing down work rates etc.), reformist demand, or revolutionary demand. This last alone derives not from an empirical apprehension of the effects of exploitation, but from a scientific analysis of its causes. By seeing demands as so many objective necessities of the mode of production, revolutionary theory also makes it possible to demonstrate the objective possibility of their satisfaction, provided that the workers mobilise. It is by establishing that today the sole responsibility for the logic of exploitation lies with the crisis of capitalism, and thus showing that the satisfaction of needs constitutes a necessary condition of its resolution, which is consequently and all the more emphatically possible, that the organisations of the class struggle – whether unions or political organisations – can, while setting higher objectives of struggle, help the workers resist the blackmail of big capital and wrench them out of resignation.

Capital, of course, does not remain inactive, and constantly seeks to influence the individual perception of needs: first of all by presenting the existing forms of exploitation as the objective necessities of 'the economy', to hinder the emergence of that perception; and, if this fails, by giving it a reformist expression and orienting it towards a mode of satisfaction that can be integrated into the logic of exploitation, implying a modification of its forms rather than of its degree. Thus the 'quality of life' makes austerity palatable, 'anti-hierarchical' measures allow the rate of profit to be maintained, and 'participation' diverts the perception of the need for democratic management and so on.

The intervention of class organisations – various associations and movements, unions, parties, the state, the practice of the ideologists of the confronting classes – thus contributes actively to the setting up of new 'systems of needs', and not simply to the clarification of existing needs. However, one cannot simply reduce relations of production to more relations of power, and, in the final analysis, to an ideological relation. In whatever form they are represented, needs always refer back to the necessities inherent in the production process. Class organisations cannot formulate slogans at random, and their effectiveness depends on their ability to grasp both the objective moment and the spontaneous expression of needs and class interests.

Besides, history shows that it is always on the basis of immediate forms of exploitation, and especially over-exploitation – on the basis of obstacles opposing the reproduction of labour *as such*, and thus of the contradictions of capital itself – that class struggles arise and that class organisations can play their part to greatest effect.

The state today plays a particularly important part in defining the general conditions of exploitation, as well as in defining and establishing the conditions of reproduction of labour-power: experience helps to develop the capacity of the dominant class to define its own interests and common needs (however much they may be stamped, as we have shown, with the contradictions inherent in that class) in terms of consumption and of reproduction of labour-power. The development of the economic role of the state, the diversification and the growing precision of its intervention are accompanied by the development of the struggles engaging the content of its 'social' policies and a modification of their context.

Relations of production and relations of consumption

First of all, in considering social needs, the objective constraints of the reproduction of labour-power preclude (in contrast to non-Marxist economics and sociology) the autonomisation of the spheres of production and consumption. The conditions of the use of labour-power define certain demands concerning its reproduction outside work: the evolution of the process of production, as we have suggested in relation to the question of housing, is necessarily accompanied by transformations in the process of consumption. These transformations in turn play a specific and active part in the formation of new needs. The concrete forms and social conditions of labour, the practices of consumption, and the lack of correlation between the one and the other, are thus the fundamental elements that constitute the historically determined configurations of social needs.

We will give a more precise account in later chapters of the evolution of the practices and needs of consumption, and the types of social struggle in this sphere. At this point we will simply make a few general remarks.

The characteristics and demands of the process of capitalist production have changed a good deal over the last century. Precapitalist forms of production and, by the same token, precapitalist forms of consumption have considerably contracted. Capitalist market relations have imposed themselves increasingly at all levels of production and the transformation of use-value, taking the place of both small-scale market production and personal work: the traditional domestic activities (cooking, making and mending clothing, even the socialisation of children) tend more and more to fall outside the province of the family. This development favours female labour, which in turn spurs it on; the forms of family life are in consequence profoundly altered. The concentration of industrial production assumes a massive urbanisation of the population, with the labour force having at its disposal adequate housing, public or private transport, and so forth. The raising of the average qualifications required of the labour force, combined with the disappearance of individual means of transmitting knowledge, implies a generalisation and extension of state education. The modification of forms of industrial labour, the increase in the rate of work, the greater mobility of the work force and the deterioration of the urban environment links the reproduction of the labour force with new forms of rest, leisure, sanitation measures and so on.

This whole *way of life,* this complex of needs and related practices of consumption, is continually modified by the development of capitalist production.[34] One cannot object too strongly to the assumptions implicit in non-Marxist analyses which, from Condillac to Baudrillard, have postulated the possibility of dealing directly with consumption practices without analysing class situation and relations with the sphere of production. The true difficulty of a scientific approach is that of considering *the specificity of the modes of consumption in their dependence on the concrete modes of production,* as so many specific moments in the whole process of social production.

A few remarks will suffice to show that this specificity is an essential feature of consumption relations. Firstly, consumption practices are linked to forms of sociality: family relations, neighbourhood relations and so on, which are in the final analysis determined by the mode of production, but which translate its demands in specific ways and evolve in a different social time.

Secondly, these practices are implicit in cultural and symbolic relations and traditions, whose links with the forms of production are also more or less strongly mediated. For example, merely to note the slow rate of change in French eating habits over the centuries is to be made aware of the hold of national traditions in this area.[35] In another instance the extent to which consumption can be seen as a cultural product has been shown, particularly by Pierre Bourdieu and his team, to be decisively related to the length of schooling which, as we know, occupies an ambiguous position in relations of production.[36] In addition, as we have shown in the previous chapter, differentialist sociologists have been able to distinguish the existence of an unconscious symbolic logic by which class differences are manifested in consumption behaviour. A logic to which one could certainly not reduce, as Patrice Grevet has suggested,[37] all behaviour arising from the collective unconscious: the study of the development of new social mythologies (fear of progress, the return to nature, obscurantist superstition etc.) and of the behaviour related to them in the face of the deepening crisis would doubtless provide some excellent illustrations.

[34] This way of approaching needs makes it possible to avoid the old argument between 'relative' and 'absolute' pauperisation. In fact, that argument posed the problem of capitalist exploitation in a very general way and, in the final analysis, provided little insight into its concrete mechanisms, e.g. in terms of the degree to which the workers' needs were really satisfied or not, because it overlooked *the development of the content and form of needs* which accompanied and reflected the development of the process of capitalist production. (These remarks are not, of course, intended to question the importance of the concept of pauperisation itself, only the way in which the problem has been tackled.)

[35] See in particular 'Histoire de la consommation du XIVe au XIXe siecle', *Annales ESC,* Nos. 2–3, 1975.

[36] See for instance P. Bourdieu and A. Darbel, *L'Amour de l'art* (Editions de minuit, 1966).

[37] Patrice Grevet, 'Le moment objectif et la moment subjectif des besoins', *La Pensée,* No. 180, 1975.

Thirdly, the different moments in the process of the reproduction of the labour force are interdependent. The modification of one of these moments, in response to the demands of production, will necessarily have repercussions at other levels of the consumption process (see below, chapter III).

Finally, the direct (as well as the mediated) determination of consumption practices by the demands of the production process does not make these into class practices *stricto sensu*. Francis Godard has put forward four main modalities for this determination: the place in the work process regulating the forms of use and recuperation of labour-power; the place in the social relations of distribution regulating the form and extent of return on capital; spatio-temporal restraints on the consumption process (types of products and services available, possible forms of their appropriation etc.); the demands of the development and maintenance of skill in the worker and his family, which regulate not only access to professional knowledge but also to the cultural environment, leisure and so on.[38] Now it is obvious that individuals identically situated in the production process, and thus belonging to the same social class, might well experience different combinations of these four types of determinants; whereas, conversely, individuals belonging to different social classes will, either because they are members of the same family, share in the same national culture or have at their disposal the same individual or collective means of consumption, participate at least to some extent in the same consumption practices.

It is thus impossible to draw a mechanical correlation between consumption relations and production relations.[39] But it is still necessary to show how class situation and the relations the classes maintain within production are present in the very specificity of these consumption practices; for it is only on the basis of a materialist analysis that this specificity can be accorded its proper place and full significance.

Michel Verret has noted of Richard Hoggart's work on the cultural practices of the English working class:

> An awareness of the culture implicit in the workers' production practices
> can in effect give a much better and fuller picture than the culture of
> consumption of the specificity and autonomy of working-class culture.

[38] Francis Godard, 'Classes sociales et modes de consommation', *La Pensée*, No. 180, 1975.
[39] Especially since that approach would make it impossible to assess the real effect of specific differences in consumption relations on production practices. This is demonstrated, for instance, in the case of employers' strategies in relation to the labour market which rely on the insertion of workers of a similar productive capacity into different consumption processes (immigrant workers, women, peasant workers, etc.).

Though this must be, it is true, at the price of a total redefinition, since it would lead not only to the inclusion in this culture of the cultural characteristics involved in technological practice and in the practice of the economic, political and ideological class struggle, but also to seeking out in these practices the organising principles of working class culture, right up to and including the culture of consumption belonging to it. [40]

An examination of the modalities of the insertion of the working class into the process of production reveals that categories are engendered there, perhaps in a more fundamental way than in the practices of family and neighbourhood, and take on a quite different dimension when, as Richard Hoggart thinks possible, one deals directly with practices outside production. The aspects of working-class culture which derive from its production practice, as Michel Verret has shown, illuminate cultural practice outside the sphere of production as well as the relations of the working class with other classes and their specific cultures or subcultures.

We may recall the major types of determinants referred to above; these are related to the *class situation,* which regulates consumption behaviour, and show how the logic of exploitation and thus class relations and *class position* are present at all times, whether directly (in the nature and form of the objects of consumption, in state intervention in the organisation of exploitation outside the sphere of production), or in the form of the resistance and struggles of the dominated classes.

It is inevitable that capital, at each stage of its development, should seek to intervene in the structures of reproduction of the labour force, so as to exert pressure on the contradictions that arise between on the one hand a determined way of life, its constraints, the types of personality and representations that correspond to it and, on the other hand, the development of the requirements of the mode of production. The bourgeoisie, as Gramsci remarked, has been led historically to exert considerable coercive pressure in order to mould the labour force 'to the habits of order, exactitude and precision which make possible the increasingly complex forms of collective life, the necessary consequences of the development of industrialisation'. [41] Gramsci notes the importance, in this context, of an analysis of 'Fordism' in the United States, 'the biggest collective effort to date to create, with unprecedented speed, and with a consciousness of purpose unmatched in history, a new type of worker and of man': such an effort bearing startling witness to the manner

[40] Michel Verret, 'Sur la culture ouvrière', *La Pensée,* No. 163, 1972; Richard Hoggart, *The Uses of Literacy* (Chatto & Windus, 1957).
[41] A. Gramsci, *Selections from the Prison Notebooks.* ed. and trans. Quintin Hoare and Geoffrey Nowell Smith (Lawrence & Wishart, 1971).

in which the new forms of labour and of exploitation (in this case, Taylorism) 'are inseparable from a specific mode of life, a specific way of thinking and feeling'. As well as to a remarkable awareness on the part of the employers of the impossibility 'of achieving success in one sphere without having tangible results in the other'.[42] The prohibition of alcohol, sexual repression and the Puritan ideology appear here as so many aspects of 'the exercise of coercion over the working masses in order to make them conform to the needs of the new industry'.[43] In this way, the public means (Prohibition) and the private ones (see Ford's attempts, described by Gramsci, to 'intervene, through a corps of inspectors, in the private lives of his employees, and to control the way in which they lived and spent their wages'), combine together to bring about the necessary development in the modes of life and of consumption.

This struggle by capital against the workers in the sphere of consumption is, however, not carried on without a certain amount of resistance, nor without giving rise to fresh contradictions. Its first obstacle is the natural inertia of cultural traditions and of the complex forms of family environmental/communal habits of seeing and feeling. It has to exert pressure in a coordinated and simultaneous manner on all levels of the material, social and ideological conditions of the reproduction of the workers. This need for an organised management of the social reproduction of the labour force cannot easily be attained in an environment dominated by the logic of private production and the anarchy of competition. A high level of socialisation of the productive forces, through a considerable growth in the complexity of the variables which have to be taken into consideration (internal differentiation of the social labour force, diversification of the market for consumer goods and socialisation of consumption, the management of urbanisation, of transport, of leisure etc.) and of their inter-relationships, renders the whole question yet more delicate.

Even more fundamental, perhaps, is the strategic ideological role of 'private' consumption, which has to be tackled in any attempt to intervene directly in this sphere. For capital cannot at one and the same time present free market consumption as being the very essence of freedom itself, promoting it as the symbol of advanced liberalism, and openly manifest its totalitarian desires in this domain. This is a crucial point if it is in fact the case, as seems more than likely, that such freedom as exists, however limited it may be, in the sphere of consumption, and makes it the site where the exploited worker finally recovers himself as

---

[42] Ibid., p. 302.
[43] Ibid.

sovereign subject and can act as the boss's equal, is a significant factor in the adherence, even if only a passive adherence, of a good many wage-earners to bourgeois society, and for their resistance to the notion of a socialist transformation. It is not just a piece of superficial window-dressing as far as the dominant class is concerned: in this sphere it is more profitable for it to operate by ideological moulding than by authoritarian-ism and open coercion.[44]

This point of view is given added weight from another direction by the private character of commodity consumption, which tends to fragment the workers. Among other studies, the work by Hoggart mentioned earlier shows this clearly: certain practices outside production particularly favour the hold of bourgeois culture and ideology, and here working-class culture shows itself to be more permeable and less robust than in other areas. Consumption is certainly not an innocent affair: through the forms it takes and through advertising – and it is prepared to use certain ideological categories and schemes belonging to the dominated classes to this end – capital imposes practices (and the values implicit in them) which reinforce its ideological and practical dominance; the objects of consumption can be seen as representing so many ideological messages, which have underlying them as many constraints leading to competitive individualism, to the depoliticisation, fragmentation and opposition of the dominated classes.

That consumer goods, as differentialist sociologists maintain, function here as 'signs', that their symbolism in its turn governs consumer practices, and that capital makes use of this symbolism to commercial and political ends, is not in doubt. Nevertheless, this play of signs and their manipulation occurs only within very well-defined limits, set by the constraints and demands of the reproduction of the labour force. To miss perceiving these limits, in the misty vision of a dominant class with total control over the code of symbolism of these objects, would mean that through the screening of the internal contradictions of capital, the real basis for the possible development of struggles in the sphere of consump-tion were not perceived.

It is only in this area, as we have seen, that the producer can realise himself and identify himself as subject within the practice as well as the ideology of the bourgeois society. By making use of this state of affairs, though the 'differentialists' maintain a certain silence on this point, the

---

[44] The crucial factor is respect for the *formal* freedom of consumption practices, which would be expressed through the spread of available products, the differentiation (economic, geographical, cultural etc.) of markets, and so on; that is, through modalities imposed by the employers and, above all, by the state's 'social' policies for the reproduction of labour-power.

manipulation of the logic of signs tends also to reinforce it, as well as reinforcing the implicit masking of the dispossession of the subject in the sphere of production. Even at this level, however, contradictions appear: the frustration of desire in consumption cannot but lead back, through its bearing on the market value of the labour force, to the realities of exploitation.

If the glitter of the sign cannot hide the harsh realities of credit payment for long, its effectiveness is further undermined, at a second level, by the equally imperative constraints of use-value. Denis Duclos has demonstrated this with regard to suburban consumption in a new town in the Paris region. The manipulation of signs, in relation to a subject that suits it particularly well, is shown to be very effective in analysing the level of house sales; but consumption of the object itself, the *use* of the suburban environment, reveals a whole series of contradictions (beginning with the limits imposed on this use by the characteristics of the whole cycle of the labour force: distance from the place of work and collective organisation, duration of work, problems of transportation and so forth) which end by calling into question the effectiveness of the sign – and the outlines of the famous 'suburban ideology' – while building up the basis for a series of struggles making new demands of the conditions of consumption.[45]

In the long run, consumption practices cannot avoid, and will in fact be less and less able to avoid, the class confrontations which owe their meaning and bearing to the logic of relations of production. Even if, due to specific differences in practice, the conflicts provoked here are more spontaneously open to reformism than others, the progress made by working-class organisations and the influence of the working-class outlook will finally show themselves in this area too, so that it will become both the site and the goal of overt struggles for the achievement of class hegemony. Whether they occur within local, municipal or cultural organisations, or are centred on the school or the family, these struggles end by imposing daily practices and forms of consumption which break away from the dominant culture and are the bearers of new values.

---

[45] See Denis Duclos, *Pavillonaires d'une ville nouvelle* (CSU, 1975). One should note that according to the 'differentialists', the effectiveness of the 'code' lies in the significatory possibilities of the effective use of the objects. But it would be a highly abstract approach to reduce this use to the *exhibition* of the objects. For it is precisely in actual practice that the effectiveness of the code or the hold of the 'cultural models', as evidenced by the *projection* of use, finds its limitations. And it is also precisely these unavoidable 'returns to reality' which force the imaginary constructs of consumption to a perpetual renewal. Nonetheless, an awareness of these contradictions between sign/value and use/value assumes that an analysis of consumption does not disguise the wealth of determinants which insertion into the complex cycle of the reproduction of the labour force confers on the concrete appropriation of the object consumed.

Finally, and by no means unimportantly, they may constitute a privileged moment for the concretisation of certain class alliances (especially with the non-wage-earning strata), a point we shall return to in later chapters.

Thus it is easy to understand why, however interesting one may find the ideas of culturalist or differentialist sociologists who declare themselves to be dealing exclusively and directly with daily practice outside the sphere of production, the values invested in it and their symbolic logic, these propositions will never cover the whole reality. If it is true, as for instance Pierre Bourdieu suggests, that the make-up of the 'class ethos' is far from being unaffected by the 'social trajectory' of the class in question, how could one maintain a coherent argument of the consumer practices of the middle classes without looking precisely at the evolution of production relations, without posing the question of the effects of wage-payments and the possible proletarianisation of these social strata, their contradictory openness to both capital and revolutionary values, the alliances which might make them tend more in the direction of capital than of the working class, and so on? If there is a cultural or symbolic specificity in consumption relations, as suggested by certain sociologists, a complete understanding of it must include a recognition of the primacy of relations of production.

Individual consciousnes of needs

Consumption, whose class determinations (under a number of different forms) are revealed by theoretical analysis, is largely reduced in bourgeois society to individual practices which appear to have as their principle of differentiation nothing more than particular individuals and their different desires.

While substituting the collective worker for the individual in the production process, creating greater and greater *socialisation* of the productive forces, the capitalist mode of production makes consumption into a 'private affair' (within certain limits, as we have seen), the concern of individuals and of households, isolated units for the reproduction of the labour force.

One might suggest that its development is accompanied by a certain homogenisation of individual modes of consumption, linked with that of class situation (extension of wage-labour), of disposable goods (development of large-scale mass production, standardisation of the national market, concentration of the means of distribution) and with the relative development of collective organisations. However, this trend tends to reveal the social character of consumption as much as it disguises class determination under the misleading notion of 'mass consumption'. Nevertheless it leads to a distinction being drawn between the social practices of consumption (involving units larger than the household due to their place in social (municipal, state) organisations of consumption) and individual consumption practices; and equally to a distinction between the practical social ideologies of consumption drawn from these socialised practices and carried through in the corresponding organisations, and the individual forms of the consciousness of needs.[46]

Individual consumer practices within the restricted framework of the family unit nonetheless remain largely dominant, and even include the form of 'mass' consumption. It is to this phenomenal reality of consumption that psychosociologists refer when, in the name of a pseudo-democracy, they claim to be able to ascertain needs through public opinion polls; and in consequence set themselves up as holding the individual forms of the consciousness of needs and the sole repositories of the essential truth of needs.

However, such enquiries are by no means uninteresting since, unusually in this field, scientific concerns have not here become overlaid by commercial or politico-ideological demands. The results of these enquiries constitute an index of to many real problems, pose a number of questions for the researcher and represent, for class political practice, a range of indications of the level of consciousness of the masses. But they must be taken for what they are: data to be processed, questions to be subjected to theoretical investigation, and not a definition of the ultimate reality of social needs. To take a very basic example, no survey can bring out the individual need for a balanced development of social production, although this demand affects the daily life of every member of society.

It must be re-emphasised that only class organisations, which have at their disposal the experience of a class, the experiences of the whole class, and a suitable theoretical apparatus, are in a position to formulate, in the shape of union demands or of aims in the political struggle, the objective demands of the process of social production and the process of reproduction of the labour force. Thus in the final analysis one can distinguish between three levels of the consciousness of needs and their complex interrelationship: the class consciousness of social needs, based on the practice of class organisations; the practical social ideologies of consumption; and the individual consciousness of needs.

Though this last cannot be a point of departure, the fact to be explained, it nevertheless should be explained by the materialist approach

---

[46] This is a distinction previously put forward by Preteceille in 'Besoins sociaux . . .', *La Pensée*, 1975.

and not left to the arbitrary mercies of the infinite contingencies of the empirical. To abandon this field to abstract psychology and psychosociological empiricism would amount to a *de facto* recognition of their theoretical legitimacy, and would finally leave the way open to the Trojan horse of essentialist humanism embodied in the opposition between society and individual. The materialist assertion of the fundamental sociality of the individual cannot be translated into a denial of the effective diversification of individual forms of consciousness of needs, but instead results in an approach to the individual as the specification of a variety of social determinants.

The individual consciousness of needs has its roots in the combination of a production practice and a consumption practice, and is built up on the basis of an individual biography through contradictory demands and social relations. There is no question, in any attempt to recover the concrete in all this wealth of determinants, of abandoning the solid ground of an analysis of the demands of the mode of production with regard to its agents; on the contrary, the concern is to develop this analysis so as to take account of the way in which the multiple social determinants fit together to make up the individual consciousness.[47]

We have described the diversity of the variables capable of intervening in the progress of consciousness of the class situation, in the awareness of a production as much as of a consumption practice. The variety of concrete biographies and individual experiences is linked to the development of the social and technical division of labour, to the extent of social mobility and the complexity of social trajectories. The experience of a common work situation and the intervention of class organisations tend to reduce the gap between individual life experience and class consciousness – without this implying a move towards the lowest common denominator, but rather the possibility available to each person to 'lift his eyes beyond the horizon of the single self to the horizon of all'. Class consciousness, in turn, is enriched by the multiplicity of individual experiences which nourish it and play an important role in promoting its development: consider, for instance, the widening of the experience of the French working class represented by its awareness of the problems posed by the growth of multinational immigrant labour or the increase in female paid labour, or, yet again, the growing participation in the revolutionary struggles of the intellectual social strata whose most advanced fraction has joined its class organisations.

---

[47] It is obvious – though we are doing no more here than *indicating* an important, even crucial field of inquiry – that an understanding of the way a concrete individuality and its particular needs structure themselves through a body of social determinants must include a consideration of psychological and psychoanalytic research.

Consumption practices play an active part in the process of differentiat-
ing individual forms of the consciousness of needs, even if only through
unification within the same concrete units of consumption (households) of
the reproduction of labour power that occupy different positions in the
division of labour, and thus set up tension between different class
practices and cultural traditions.

The domain of 'cultural' practices and needs constitutes a privileged
locus for individual differentiations. It is all the more necessary here to
beware of the pitfalls inherent in the opposition of the individual and
society, which can appear in the form of a distinction between economic
needs, seen as class needs determined by position in the sphere of
production, and cultural needs, which take on the arbitrary form of
individual 'preferences' and 'opinions'. On the one hand, sociological
studies (we have already referred to the work of Pierre Bourdieu) have been
able to distinguish the class nature of the unwritten rules which to a great
extent govern cultural consumption behaviour. But we have also
suggested that it is necessary to go further and to attempt a more precise
conception of the unity of production and consumption practices, a unity
in which cultural practices also share. This, we repeat, is an important
field for scientific research, so long as one avoids the reductionist,
narrowly concept of the demands of the reproduction of labour-power.[48]
There can be no *material* appropriation of the world without objective
knowledge, specific demands, and a particular understanding on the one
hand, without determined modes of sociality on the other: without,
therefore, a *cultural* appropriation of the world. 'Culture' is the essential
modality of the relationship of men to nature and society, at one and the
same time a dimension of all social practice and the domain of specific
practices. It would be absurd to separate and oppose the material and
cultural needs of the reproduction of labour-power. Such a separation
could only be the ideological effect of the strictly utilitarian practice of
capital and its natural tendency to devalue living labour and hamper its
development, and thus to reduce 'culture' for the masses to a 'supplement
for the soul', a mere diversion with an insignificant cultural (not to
mention ideological) content. Undoubtedly, certain cultural needs that
correspond objectively to the development of living labour may be
misunderstood for longer than others without calling into question a
certain reproduction of labour-power; and no doubt an awareness of their
reality assumes, such as the *animateurs* of popular culture for instance

---

[48] This attitude marks the arguments of, for example, Baudelot, Establet, and Malemort, *La petite
bourgeoisie en France* (Maspéro, 1974): enquiring into the nature of the needs that define the values of a
more or less skilled labour force, they hold the unequal duration of schooling to be the only objective
criterion of differentiation.

experience it, highly complex modalities of practical learning. Finally, although it is objective, the determination of these needs by the development of the mode of production leaves room for a good deal of scope – which is precisely the basis for individual differentiation. These factors combine to make the reality of capitalist exploitation less visible in this domain, but also make its weight especially onerous here. However, that is no reason for concluding that needs which are at particular risk today are not objective in character, that they are not *socially* contradictory, for this would be to acquiesce in the mutilated development of the individual under a capitalist regime.

The limits imposed by the logic of exploitation on the development of such human potential as does not immediately appear to be linked to the appropriation of short-term profit and on the satisfaction of the corresponding needs which, *nolens, volens,* appear alongside the development of the productive forces, carry a twofold consequence. First of all, they hamper economic and social development, laying down obstacles which are all the more weighty in proportion to the degree of development and the complexity and socialisation of the productive forces involved. Whereas historical development elsewhere is accompanied, as Marx suggested in several places, by a growing individualisation of the members of society, and thus by a growing differentiation of the forms of an individual consciousness of needs, the limits set by the logic of capital act more and more as a brake on this process. They constantly bring back to their lowest common denominator the possibilities open to the great mass of individuals for access to the social heritage, to both the material and the cultural wealth whose creation and accumulation has been historically permitted by the capitalist system. The denial to individuals and groups of a 'right to difference' thus appears integral to the bourgeois order. The impulse which is now being felt, in however confused a way, to resist the reduction of individuals to the exploitable dimension of their labour-power testifies to the increasing difficulty of controlling the access of members of the dominated classes to this heritage, to cultural and scientific knowledge in excess of the strict demands of the reproduction of labour-power. The appearance of these new needs, individually diversified, though still limited and deeply imbued with the dominant ideology, is nonetheless if not ahead of their time, at least ahead of the state of social relations, an advance sign of the revolutionary thrust of the productive forces. This is an almost untouched field for materialist research.

It is clear in any case that from this point of view the social homogenisation assured in a socialist society by the removal of capitalist hindrances to the development of living labour and thus the full development of the physical and intellectual capacities of each individual, far from leading to standardisation and uniformity, provides the opportunity for the mass of individuals to escape the cultural poverty and dreariness of daily life in bourgeois society, through a many-facetted development of their personalities and a significant differentiation of their capacities and individual needs. Such a differentiation is in the first place an effect of the new mode of applying productive forces and the consequent changes in the division of labour.

This leads to the systematic modernisation of the productive apparatus, a general improvement in the skill of the workers, and a questioning of the separation between manual and intellectual work. On this basis, particular fields of knowledge and the specialisation of social activities, and thus of individual practice, can develop. The building of socialism thus leads, simultaneously and without contradiction, to a diminution and development of the social division of labour. In any case, the diversification of individual concrete biographies and particular needs is its inevitable consequence. And, it becomes clear, it is also its major condition.

FROM STATE MONOPOLY CAPITALISM TO SOCIALISM

When Plekhanov, in the draft of a programme for a Russian Social Democratic Party, defined socialism as 'the planned organisation of the social process of production for the satisfaction of the needs of society as a whole and of each of its members in particular', Lenin replied, in 1902, 'This is not enough. The Trusts could come up with an organisation like that.' He thus forcibly underlined the crux of the materialist and historical concept of needs: the social formation to come cannot be defined simply in terms of the satisfaction of present needs, since these derive from the economic and social conditions of today; socialism, besides satisfying the needs born of and within capitalism, changes them and creates new needs, and so on. It would be more exact to say, added Lenin, that the aim of the social revolution is 'to ensure the *complete* welfare and the free and *total* fulfilment of all members of society'. This clearly assumes the satisfaction of needs other than those of today.

The notion of a possible temporary capacity in capital to respond to needs relates first of all to the fact that these needs are fundamentally those of the reproduction of labour-power, and thus those of capital itself. If capital is not to founder, it must somehow, through its trusts, through the state organisation, afford them at least a minimal satisfaction. In this sense, the only need of the workers which capital could not meet would be their need to no longer reproduce themselves for capital. But this presupposes the perception of that need, and is another dimension of the question Lenin raised: the capacity of capital to limit the workers' consciousness of the objective content of their needs,[49] and in particular of the most crucial of all, the need for the abolition of exploitation.

Paradoxically, it is necessary to understand that the needs arising *within* capitalism are those *of* capitalism, and that capital therefore *could* satisfy them, in order to understand why, having reached a certain stage in its development, capital finds their satisfaction more and more difficult.

So let us abandon the abstract and the conditional. Organised resistance by the workers has in fact always been an active condition of the satisfaction of their most minimal needs. Their intervention may remove for a while the barrier represented by that concrete form of exploitation. The gains won in the struggle can never be definitive, at least until the social revolution, since they themselves constitute the basis on which new forms of exploitation will be constructed.

Thus, in the economic crisis of the 1930s which affected all developed capitalist societies, it was the new forms of state intervention, which arose through a wide variety of social struggles in different countries, that made it possible to overcome the problems of the reproduction of labour-power (unemployment, buying power) as well as the difficulties in the accumulation of capital. And it was in that way that there arose the monopolist state which has become an essential element in the forms of exploitation carried out by state monopoly capitalism and is today an essential element in its crisis.

Thus the crises of the capitalist system follow one from another, and are dissimilar only insofar as the fundamental contradictions inherent in the system manifest themselves in a different way on each occasion. And not only in a different way, but on a larger scale, since every crisis occurs at a new stage of the accumulation of capital, and thus in the context of an increased development and socialisation of the productive forces and in the context of an altered state of the social relations of production.

From this point of view it is possible to see why the present crisis in state monopoly capitalism, the expression of a confrontation between the logic of monopolistic exploitation and highly developed and socialised productive forces, although it may appear less severe in its economic effects than the crisis of the 1930s, is in fact much more profound, assuming the dimensions of a world-wide, structural social crisis, with effects which transcend momentary variations of time and place. It is in fact developing within an entirely new and unprecedented context of technological, economic, social and international relations.

---

[49] By manipulating for a time, and within particular limits, the elasticity of human needs.

The very power of the monopolies today threatens their dominance. The concentration of the ownership of capital, the size and interdependance of the units of production, the direct or indirect submission of productive sectors and social activities to major capital are signs of this power. So also is its direct hold over the state, but so too is the concentration and growth of the working class, and of the non-productive salary-earning classes whose members have been uprooted from independent undertakings.

The struggle against the falling rate of profit, which is itself related to the development of the productive forces, by an intensified reliance on the methods of state monopoly capitalism (public financing of monopolist accumulation, inflation, 'industrial redeployment' etc.) and to the classic means of production of relative surplus value (intensification of labour, lowering of wages), by maximum reduction of unnecessary costs (education, health, community property, research etc.), entails in these conditions an awful confusion in the material productive forces and a huge waste of the human powers and intelligence of a whole generation; it touches every category of the population in one way or another, and no social activity is immune.

Now it is precisely in this context of a general threat to living and working conditions, and of extreme suppression of the workers' needs, that qualitatively new demands have appeared, among the productive forces. The pursuit of their development entails greater and greater control over the whole process of social life and cooperation between production units, as well as changes in the work process, which imply in particular a progressive disappearance of the distinction between manual and intellectual work, and the emergence of workers of a new type: capable both of adapting themselves to the new content of work and of modifying it, and able to grasp intellectually the whole of the work process and to participate in its management and organisation – workers endowed with advanced professional training, and with a high level of education and social consciousness.

Now these are needs (as we will show in greater detail in the next chapter) that capital cannot satisfy. Abolishing the anarchy of capitalist production, and making possible the training and valorization of the labour force on a massive scale, even in terms of its most 'cultural' aspects, are demands which the logic of exploitation is scarcely equipped to cope with.

Yet they are needs inherent in the development of capitalism, and born of the movement of its own reproduction: needs which today pose a direct threat to capitalism, and which can be satisfied only through its abolition. They are also the very same objective needs of the development of the productive forces under the specific conditions of capital which partici-pants in the contemporary social struggle, whether semi-skilled workers, students, researchers or women, feel and express as their own particular needs.

Of course, though signs of the crisis multiply immediate reasons for the struggle, they also encourage a complete renunciation of the struggle and of all reformist illusions. One must not, however, overlook the fact that the same development that has reduced the real gap between the needs arising from the expansion of capital and the need for its abolition has produced the material and social conditions promoting consciousness of that situation. The significance of the contemporary struggle, at the heart of the crisis in the problematical context of France, where the working class has provided itself with class organisations and with a mass revolutionary party, as well as the growing consciousness of the necessity for political struggle in the factories, bears witness to this. There is an increased consciousness that the securing of demands, the satisfaction of the most immediate needs, is closely linked with a radically anti-monopolist policy and, finally, with the setting-up of an improved economic, social and political order.

Socialism thus appears, under the magnifying effects of the crisis, in all its materialist significance: related not to the construction of some readymade model of the perfect society, but to the practical resolution of the internal contradictions of capital and the problems posed by its development. The concrete necessity for socialism in France today, evident from the fact that it has become a mass question, a mass idea, derives from its greater capacity to cope with the most pressing problems of the modern world. As well as developing and transforming needs, socialism cannot be socialism unless it begins by satisfying them.

Capitalist production has considerably enriched the human social heritage, but it has made it impossible for the great majority of people to have access to that heritage. Alongside capitalist development and the growth of class antagonism, there has emerged the initially objective, but increasingly subjective need for the appropriation of that heritage by the dominated classes. Socialist society simultaneously enriches that heritage by transforming it in response to existing needs and, above all, by producing in each of its members the need for its appropriation.

The social appropriation of the means of production makes possible the reorientation of production and accumulation in terms of *historically defined existing needs*. But expanded reproduction is no longer the accumulation of capital, it has become the need of the producers: it can then no longer be carried to the detriment of living labour, since the satisfaction of the needs of the producers is equally applicable in places of work. An increase of productivity under socialist conditions thus implies a profound change in the application of the productive forces within the work process, and a concrete reappropriation by the socialist producer – who has been substituted for the capitalist worker reduced to the state of a mere 'appendage of the machine' – of the collective means of production, a general development of the totality of his abilities, and the gradual elimination of the distinction between manual and intellectual work. The development of the producers and their needs is a demand of socialist production itself, and the more the technological complexity of the productive forces increases, the more imperative that demand becomes.

The needs of socialism remain the needs of production, but because the production is different, the needs are different too. As Lucien Sève has said:

> This is the answer to the ideological objection which is constantly made to communism: how could one ever give 'to each according to his needs' if those needs had the characteristics observable in a non-communist society? Naturally, the needs satisfied by communism are the needs of *communist* man . . . and if, under communism, work has become the most important need, then in the same way *need becomes the most important work,* in the sense that the production of the *rich* man, with richly developed needs, is the production of the most important of *social riches*.[50]

Thus under socialism the apprehension of social needs in their concrete forms proceeds through an analysis of the complex process of the internalisation of the needs of production. But the modalities here are markedly different. Cultural and ideological social relations sharply characterised by antagonistic production relations and class struggles make up the determining moments of this process in bourgeois society. The social appropriation of the major means of production and exchange makes it possible to substitute for that the democratic confrontation – in different forms and at different levels – of the interests of the old exploited classes and of various categories of workers, on the basis of a cultural revolution and of the social knowledge of the laws of the development of socialist formation; and then of that of all the members of the communist society. The traditions of the past weigh heavily on the heads of the living, and can for a long time impede the setting up of social needs adequate to both the possibilities and the demands of socialist production. This should not be underestimated if it is true that the transformation of

---

[50]See Sève, *Marxisme et théorie de la personnalité*, p. 406.

production relations, while suppressing the material basis of bourgeois ideology, does not of itself produce new ideological relations ready formed, and is not able to reduce ideology to scientific knowledge, the importance of the cultural revolution and the imperatives of the ideological struggle.

3

Social needs and
state monopoly capitalism

THEORETICAL CONCEPTIONS OF NEEDS

From the point of view of the dominant ideology

Some years ago, when learned gentlemen were declaring the final embourgeoisement of the working class through the delights of the consumer society, the official ideology promised the imminent satisfaction of needs thanks to growth. Every day in every way the cake was getting bigger and bigger, and soon everyone would have their share.

The reality of the expansion of capitalist production after the Second World War lent substance and some political credibility to these promises. Among the material forms in which this ideology manifested itself, the real dimensions of this notion of a march towards the satisfaction of needs are apparent in the ideological direction of the machinery for economic planning.

Where the planning of 'public' investment was concerned, the argument consistently put forward – though not always completely followed through – was explicit: on the basis of an assessment of the current situation, and working from an 'expert' definition (arrived at in what way?) of the norms to be satisfied, the planners would measure the distance between the present situation and one in which the norms were satisfied, and would deduce the size of public investment necessary. There is a great deal to be said about the way these calculations were carried out, the concrete content of the normative definitions of needs thus established, and the types of answers put forward. But for all that, social needs were explicitly present; disdained, distorted, averaged out to be sure, but to some degree recognised.

This was also a time which saw the development of the social sciences: urban sociology began to take shape in France, seeking to demonstrate, through a humanist approach to needs, the most keenly felt social distortions and point to areas of necessary reform in urban planning. We were on the threshold of the leisure age, and experts were beginning to look at the implications of a sudden, huge expansion in free time, how it could be used, and what effect it would have on our way of life.

In the academic sphere, short-sighted 'radical' critics, misled by the mirage of 'expanding' industrial societies, declared the exploitation of labour by capital to be a nineteenth-century cliché which had been overtaken by the age of organisation, the age of bureaucracy and management, and concentrated their fire on alienation within and through consumption.

These critics, incidentally, were quickly caught out by the development of the crisis in capitalist societies, since the most highly worked out and most interesting manifestations of this line of thought (for instance, the work of Jean Baudrillard) gained prominence at precisely the time when the official ideology was changing direction because of the crisis, and reorganising itself around the notion of austerity, the only capitalist response to the crisis. An austerity to be imposed on and, if possible, to be accepted by the workers.

Reflecting the crisis before it had even been officially recognised, the state apparatus had, it seemed, suddenly discovered the 'validity' of the criticisms – particularly the most radical, the most 'far left' – levelled against the concept of need and, apparently abandoning the psychologising humanism which had traditionally been mixed with its econometrics, it abandoned all attempts to evaluate needs and measure the means of satisfying them. Norms were quantitative, they smacked of dominance. Now it was long live the right to be different, and the quality of life – in other words, freedom in austerity. One may note in passing that one remarkable but officially little emphasised effect of the organisation of the French Fifth Plan was the extent to which the public investment aims presented as the indispensable minimum to meet needs failed to be realised.

As for the Seventh Plan, there was no longer any reference to needs or quantified objectives, but merely priorities for 'action' and 'programmes' to deal with this problem or that, the site for the articulation of social demagogy in terms of monopolist policies. Parallel with this, a whole 'leftist' critique grew up, whose main points have been outlined in the preceding chapters. Let us concentrate here on one of their most important aspects which, incidentally, only reproduces in other forms the traditions of bourgeois economy: the dichotomy between production and consumption which made it possible for Michel Rocard, for instance, to advocate a revolution in our way of life at the same time as showing his admiration for the 'production machine' of capitalism.

On the one hand, unemployment is on the increase, inflation is high, and the buying-power of large sections of the population is going down. On the other hand there is the gospel of austerity, frugality, good-neighbourliness, and the cry that consumption is waste. The title of an article which appeared in *Le Monde,* written by the banker and director of the UDR, Albin Chalandon, shows clearly how capital sees the way out of the crisis: 'Produce more, consume less'.

From the Marxist view point: antihumanism against economism?

In the period preceeding the crisis, as has been said, the dominant discourse was that of partnership between technocracy and humanism, promising, thanks to rapid economic growth and specific reforms, a speedy (though always, be it noted, a future) satisfaction of social needs. As far as this period is concerned, one must concede a certain usefulness to the Marxist movement which has been called 'theoretical antihumanism', simply because it challenged the validity of 'soft humanism' and brought out its latent or explicit political ambiguities; its critique opposed an idealist psychologising of needs, in which the social is reduced to the transmission and the effects of 'cultural models'. To make needs so conceived the projected motor for a new drive for economic growth, is to surrender to an idealist problematic of the individual and his needs.

But that same theoretical movement to some extent weakened itself by its excessively one-sided insistence on the directions of class domination, as well as by its theoretical underestimation of the fundamental economic movement and its contradictions (it is not enough to repeat that economic factors are the ultimate determinant without theoretically working out their concrete content). Though it may be right to condemn any mechanistic conception which treats a spontaneous and inevitable devel-opment of the productive forces as the cause that automatically shatters a mode of production too old to contain them, it is only by an extraordinary caricature that Etienne Balibar[1] opposes this critique to those who have contributed most to the development of a theoretical analysis of state monopoly capitalism and its crisis.

Balibar ascribes to them indirectly the thesis of the primacy of the forces of production, which would be the privileged form of economism within Marxism, a thesis which 'leads inevitably to the pure and simple

[1] We have chosen to engage with Balibar here because among the theoreticians of this somewhat heteroclitic 'movement' he seems to us to be the writer who presents, in a text such as 'Plus-value et classes sociales', the least one-sided position, and provides the most interesting ground for discussion. A good many other 'Althusserians' or 'neo-Althusserians' hold a much more summary view, in which the invocation of the ultimate determination is no longer anything but a preliminary ritual.

elimination of relations of production and their scientific study (usually replaced by a reference to the juridical forms of ownership of the means of production)'.[2] In so doing, he overlooks the relevance of analyses of state monopoly capitalism and its crisis from precisely the point of view of a scientific analysis of the concrete movement of the mode of production, and the forms and transformation of the dominant relation of production. At the same time, in another essay in the same work,[3] he himself states that 'every mode of production is characterised by the tendencies of the transformations that the existing forces of production undergo as the result of determined relations of production', and he emphasises, referring to *Capital* and *Imperialism, the Highest Stage of Capitalism,* that 'what they analyse is the contradictory development of the forces of production, the contradiction in the development of forces of production, as the result of the relation of production and the fundamental exploitation historically realised in it, a contradiction which is thus practically inseparable from specific class struggles.'[4] In the same essay he puts forward some suggestions for analysing this contradictory development in the social formation of France. These are interesting suggestions, which could only benefit from a dialogue with, for example, the collective publications on this subject in *Economie et politique.* In fact, however, Balibar contents himself once again with a caricature condemning the authors of the *Traité marxiste d'économie politique,* who stand accused of 'concentrating exclusively on the importance of juridical differences in the form of ownership', and of tending to 'define capital not as a social relation of exploitation, but as a calculable magnitude . . . analysing the history of the capitalist mode of production not as the result of the class struggles which *determine* it, but as the result of the "logic of profit".'[5]

Over and above this 'reading', which is, to say the least, schematic and in which the analyses in question are scarcely recognisable, let us consider the concept of the determining character of class struggles. Is it sufficient simply to assert with Balibar that 'there is no social process existing above or below the class struggle'?

Balibar emphasises that this is not simply a question of invoking the class struggle, but of analysing it in its concrete forms and, in the first place, in the determinant forms of the class struggle within material production. But in order to analyse these struggles and their historical transformation, is it sufficient to rely on a constant reiteration of the primacy of relations of production? 'Provided that it *never* forgets the

---

[2] E. Balibar, *Cinq études sur le matérialisme historique* (Maspero, 1974), p. 232, note 27.
[3] 'Plus-value et classes sociales', op. cit. p. 119.
[4] Ibid., p. 188.
[5] Ibid., pp. 163–4.

existence of the relation of production, and its material effects, and the forms of its effective realisation within the work process, such a definition cannot fall into subjectivism and idealism.'[6] To be sure; but what is materialism, ignoring that 'forget', if it is not a concrete analysis of material effects and their movement, and thus of the movement of the forces of production within relations of production?

Having gone to such lengths to exorcise the demon of economism, this last remark of Balibar's seems an almost ritual warning. But it is precisely at that point that an effective possibility of producing a materialist analysis of the class struggle occurs, or else one may find oneself condemned to a subjectivism which would end in the autonomisation of 'instances', in economic, political and ideological categorisation, and the over-politicisation of analyses.

The concrete study of the history of the capitalist mode of production as a process of class struggle implies an examination of the concrete forms of the movement of the forces of production within relations of production, a movement necessarily contradictory to the dominant relation of production. Such a movement may be called the reproduction of the mode of production: its internal contradiction is manifested in the form of contradictory objective necessities which by their very existence determine the concrete content of the class struggle. And it could be claimed that an examination of the relation between objective demands and needs, as the subjective forms of these demands, is an integral part of the examination of the relation between class situation and class consciousness.

Thus, far from being some out-dated idealist cliché, the question of needs is at the heart of the study of the class struggle. Not in terms of providing a 'motive' fuelling that struggle from the outside, but rather because that struggle is the developed social form of the contradiction of the mode of production, the social form in which its reproduction, and thus also its transformation and confrontation, occurs. To put aside the question of needs is to put to one side the concrete content of the class struggle, to retain only the abstract form of the confrontation while forgetting what is at stake. Let us examine, for example, the demands and objectives advanced by the labour movement in the class struggle. What we call over-politicisation is to see in them only the result of a purely political and tactical process, whose unique aim is 'political effectiveness' in terms of an immediate political contribution to the overthrow of the power of the bourgeois state. Whereas the actual production of the demands and objectives of the workers' struggle links this aspect of the political situation to the objective demands that arise from the repro-

[6] Ibid., pp. 182–3.

duction of the productive forces from the workers' point of view, demands that are in no way tactical.

This is what is fundamentally at stake in contemporary political debates and struggles in the face of the crisis. For what characterises the crisis is something other than a straightforward repetition of the constant tendency of capital to reinforce the rate of exploitation. The policy of austerity and pressure on popular needs manifests, in the aggravation of the conditions of life it produces, something other than a simple extension of previous tendencies. It reveals a new situation, involving the diversion, the blocking, the wastage, even the regression of the forces of production. And today, more clearly than ever, the demands of the reproduction, reorientation and development of the forces of production have revolutionary implications; for if their satisfaction appears to be a necessary condition for the improvement of living conditions, that clearly entails the elimination of the dominance of monopoly capital, the dominant form of capitalist relations of production.

Let us add one final remark about the negative effects of certain 'antihumanist' positions regarding needs. An over-restrictive interpretation of Marx's sixth thesis on Feuerbach appears to us to eliminate the consideration of anything except the general question of social relations, without examining the specific articulation of these relations by concrete individuals. This concrete specificity, which as Lucien Sève has suggested can be studied in the biographies of individuals and cannot be confused with metaphysical abstraction, is an indispensable element in the analysis of concrete social processes and, so far as our present purpose is concerned, in the analysis of the individual experience of the forms in which needs are socially determined, the individual forms of the contradiction between needs and conditions of life and work, the relation between individual needs and the social consciousness of needs, between individual consciousness, class consciousness, and the collective consciousness of an organised class. Moreover, the specific articulation of social relations represented by individuals is supported by a fact that cannot be overlooked in any consideration of manual or intellectual work; the contradictory unity of the concrete life of production and reproduction, the individual unity of the body.

OVERACCUMULATION OF CAPITAL, PRODUCTIVE FORCES AND
NEEDS IN THE CRISIS

Is a solution to the crisis possible? Or does the crisis unavoidably imply austerity for the workers, the only way of restoring necessary economic profitability (according to the right), the only way to cease to be alienated by the headlong consumption of 'signs' whose underlying logic is the reproduction of domination (according to one faction of the left)? There are some who take this logic to its conclusion and say that one should not work at all, except for oneself. Does not the sale of labour-power mean becoming part of the system?

Or, on the contrary, is the only real way out of the crisis through the satisfaction and development of social needs, the development and transformation of both production and consumption? Does not the satisfaction of needs imply a policy of complete change, as described above when discussing the contradictory relation of capital to social needs and the reproduction of the labour force?

The central elements of the crisis

To answer these questions, one must start by analysing the crisis itself, so as to establish its nature. One must examine how the question of the relations between production and consumption comes into it. Let us consider the main points.[7]

The crisis is due neither to external factors (the oil 'crisis', or the exhaustion (?) of raw materials), nor simply to a historical depression linked to more or less technical, esoteric and reputedly 'worldwide' imbalances and instabilities. It is a universal crisis of capitalist society, a profound crisis arising within the very heart of that society from the dominant social relations which define it: the exploitation of labour by capital and the process of capital accumulation. The heart of the crisis lies in the *overaccumulation* of capital, the structural result of the recent period of rapid capital accumulation which continued until the late 1960s. Characterised by an acceleration of monopolist concentration of increasingly international character, by the establishment and improvement of the political and economic mechanisms of state monopoly capitalism through the transformation of the state apparatus, by direct or indirect investment by major capital in sectors of activity such as agriculture and building which had previously been dominated by small or medium-sized industry and small-scale commodity production, this period ended in an overaccumulation of capital which today threatens monopoly profit itself.

Recent work by the INSEE (Institut national des statistiques et des études économiques) on trends in the development of productive fixed capital,[8] despite its somewhat different conceptual basis, nonetheless

---

[7] For an extended analysis of the different aspects of the crisis, see *La Crise* (Editions sociales, 1975).

[8] *Fresque historique du système productif*, Collections de l'INSEE, October 1974; *La crise du système productif*, Collections de l'INSEE, December 1981.

confirms in general outline the principal elements of the Marxist analysis of the movement of the overaccumulation and devalorisation of capital, which forms an essential element in the theory of state monopoly capitalism developed from the 1950s onwards. But it is necessary to go beyond a recognition of the structural fall in the *profitability* of capital – the principal aspect of the crisis from the point of view of capital – to grasp what it reveals about the principal contradiction of the capitalist mode of production, the contradiction between forces of production and relations of production.

If there is a tendency for the rate of profit to fall – not only on average but, during the crisis, in monopolist terms as well – this is due to the excessive accumulation of capital in relation to the surplus-value which can be appropriated. However, this accumulation of capital should not only be considered in its value-form, but primarily and above all in its form as real capital – labour-power and means of production – where the increase in organic composition, i.e. the relation between constant and variable capital, between dead and living labour, is precisely where the problem lies. It also embodies, as the social relation of appropriation, the determination of the content and form of concrete labour, and the exploitation of that labour.

In other words, at the heart of the crisis there is a crisis in the relation of the productive forces to capital. During the preceding period of growth, capital, in its search for relative surplus value, developed the productive forces – in its own way, as we will see later. This development was carried out in two ways: by the expansion of capitalist production into new spheres, and by the transformation of production processes through the application in all sectors of new technology, with automation as the most advanced point of this movement. Throughout this period, capitalism, growth and technological progress seemed to go hand in hand. The principal characteristic of this movement of the productive forces was the systematic tendency for the accumulation of dead labour to replace living labour. If capital bought new, more complex and more efficient machines, it was to economise on living labour, and above all on skilled labour, which was the most costly. But such a movement is contradictory, because in order to produce, operate and maintain the new machines which would make it possible to employ a less skilled labour force, it was necessary, at other points in the process of social production, to have a more skilled labour force.

Thus the movement of productive forces was to transform both the means of production and the nature, volume and skill of the labour force.

Transformations in the labour force

From this point of view, changes in the structure of the working population in France clearly reflect the changes that have taken place in the mode of production and the productive forces.

The expansion of capitalist production and circulation has led to a marked reduction in 'independent' categories, the traditional non-salaried petty bourgeoisie: farmers (down 58 per cent between 1954 and 1975), craftsmen (down 30 per cent), small shopkeepers (down 27 per cent). At the same time, wage-earners have increased by 47 per cent, representing now over four fifths of the working population.[10]

Among wage-earners, the working class has continued to grow, in absolute (up 26 per cent) and relative terms (from 33.6 per cent of the active population in 1954 to 37.7 per cent in 1975), contrary to the theses of post-industrial society and the progressive replacement of the working class by white-collar workers (making use, it must be admitted, of some fairly doubtful definitions of social categories in the statistical data produced in many countries).[11] The number of skilled workers has increased slightly more than the number of the unskilled. But the changes in the structure of the class are deeper than is shown by those overall figures. Some traditional categories, such as agricultural employees, miners, sailors, fishermen and apprentices, have decreased greatly. The proportion of semi-skilled workers has gone up by over 50 per cent in the steel industry, and by over two-thirds in the motor and electronics industries. It has been said that the development of productive forces in the capitalist mode of production is marked by the accumulation of dead labour and the intensification of the contradiction between dead labour and living labour. The changes in skills are evidence of this, since one can see on the one hand an increase in the number of semi-skilled and unskilled workers, servants of machines whose operations rule their work, and on the other hand a marked increase not only in the number of skilled workers in the traditional definition, but also of other categories closely

[9] See Paul Boccara, *Etudes sur le capitalisme monopoliste d'Etat, sa crise et son issue* (Editions sociales, 1975).

[10] Corresponding figures for the 1982 census were not available at the time of writing.

[11] Contrary to the empiricist point of view, social facts do not spontaneously present the adequate categories to grasp them, and the definition of these categories, preliminary to any statistical analysis, is in itself a social stake and process. In France, specific historic and political conditions have led to categories used by the INSEE for the analysis of census data and many others surveys, the 'catégories socio-professionnelles', which although of a different status than the concept of social class allow a better empirical study of class structures than most statistical systems. See Alain Desrosières, 'Eléments pour l'histoire des nomenclatures socio-professionnelles', in *Pour une histoire de la statistique*, Vol. I, INSEE, 1977, pp. 155–232.

related to directly productive work through their predominantly intellectual skills.[12] This last group includes most technicians (up 115 per cent between 1962 and 1975) and many engineers (up 81 per cent). This extension of productive work beyond the traditional definition of the industrial working class has led Claude Quin[13] to a figure, for 1974, of 9,650,000 workers, 44.5 per cent of the total working population (see table 1).

TABLE 1 DISTRIBUTION OF THE WORKING POPULATION IN FRANCE BY SECTOR, 1954–75

	1954	*1962*	*1968*	*1975*
FARMERS	3 966 015	3 044 670	2 464 156	1 650 865
AGRICULTURAL WORKERS	1 161 356	826 090	584 212	375 480
INDUSTRIAL AND COMMERCIAL ENTREPRENEURS	2 301 416	2 044 667	1 955 468	1 708 925
Industrialists	91 067	80 660	80 720	59 845
Craftsmen	757 380	637 897	619 808	533 635
Fishermen (owners)	18 747	19 312	18 380	15 835
Large scale traders	181 717	172 833	210 344	186 915
Small shopkeepers	1 252 505	1 133 965	1 026 216	912 695
INDEPENDENT PROFESSIONALS AND UPPER MANAGEMENT	553 719	765 938	994 716	1 459 285
Independent professionals	120 341	125 057	140 572	172 025
Professors, literary and scientific professions	80 380	125 126	213 420	377 215
Engineers	75 808	138 061	186 184	256 290
Upper management	277 190	377 694	454 540	653 755
MIDDLE MANAGEMENT AND EMPLOYED PROFESSIONALS	1 112 543	1 501 287	2 005 732	2 764 950
Schoolteachers	384 984	421 189	562 096	737 420
Health and social services employees		110 101	172 718	298 455
Technicians	193 206	343 986	530 716	758 890
Middle management	534 353	626 011	740 172	970 185

continues

[12] This evolution has led the specialists to reconsider the statistical measures of skilled work (see Michel Cézard, 'Les qualifications ouvrières en question', *Economie et statistique*, No. 110, April 1979), and on a more general level to a reconstruction of the whole system of social categories for the 1982 census. See Alain Desrosières, Alain Goy and Laurent Thévenot, 'L'identité sociale dans le travail statistique: la nouvelle nomenclature des professions et catégories socio-professionnelles', *Economie et statistique*, No. 152, February 1982.

[13] Claude Quin, *Classes sociales et union du peuple de France.* (Editions sociales, 1976), p. 56.

Table 1 *continued*

	1954	1962	1968	1975
EMPLOYEES	2 068 118	2 396 418	2 995 828	3 840 700
Office employees	1 627 548	1 885 506	2 371 128	3 104 105
Shop assistants	440 570	510 910	624 700	736 595
WORKERS	6 489 871	7 060 790	7 705 752	8 207 165
Foremen	3 052 953	306 142	363 216	443 305
Skilled workers		2 286 459	2 630 040	2 985 865
Semi-skilled workers	1 816 265	2 394 102	2 670 328	2 946 860
Miners	239 155	191 588	144 696	73 440
Sailors and fishermen	54 865	48 061	43 344	38 280
Apprentice workers	201 310	251 044	256 206	106 690
Unskilled workers	1 125 323	1 583 394	1 597 920	1 612 725
SERVICE PERSONNEL	1 017 789	1 047 312	1 166 252	1 243 490
Domestic staff	320 758	306 602	280 876	234 355
Charwomen	239 406	222 467	227 328	154 100
Other service personnel	457 623	518 243	658 048	855 035
OTHER CATEGORIES	513 937	564 023	525 860	524 000
Artists	45 089	42 184	50 196	59 075
Clergy	171 394	165 634	137 124	116 945
Army and police	297 454	356 205	338 540	347 980
TOTAL	19 184 764	19 251 195	20 397 976	21 774 860

And it must be added that the degradation of work and its dequalification in terms of skill, which for the workers are the consequence of a development dominated by the search for profit, are not simply confined to an opposition between skilled and unskilled workers, between manual labour on the one hand and intellectual work on the other (as the demagogic campaign on the 'revalorisation of manual work' would have had us believe in the last years of the Giscard period).[14] On the contrary, it affects every category of worker, whether they are involved in production as engineers, technicians, programmers, skilled and semi-skilled workers, or in circulation, as has been highlighted recently by the struggles and demands of employees in banking or commerce, or are

---

[14] A commentary broadcast by France-Inter echoed our own thoughts on the slogan which appeared on the poster for the revalorisation of manual work, which went roughly: 'Whoever gives of his best has a right to a fair share too.' That 'too' implies that he does not always get a fair share, that perhaps he has not always had one. But if he had an unfair share, how could the other shares have been fair? That small logical difficulty sums up fairly well the ideological principle which states that basically everything is all right ('basically' meaning the relation between profit and wages) but that perhaps some are doing a bit less well than others (the wage-share needs adjusting) and that fundamentally distribution is a question of justice (and not of the determination of wages by the value of labour-power, and thus in the end there is no reference to needs, except perhaps the need for *dignity*: and that's how we are always brought back to the social signified . . .).

involved in the sphere of reproduction of the labour force as health workers, social workers or teachers.

These non-working-class categories of wage-earners have increased even more rapidly, leading to the expansion of the commodity character to all types of work force, and therefore to their reproduction processes. But this rapidly growing number of 'white collar' workers can neither be interpreted as a decline of the working class replaced by the 'new middle classes' – a general embourgeoisement of society – nor simply as an extension of working class conditions – a general proletarianisation of society. It is partly a result of capitalist development and the socialisation of productive forces leading, as we have seen, to the growth of new categories of skilled white-collar working class (producers of surplus value); but it is also due to the growth of management and control bodies (in private firms and in the state) whose staff act, for at least part of their work, as agents of capitalist exploitation and domination. Part, too, is due to the expansion of the circulation of capital and commodities, where the development of work conditions and relations has gradually brought about a situation similar to that of the working class for many employees and technicians, but where the hierarchical pressure of capital weighs on and mobilises both top and middle management. Finally, it also results from the socialisation of consumption, a movement largely organised by the state, in education and health services, public transport, public housing and so on, where work relations are more distant from capitalist domination but are nevertheless subject to similar trends in the division of labour and the power relations that create objective differences, as well as potential solidarities between categories such as doctors and nurses, or university professors and secretaries.

The needs that have to be met to ensure the overall reproduction of society basically reflect this complex structure of labour processes and power relations. They cannot be seen simply as the addition of the individual consumer's preferences, or as the homogeneous needs of the reproduction of an undifferentiated labour force opposed to capital accumulation and the luxury needs of the bourgeoisie. The social processes of the definition of needs are built on the growing variety of skills and work processes. And the contradictions in the definition and meeting of needs express the conflicting class interests in the definition, use and possible developments of all types of skills, both individual and collective.

The monopolist mess

If the crisis is the result of the changes that can be observed in the preceding period of rapid growth, and is to some extent the aggravation of tendencies which were already apparent then, it must also be seen as a

complete break, a new stage, a reorientation. The 'redeployment' sought
by monopoly capital reveals this clearly. This new orientation of investment in the crisis is characterised by its openly contradictory relation to
the development of the productive forces. Thus the desire to concentrate
production in selected places for greater profitability has as a corollary a
'redeployment' which is a contraction, a concentration on certain units of
production while others are abandoned and destroyed. This devalorisation
does not arise from the declining economic utility of these units of
production through obsolescence or the poor quality of the goods they
produce – indeed, it often applies to modern factories, even those using
the most up-to-date technology – rather it is 'simply' their adaptation to
the conditions of the search for monopolist profit in the crisis, bringing
together every aspect of the imperialist relations and strategies of the
multinational groups, along with every viable form of speculation, and
the class struggle too, in the different forms and intensities appropriate to
different countries. The early and significant cases of Lip and then Rateau
had already shown the extent to which the criterion of profit could diverge
from criteria relating to the social utility of a firm economic potential.
Modern units of production, with a highly skilled work force and high-
quality means of production, producing materials appreciated for their
quality and relating to key sectors, with the promise of expansion
and vital to the economic independence of the nation, saw themselves
under threat. And in the last years of the Giscard-Barre government it was
no longer a case of one or two typical but isolated cases: the entire
economic potential of our country was under threat, including crucial
sectors such as the steel industry, whose dismantling had been decided by
big business within the framework of redeployment and the new
international division of labour, or the information or the nuclear
industries, which were falling under the dominance of American imperialism. At the same time, research was receding and finding itself more
and more closely linked to criteria of immediate profitability, or was even
being sold off directly to private groups, as in the deal between the Centre
National de la Recherche Scientifique and Rhône-Poulenc.

Related to these characteristics of redeployment, the growth of
unemployment, which is now taking on dramatic proportions in all
capitalist countries, shows the universal inability of capital to make use of
all the productive forces, although the labour of all the unemployed is not
only useful, it is indispensable to the development of the societies in
which we live. All categories of workers, including the most highly
skilled, are affected by unemployment, and the young, the future
productive forces, are the most severely affected of all. As for those in
work, the characteristics of the previous period appeared even more

strongly marked: a decrease in skilled work, an increase in the work-load and in the rate of working, long working period, an increase in working two or three shifts, particularly in large factories, in order to accelerate the profitability of a considerable amount of fixed capital.

In this way the very level of development of the productive forces which accompanied the movement of accumulation is today in open conflict with the domination of monopoly capitalism, in production as much as in social life generally. This is manifested by disorganisation and waste in the means of production and in human productive forces, and in the sterilisation of their possibilities for growth. Thus, for instance, automation is only put into practice by capital in a partial, trimmed and mutilated way, because capital seeks to utilise it while keeping down employment of skilled labour, whereas the full use of automation on a large scale would mean a major growth in employment of skilled workers, and would be incompatible with the growing instability of capitalist production and its outlets.[15]

State policy in the crisis

This blocking, this widespread social disorganisation, far from being tempered or restrained by the policies of the state, was, on the contrary, reinforced by them before May 1981. The main lines of the Seventh Plan, following those of the former 'plan of revival', confirmed all the existing trends.

Firstly, in the name of 'selectivity', certain giant capitalist groups were reinforced, increasing the degree of concentration in sectors judged 'backward' and the elimination or increased domination of small and medium-sized firms.

Secondly unemployment was kept at a high level: 800,000 unemployed on the optimistic assumption of a resumption of 'growth'. Because direct aid to the accumulation of monopoly capitalism is more and more obviously an aid to confusion, speculation and the suppression of jobs, and not to the real development of the productive forces: according to this optimistic hypothesis, there was to be no more industrial employment in the 1980s than there had been in 1974. And this 'aim' was more than achieved when, in 1982, real unemployment went up to 2,000,000.

Thirdly, there were rising prices and the increased plundering of public funds, as well as increased pressure on all forms of popular consumption.

[15] See Paul Boccara, 'Inflation, chômage, ressources naturelles, automation' in *La Crise,* and Jean Chatain, 'A propos de l'automation, exigence de nouveaux rapports sociaux à l'échelle nationale et dans l'entreprise', *Economie et politique,* No. 258, January 1976.

For the corollary of increased support for monopolist profit in the crisis is undoubtedly the reinforcement of the austerity imposed on the workers, and this is applied in all domains relating to the social reproduction of the labour force:

– Pressure on wages through inflation, unemployment, decrease in skilled work, and fierce resistance by management and the state to any increase in wages, except in terms of certain demagogic measures of strictly limited range, concerning only the 'most disadvantaged', and which it was made clear could only be financed by a redistribution of the 'total wage bill'. Unemployment, inflation and stagnation or a very low increase in wages, in comparison, for instance, with the official retail price index, which substantially underestimated the rise in prices, led to a stagnation or fall in the buying power of large sectors of the population. This was exacerbated by an increase in the burden of taxes, whether direct, indirect, or local, an increase in social security contributions and a decrease in allowances as they were transferred from the state budget, a fall in the buying-power of the family allowance and various social security benefits, as well as of pensions and sickness benefits, and an increase in public costs.

Housing policy was typical of this policy of aggravating the crisis at the expense of the workers. The cost of subsidised housing, *Habitations à loyer modéré* (HLM), (both rent and maintenance charges) has gone up steeply, putting this type of housing further and further out of the reach of the least well off; furthermore, the production of housing in the public sector, while still remaining the cheapest available accommodation, has gone down. The prospects set out in the Barre report, and subsequently implemented, went even further. The progressive abolition of the HLM sector and of public aid to the construction industry was undertaken, thus opening the entire housing market to private enterprise while 'supporting' the 'most disadvantaged' members of society through a 'personal housing grant'. Because, you see – and this was one of the conclusions of the Barre report – the state was wasting money in helping to house too many people who did not need it!

Now housing problems, while affecting most severely the least well off, concern all social sectors except a very small minority. Thus, for all those whose income is above the ceiling for access to subsidised housing, but who are not wealthy, the gradual decontrol of pre-1948 rented accommodation, the increase in interest rates, the rapid rise in construction costs and intense speculation in housing have made the cost of housing, whether rented or bought, increasingly difficult to meet.

At a time when statistics showed that the need for housing, in France, was still acute, when the percentage of small, poky, ill-equipped, badly sound-proofed and over-crowded housing had gone up, several thousand flats and houses in the Paris region (88,000 for the city of Paris alone, according to the results of a 1974 survey) remained empty because they were too expensive, while at the same time evictions and foreclosures were on the increase: that was the 'social' content of this policy.

Education policy was going down the same road: adaptation to the demands of a management seeking cut-price training and an increased distinction between wage and skill. With the setting up of short-term training projects, the reform of the second 'cycle' of university education, the general shortage of posts and funds which brought the universities to the brink of bankruptcy and were leading to a rapid decline in educational standards, the systematic search for selection by elimination, all these meant imposing on the young a choice between unemployment and unskilled and badly paid work: was this not one of the meanings of the campaign for the 'revalorisation of manual labour'?

The same could be said of all the other public sectors where policy is linked to the reproduction of the labour force. Whether it was a question of health, transport, sport or cultural activities, one found the same thing at every point: a decrease in available funds, a reduction in the equipment, services and personnel to keep them going, with controls enforced on the grounds of profitability by the monopolies and the increasing authoritarianism of the state.

Larger and more pressing social needs

It was a policy of crisis, but also a policy which aggravated the crisis and could not be seen as a functional answer opening the way to a real solution. For although it might have been, to a certain extent, an immediate response to the demands of monopoly profit, this policy also directly aggravated the contradictions which threatened that profit. The state of development reached by the productive forces, and the workers' concrete situation, produce objective necessities which are expressed more and more clearly in the workers' struggles and the social and individual consciousness of needs, in a way that comes into direct conflict with capitalist domination. These objective necessities, these social needs, are expressed in an increasingly closely linked way in both the sphere of production and in the reproduction of the labour force. In a concrete way, they show the impossibility of isolating the 'economic' and the 'social', production and consumption, as if they belonged to two separate worlds, determined by separate factors. They provide concrete proof of the unity of productive forces and social needs, of the development of living labour and the satisfaction and development of needs.

Excessive exploitation of the labour force produces a twofold demand for a slower pace of work and for better conditions of work, and also for better living conditions in order to reduce fatigue outside work and allow more rest and the enrichment of daily life: diminution of travelling time and an increase in comfort, better housing, leisure facilities, holidays.

The struggle to defend the workers against poor safety arrangements and accidents at work, as well as against occupational diseases, whether they are recognised as such or not, is closely related to the general social need for an improvement in the health system, the development of preventive care, better living conditions and anti-pollution measures.

The movement towards an unskilled labour force and tighter control of the work processes has entailed a demand for a change in the content of the work, the application of technical progress to the benefit of living labour and the development of skills for all, expressed the more forcibly as the technical and social potential is more clearly apprehended.

This demand by the workers is increasingly converging with the demands put forward by students and teachers for the maintenance and improvement of the educational system, by research workers for the safeguarding of the scientific potential of the nation, and by artists, film-makers and creative artists of all kinds for the freedom and means to create, and also for the widest possible popular access to every kind of cultural activity. There is no question here of 'productivism' or 'utilitarianism', with social development subordinated to the production of things. For to speak of the development of the productive forces and the development of living labour in this way is to take into account, without setting up a hierarchy or ranking one above the other, every aspect of society's relations to itself and to nature, every mode of appropriation of nature by man. In this way the development of productive forces must, for instance, include the expansion of all forms of cultural activity. Not in order to subordinate and direct cultural activity towards making a direct contribution to the progress of productivity in industry, which would be the utilitarian vision, but because culture, as an essential mode of the relationship of society to itself and to nature, is a constituent part in human productive forces.

It is the capitalist mode of production which, by establishing production as the production of surplus value, fails to recognise as socially useful any work which does not contribute to capital accumulation. This gives rise to the objective reduction of all human activities to the expanded reproduction of capital, reflected in the subjective reduction operated by bourgeois economics, the organising ideology for the accountability of capital.

In that reduction, the basic opposition is between dead labour and living labour. Capitalist accumulation tends to lead to the accumulation of dead labour and a relative elimination of living labour, and to increase the productivity of living labour by rendering it subservient to dead labour. The satisfaction of social needs and the development of popular consumption are an aspect of the development of the productive forces which necessarily depends on according primacy to living labour.

This primacy of living labour cannot be achieved, as is sometimes suggested today, by denouncing science and technology as the guilty parties, so avoiding according any responsibility to the dominant production relation. That sort of attitude is not dissimilar to the obscurantist ideology now favoured by capital when its demands for profit are seen to be openly contradictory to scientific and technological development. Nor can it be achieved by a return to earlier forms of production, to more 'human' forms of craft and pastoral organisation. To suggest that sort of regression of the productive forces is nothing but an individualist flight on the part of petit-bourgeois elements edged out by the crisis.

On the contrary, it is scientific and technological progress that can help to provide the answer. But a new kind of progress, which must break away from the present orientation of scientific policy and technological selection. For science and technology, like the totality of productive forces, are not 'neutral', but are stamped in their very mode of existence, in the choices made in their development, by the social relations in which they function. In this way, in order to oppose the current domination of big capital and the state, the former seeking the means for increasing its profit, the latter the means for increasing its power and its control over society and of developing to an ever greater extent the military machinery of destruction and repression, one must both liberate research from the utilitarian aims which shackle it and undermine its potency, and throw open the whole range of scientific and technological research to the widest possible awareness of real social needs. That kind of growth is only possible through a growth in living labour, through an expansion of the number of skilled workers, research workers, engineers, technicians, who at once make this growth possible by providing the means for liberating the least qualified and most subordinate members of the human productive work force and make them available for more skilled and rewarding activities, both within social production and in the spare time available to them, which would also be increased.

But in order to achieve this, other demands which are being asserted must also be met. In the face of unemployment, lack of job security and the major upheavals caused by the movement of capital, there is a rapidly growing demand for job security and the right to work for all, as well as, above and beyond this, a consciousness of the need and a demand for some sort of social control over production by the workers themselves. In this way there has come into being a social need radically opposed to the domination of capital, a need for the workers to control themselves, for themselves and for the whole of society, their own work, the process of social production. For themselves as workers and as consumers: in effect, the necessary transcendance of the contradiction between economic logic (the accumulation of capital) and the logic of needs (in work as much as in the expanded reproduction of the labour force, in social life as a whole) implies control by the workers themselves, and so the necessity for a new mode of production.

It is one effect of the crisis that it underlines, negatively, the unity between the sphere of production and the sphere of consumption. Unemployment, economic upheavals, pollution, devalorisation, on the one hand, decline in the standard of living and living conditions on the other, all under the aegis of domination by the multinationals and a state policy of austerity and 'redeployment', show that the contradiction between the productive forces and production relations today has produced blockages, in both production – productive consumption – and in consumption – the reproduction of the labour force. There can thus be no question of making needs into a 'social' question, contained solely within the sphere of consumption, to which there could be an 'economic' answer, conceived in instrumental terms. There can be no 'revolution in our way of life' without a revolution in the 'machinery of production'. The only way out of the crisis must involve the development of living labour and of skilled human activity in all its forms.

Social control of the principal means of production and exchange, wrenched from the monopolist groups and applied to the struggle against waste and devalorisation to bring about the reorientation and development of the productive forces, is necessary in order to satisfy consumption needs, raise the standard of living, and improve and transform living conditions. It is also the necessary first step to the satisfaction of production needs, of needs within work, and of that crucial need for control over their work by the workers themselves.

Equally, the raising of the standard of living and the development, improvement and enrichment of individual and collective consumption, and of the whole scope of life, while being so many necessary modes of the satisfaction of needs, are also so many necessary conditions for the development of the productive forces. Not only, nor even principally, to produce a 'revival through consumption', as is claimed by the flatly economistic caricature of a Marxist analysis of the crisis and its solution, but because, as we have already said, the development of living labour and skilled human activity cannot occur without a growth in education, culture, sport, health and so forth.

Finally, the growth of democracy is at one and the same time both the necessary response to the pressing need for freedom of a people which the power of major capital seeks to muzzle and constrain more and more closely, and the necessary means for achieving a real social control of production, a real expression and satisfaction of social needs, and a widely based popular extension of the demand for socialism, over and above the first stage of the struggle and the overthrow of monopoly domination.

CONSUMPTION

Following these opening remarks on social needs in the crisis of state monopoly capitalism, we would like to discuss some points in greater depth and advance a number of hypotheses to analyse consumption and collective facilities in greater detail. Of course this is not the principal aspect of a study of needs since, as we have shown, needs express the contradictory demands of the reproduction of the mode of production; but though production is the determinant, and the contradictions and historical movement of that determination must be subject to concrete analysis, consumption cannot be reduced to these terms.

Marxist analysis has developed in a way that has tended to emphasise the central, determining aspects of the mode of production, and has primarily tackled the question of consumption through the purchasing power of wages, the aspect most directly related to exploitation and the class struggle. More recently, the increasing importance of collective consumption has principally been dealt with in the study of the public financing of consumption through the 'indirect wage'.

The appearance of non-market forms of reproduction of the labour force within the mode of capitalist production, the historical transformation of needs related to the development of the productive forces, and the significance of forms within the sphere of consumption that block and threaten the reproduction of the labour force in the crisis, have made it indispensable that we seek a deeper theoretical understanding of this field so as to develop the theory of state monopoly capitalism, its crisis, the outcome of the crisis and the socialist outlook for this country.

This is particularly important because the multiplication of more or less theoretical writings on the subject not only masks the 'heart' of the crisis, but is an expression of its acuteness and complexity. And it is no longer enough to respond with some figures on the level of workers' purchasing power or the theoretical determination of consumption by production. It is impossible to evade a concrete analysis of that determination, of the specific characteristics of this sphere of social life and its specific relations with other spheres, or to abandon the theoretical field to econometricians or the psycho-sociologists with their investigations into consumer 'motivation' and all the theories which dissect consumption and suggest that the key to understanding may be found in social status, value systems, imitation, the sign, differentiation etc.

The following discussion does not claim to put forward a finished theoretical system, nor to have dealt with all the aspects that need to be considered. It is simply a contribution to the current debate and takes it, we hope, a little further forward.

Consumption and purchasing power

The term consumption – defined by the dictionary as 'to make away with, destroy, use up, spend', and related to the notion of consummation, 'completion, conclusion, the action of perfecting' – covers a wide variety of social practices. Whereas vulgar economics sees consumption as the goal and end-point of a chain which starts from production, passes by way of distribution and exchange, and ends up at consumption, Marx's classical analysis, among others, has shown that production and consumption are very closely linked, and that it is important to distinguish productive consumption from individual consumption:

> The labourer consumes in a twofold way. While producing he consumes by his labour the means of production, and converts them into products with a higher value than that of the capital advanced. This is his productive consumption. It is at the same time consumption of his labour-power by the capitalist who bought it. On the other hand, the labourer turns the money paid to him for his labour-power, into means of subsistence: this is his individual consumption.

In the capitalist mode of production, the production relation separates these two kinds of consumption, with the individual consumption that ensures the reproduction of the labour force taking place outside the process of production through the purchase of necessary commodities by means of the wage:

> The labourer's productive consumption, and his individual consumption, are therefore totally distinct. In the former, he acts as the motive power of capital, and belongs to the capitalist. In the latter, he belongs to himself, and performs his necessary vital functions outside the process of production. The result of the one is, that the capitalist lives; of the other, that the labourer lives.[16]

[16] Karl Marx, *Capital* (Lawrence & Wishart, 1954), Vol. II, Part VII, Chapter XXIII, p. 571.

One must thus distinguish productive consumption and individual consumption, the latter being nothing but that part of the reproduction of the labour force which occurs outside the labour process and outside the time bought by the wage. There must also be added a third category, consumption by the dominant class or luxury consumption, where the dominant class is involved in spending its share of surplus value.

The separation of productive and individual consumption is characteristic of the capitalist relation of production, and involves not only the working class but all wage-earners. The expansion of the dominant mode of production in the social formation entails, as we have seen, the progressive elimination of small independent producers and the growth of wage-earning categories: as a result, the various forms of subsistence production are progressively eliminated.

It is crucial to realise that this rift between 'work' and 'outside work' is not simply the unavoidable consequence of 'progress' and the development of the social division of labour. It is precisely because production is fundamentally the production of surplus value, in a relation of exploitation that subjugates human labour to the accumulation of capital, that this separation is becoming increasingly acute. We have already shown that the present development of the production process is marked by an increasingly sharp contradiction between the development of the productive forces and production relations. On the one hand, accumulation subjugates living labour to dead labour, breaks the work up into repetitive, unskilled tasks, and emasculates research. On the other hand, the objective necessities for the development of living labour become apparent with increasing force in demands about the conditions of work, training, skills, and the creative involvement of the workers themselves in the development and organisation of labour processes.

In contrast to the prevailing situation, the place of work should be a privileged site for the social development of the productive forces, and it could, above and beyond its immediate concerns with the increase of production, contribute to the growth and stimulation of those sectors of consumption which foster the development of the productive forces on the social scale: transport, nurseries, health care, as well as education, socio-educational and cultural activities, sport etc. Trade union demands increasingly express these needs and voice this point of view; and, within the narrow limits of the scope for action available to them and the constraints enforced by the forms of use of the labour force, so does the action taken by the unions through works committees.

We will return later to the social and spatial consequences of this separation in terms of the concrete organisation of the processes of consumption characteristic of the different social classes and strata. Here we would simply mention that this important aspect of current social consumption is not a 'historical casualty', 'the price of progress', or any similar trite phrase, but a direct effect of the dominant production relation. And yet bourgeois economics relies on this 'obvious fact' to separate the consumer from the producer absolutely, setting them up as rational subjects which have nothing in common.

From this point of view, the consumer is a subject who has at his disposal a certain amount of money, his 'income', which he employs in the purchase of a certain number of commodities available to him, his rational character being defined by the quest for 'utility maximisation', itself a function of a 'preferences schedule'. This provides us with a definition of consumption as the purchase of commodities, and studies of consumption are in fact essentially studies of consumer spending: to purchase which commodities do consumers employ their income?

The need to study consumer spending is undeniable, particularly as the commodity is the dominant form of circulation of the social product and the wage the principal means available to the labour force for ensuring its reproduction. Thus an understanding of what the workers can buy, what their purchasing power is, and what they in fact do buy, is clearly extremely important.

In scientific terms, it raises several difficulties. The first is the access to information on real wages; the second is the statistical definition of the measurements which are linked to class structure but also to sectors of activity, age categories, and social mobility. The third difficulty is the measurement of inflation, while a fourth is that of actual consumption practices. And the issues are not simply academic, they are now important elements in the political debate. Understanding of the social structure of income and its evolution has improved in recent years and is in dispute only for non-wage-earner categories,[17] but it is still a complex problem which cannot be solved by aggregate average figures: differences linked to skills, gender, age,[18] and location are crucial to an understanding of the class structure and the relations between classes. But the measurement of inflation has been much more in dispute. The price index worked out by the INSEE, although more independent of direct manipulation by the government than similar indices in many other countries, has been criticised by the unions over the years, to the extent that some unions have

---

[17] The INSEE publishes at least every year, in *Economie et statistique*, studies of the evolution of wages measured by various surveys, and so does the Centre d'Etude des Revenus et des Coûts.

[18] The age structure of wages is less known, and presents intriguing paradoxes: for various given categories, the average wage tends to decrease with age after a certain point, although for the average individual in each category wages increase with age. See Christian Baudelot, 'L'évolution des salaires: une nouvelle approache', *Economie et statistique*, No. 149, November 1982, pp. 3–11.

worked out their own price index. This sort of argument is clearly not confined to technicalities; it concerns whether the standard of living of the working class has been improved, maintained or reduced, as well as involving the causes of inflation, with the capitalist class and its experts claiming that the excessive raise of wages is its major cause. [19]

The evolution in workers' purchasing power is directly linked to working class struggles, and a careful study of its development constitutes an indispensable aspect of the theoretical and political battle. But it is also necessary to emphasise the limitations and omissions inherent in an approach that deals with this alone. The purchase of commodities is not their consumption. To see it as such is another ideological effect of the domination of the capitalist relation of production in reducing consumption to that one of its aspects which concerns accumulation, the realisation of value in final exchange. For capital, consumption is the act of allowing capital to regain the form of money in order to resume the cycle of the expansion of value. For the consumer, on the other hand, purchase is only the preliminary to consumption.

In fact, consumption presents a problem similar to that encountered in the analysis of production: the existence of a double aspect to these social processes – value and use-value – to which there correspond the two elements of the relation of production, the relation of ownership, and the relation of real or material appropriation. Just as production is both the process of production of surplus value (its dominant aspect) and the real process of production of use-values, so consumption is both the process of the realisation of value (the dominant aspect for capital) and the process of the real appropriation of use-values. This is equally true of productive consumption and workers' consumption. However, the latter differs to the extent that the social relations in which it is established are not the relations of capitalist production. In production, or productive consumption, what is produced (commodities) is produced through the domination of capital within the twofold relation of ownership and material appropriation; while so far as workers' consumption is concerned, what is produced is human beings, and the relations of production to that production are different – it is not capital which organises it directly – even though they are derived from and determined by the dominant mode of production.

Analysis of consumption practices must thus be concerned with an examination of the concrete process of consumption in its twofold aspect of distribution of the social product and the process of real appropriation

---

[19] Let us cite as an example P. Drouin, who wrote on the front page of *Le Monde*, 9 September 1976: 'Bringing down the fever of consumption is becoming increasingly possible as the standard of living of the majority goes up . . .'

of use values, and must also specify the social relations that characterise these concrete processes, as well as showing that these concrete processes are themselves products of the mode of production.

An important ambiguity in classical approaches to the problems of consumption is the way in which the question of needs as the reflection of objective requirements for the reproduction of the labour force is made to disappear, and needs are replaced by 'preferences' or 'value systems', strictly subjective terms, the ultimate free play of the behaviour of the 'rational consumer'. From the moment that 'disposable' income goes up, satisfaction increases, and the 'standard of living' rises. It is the classic argument, served up afresh at every election: look at all the cars on the roads, you can see that the French are doing better and better. Even if the argument was based on a calculation in real terms, using an accurate retail price index as a more faithful reflection of reality, the equation 'more commodities = more satisfaction' is a false one.

False precisely because it 'overlooks' two processes, the transformation of needs and the transformation of the general social conditions of the reproduction of the labour force.

The evolution of the necessities for the reproduction of the labour force

Let us look at a particular category of workers or employees, allowing that its net income, after tax, has gone up in real terms. In order to understand what the true consequences of this rise have been, one must first consider the development of the objective necessities for the reproduction of that labour force. It then becomes apparent, even if only the most direct determination is concerned, that in a substantial majority of cases there has been an increase in the work rate, the intensity of work.

It is difficult to show this increase in the intensity of work statistically: it is possible, for example, to measure the annual increase in productivity per worker, or by branch of industry. But this increase in the productivity of labour – a general and marked increase – is a result both of an increase in the speed of work, in work rates and the reduction of 'dead periods', and of the progressive technological transformation of production processes, the transformation and accumulation of fixed capital.

On the other hand, all the studies of the subject reveal the degree of this intensification, whether or not technological changes have occurred. In the same way, workers' demands, which bring out the problems being felt most acutely by the workers, have sufficiently emphasised work rates for this to be beyond question. But it should not imagined that this is only a problem affecting unskilled assembly-line workers, as is commonly maintained, in a variety of more or less useful ways, in discussions of unskilled and semi-skilled workers. They are certainly the most heavily exploited group of workers, but to concentrate on them exclusively tends to disguise the social extent of this phenomenon. Union organisations emphasise the extent to which this increase in work rates, which is a form of the intensification of exploitation, is common to all branches of work, the bank strikes of Spring 1974 having shown for the first time how even employees and white-collar workers in a sector which one might have imagined to be protected from this sort of intensification had not escaped it.

Intensification of work entails an accelerated wearing out of the labour force. This is expressed in a variety of symptoms: accidents at work, physical exhaustion, as well as nervous and mental illness and a break-down in health. This in turn makes the worker unfit to work, and leads to a tendency to dismiss older workers whose capacity has been prematurely exhausted.

The objective necessities of the reproduction of this labour force, and their subjective forms, needs, are multiplied and altered, in parallel with the development of demands increasingly focused on the intensity of work and work conditions and calling for a reduction in work rates, improvement in working conditions, a reduction in hours of work without loss of wages, and a reduction in the age of retirement.

Side by side with these demands, the increase and transformation of needs in consumption, the appearance of 'new' social needs relating to health, holidays, week-end rest and so on, are seen as manifestations of the insatiable nature of the workers who 'are always asking for more' and 'doing less'. The need for an increase in consumption, and of new forms of consumption, is only a response to the demands of this increased wearing out of the labour force, and its consequences.

Thus in order to achieve the same result, the reproduction of the same labour power, it is necessary to have a higher level of consumption, and thus a higher real income. And this conclusion is, of course, reinforced if one takes into acount the movement of the productive forces which entails increased demands for a skilled labour force, even if, at the same time, its use by capital produces a contradictory movement towards an increasingly unskilled labour force. There can thus be no increase in the standard of living without regard to the development of needs, which are not, let us repeat, an 'artificial consumer appetite' to be more or less easily manipulated, but the effect of objective necessities for the reproduction of the labour force. And it is for this reason that any analysis which isolates consumption from production is merely ideological.

One must also consider, as we have said, the general social conditions for the reproduction of that labour force. Here too, the transformations in those general conditions can be expressed as a necessary increase in consumer spending to achieve the same result in terms of reproduction of the labour force. This can be seen, for example, in the way the working population, manual and non-manual, has been forced out of the old quarters of Paris by urban renewal and shifted to the suburbs. The inadequacy of public transport often prompts the need to buy a car, even if only to get to work, a purchase which is very far from marking a 'higher standard of living' since it often represents an additional drain on income, so that spending has to be cut back in other areas. The general social conditions for the reproduction of the labour force, the socialised forms of consumption and the capitalist supply of commodities, determine the modalities of the response, in the concrete practices of consumption, to the objective necessities of the reproduction of the labour force. The transformation of these general social conditions thus entails significant changes in consumption: we will return to this point in relation to collective facilities and organisations.

The means and work of consumption

If the usual view of consumer spending as a measure of 'satisfaction' must be radically altered for the reasons discussed above – the decisive importance of the objective transformation of needs and the transformation of general social conditions – one must also go beyond a consideration of consumer spending on its own and analyse the concrete processes of consumption.

Consumption may be defined as the real process of appropriation of nature by man, through which, by transforming and destroying certain objects he reproduces himself. That is to say, every process of consumption is a process of production, the process of concrete work reproducing man himself.[20] It is important to emphasise this central characteristic of work, of labour, in the analysis of consumption. The dominant ideology, intensifying the opposition between production and consumption, presents the latter as being essentially passive. The life of consumption is said to exist 'outside work', and to be assimilated into leisure and the passive enjoyment of purchased commodities. The ideology of the consumer society takes this notion further by criticising the idleness of the consumer and describing consumption as 'push-button' work, basing this image on the stereotype of the American-style housewife (Hollywood

---

[20] We will show more precisely further on what is meant by this concept of 'the production of man'; let us simply emphasise here that it is a production, not of the isolated individual by himself, but of (re)production on the social scale.

model), completely mechanised and gadgetised, with the consumer seated passively in front of the television, his 'TV dinner', heated up in the automatic cooker, ready on his knee.

It is an image derived from myth and propaganda, far removed even from the American reality, as Jacques Arnault has shown.[21] It is even less true for French society, as statistics for household amenities make plain.

So far as amenities in the house (principal residence, by socio-occupational category of the head of the household) are concerned, only 31 per cent of farmers, 28 per cent of agricultural workers, 36 per cent of service personnel, 44 per cent of workers had both a toilet and a bath in 1978, while over 30 per cent of workers, in agriculture or industry, lived in moderately or acutely overcrowded housing conditions.

In 1979, 52 per cent of agricultural workers, 46 per cent of farmers, 34 per cent of service personnel and 29 per cent of workers did not have a vacuum cleaner. And as for automatic dishwashers, only the most well-off categories (upper management 54 per cent, entrepreneurs 40 per cent) owned one in 1981, while very few workers (12 per cent) and employees (16 per cent) had one. The most widespread household appliance is the refrigerator, partly because of the development of a way of life shaped by the organisation of work and travelling time, and partly because of the transformation of retail facilities.

Despite the fact that the number of domestic appliances is going up all the time, we are still a long way from push-button consumption. Besides, though domestic appliances may cut down on work, they do not by any means abolish it. As for the car, its use does not mean a reduction in the time and energy spent on travelling because of the worsening traffic situation, the paucity of public transport and the growing distances between home and work.

It is worth bearing in mind that there is a social form of consumption which is similar in many ways to the passivity that consumers are accused of, and that is the luxury consumption of the bourgeoisie, where the dominant class dispenses with the work associated with consumption on its own account by using the services of a specialised labour force.

It is interesting to see that it is not the passivity of the bourgeoisie employing servants to minister to its needs which is criticised by the ideology of the 'consumer society' – since this is rather a way of life validated as 'aristocratic' – but the supposed passivity of the worker, who is accused of 'letting himself be stupified by consumption'.

It is true that for the dominant ideology the only work worthy of the name is that which yields profit for capital. Any other sort of work is

[21] Jacques Arnault, *Les ouvriers americains* (Editions sociales, 1972), pp. 75–92.

leisure, and as such bears all the connotations of idleness and time-wasting. On the other hand, another contradictory facet of the ideology assimilates work and constraint, exhaustion and painful necessity, presenting the conditions of exploited labour as fatality.

If work is defined as the process of real appropriation of nature then it is possible to speak of consumption as work. The nature appropriated in it is the objects and means of consumption, generally drawn from social production (sector II) and the work of consumption realises its use-value.

Let us take food consumption as an example. The objects of consumption are foodstuffs, commodities whose use-value is not, generally speaking, directly appropriable. They have to be made to undergo a series of transformations in order to become effectively consumable, which entails work, the cooking or preparation of a meal. That work itself entails means of consumption: a cooker, saucepans, and so on which have to be maintained.

It is the development of the social division of labour which determines the social form of this process. Or else the social division of labour may separate the central task of work from the effective realisation of its use-value, and the work of the consumer is then reduced to its simplest possible expression – eating, there being two cases possible. First, that of capitalist production, where the work linked to food consumption (purchase–preparation–serving–washing up) supports the appropriation of value through the exploitation of the workers carried out in that production, a value realised in the sale of the meal – ready to eat – as a commodity. The second case is that of the socialised production of the meal as a collective service (factory canteen or school canteen, except where, as is becomingly increasingly common, these meals are purchased from capitalist undertakings). Or else the social unit of consumption is simultaneously the unit of production of the meal. Here again, two cases are possible: luxury consumption, where the consumer purchases for his personal service the labour-power actually carrying out the production, or the preparation of the meal by the consumers themselves. This latter case characterises the reproduction of labour-power, and applies to meals taken out of working hours.

It is clear that the different cases specified above are not simply 'available possibilities' among which the consumer is free to choose on the basis of his own 'preferences'. Even though the process of consumption may be an individual process, in the general sense defined above, we have already underlined the social determination of the consumption of the different social classes and strata. When analysing wage levels as being determined by the value of labour-power, which is itself defined as the value of the goods necessary for its reproduction, it is important to specify that it is the minimum value given the different social forms available for the process of consumption. This minimum value is defined by the processes which incorporate little or no value supplementary to the value of the objects and means of consumption, and which are thus the socialised production of meals, and the self-supply of the labour of preparation of meals.[22] This obviously does not mean that workers never go to restaurants, but that in social terms the working class itself is forced to provide a large proportion of the work linked to consumption. And the transformation of the social conditions of consumption can radically alter not only the cost, but also the significance of the work of consumption. This transformation has two effects on the value of labour-power. In classical terms, the focus of attention is on the increase in the cost of the necessary commodities, monitored, for example, through changes in the retail price index. But we have already shown that intensification in the wearing out of the labour-power may imply a qualitative and quantitative increase in the consumption necessary to maintain the same standard of living. In the same way, the transformation of conditions for the reproduction of labour-power may also increase its value. On the one hand, this transformation may impose an increase in the means of consumption available, while on the other hand it may entail, sometimes at one and the same time, a greater expenditure of labour-power in consumption, which will in turn raise the cost of its reproduction.

We have already cited the transport problems relating to the change of workers' living places, which may also be considered in relation to the changing forms of commercial activity.

In long-established urban neighbourhoods, where small shops are still fairly widespread, and most of the requirements for daily life can be purchased locally, it is not necessary to go far to do one's shopping, and commodities are served to the customer by the shopkeeper. But in recently urbanised areas small shops are rarer and have been supplanted by supermarkets, hypermarkets, and other kinds of shopping centre, whose prime characteristic is a more intense and larger form of commerce. The average distance from the place of residence to the shopping centre is thus much greater.

In the case of the small shop, goods are transported by specialised networks right into the immediate neighbourhood of the consumer's place of residence. With the shopping centre, there is from that point of view a decrease in the social division of labour, since it is the consumer himself

---

[22] Although capital's need to expand the field of profit impels it to become involved in developing commodity production which has as yet remained untouched, or been socialised, and thus to contribute to an increase in the value of labour-power.

who not only transports himself to the commodities in order to purchase them, but who also then transports them, over a distance of several miles, to his home. In the first case, of course, the customer pays an equivalent amount to cover the cost of transportation of the commodities. In the second case he no longer has to cover those costs, but he has to be in a position to transport the commodities himself, which implies the ownership and use of a motor car, and a certain expenditure of time and energy. This said, we are not, of course, trying to evaluate the implications of the opening of a supermarket for the inhabitants of a particular area: in a good many poorly provided suburbs, this can entail a marked improvement in living conditions so far as shopping is concerned. But in social terms, the replacement of small shops by supermarkets increases the work of consumers as a whole, even if that work is partially mechanised. And the social categories which do not have a car (in 1981, 30 per cent of total households, and nearly 60 per cent where the head of the household is not in employment, the most substantial proportion of which comprise old people) are at an even greater disadvantage.

Equally, the consumer must also provide his own facilities for storing and keeping the commodities purchased, often for a whole week, whence the obligation to have a fairly large-capacity refrigerator. Despite that, a reduction in the quality and freshness of a number of consumer products ensues.

Purchasing the commodities will apparently cost less in terms of their direct cost (theoretically at least, though there is no proof that the shopping centres pass on the full extent of these lower costs in lower prices), but additional transport costs and expenditure of energy must be taken into account. Since transportation of the commodities by heavy goods vehicle to the points of exchange is a production activity at a higher rate of productivity than the transportation of these same commodities in the private cars of a large number of consumers, it seems more than likely that in social terms these 'modern forms' of concentrated selling represent a higher cost and a higher expenditure of labour-power.

Though it is not possible to talk of exploitation, since there is no production and no appropriation of surplus value – the supplementary work of the consumer does not circulate as value appropriable by commercial circulation capital – there is nonetheless an increase in the value of labour-power, and, for the same wage, a commensurate deterioration in its capacity for reproduction. If, in the end, supermarket prices are only marginally lower than those in the small corner shop, despite the decrease in the value of the commodities, this has more to do with the monopoly situation or sharp commercial practice and is not exploitation, although it still contributes to increasing the value of labour-power.

Objections will be raised that the existence of 'free competition' and 'consumer choice' gives the lie to our analysis: the housewife tends to buy more at supermarkets than from small shopkeepers. Let us recall, in the first place, that the 'competition' is not as free as all that. The concentration of capital, the financial ties, give the supermarkets an enormous advantage which has got nothing to do with competition, quite the opposite. Then from the consumers' point of view there are all sorts of objective factors which effectively impel the housewife to shop in supermarkets: the decreasing number of small shops, lower prices in the supermarkets, the restriction of purchasing power that forces the consumer to look around for the lowest prices, even though this may entail extra expenditure of labour which does not appear as a direct household expenditure, and finally the rhythm of daily life, the length of work and travelling time, the physical and nervous exhaustion of the workers, the growing importance of female labour necessitating a reorganisation of the week's shopping outside the working week.

Free time and constrained time

This example is significant because it shows how the transformation of the social conditions for the reproduction of labour-power through the effects of the development of capitalist accumulation, can conceal under a façade of progress and modernisation an actual deterioration in the real conditions of existence. This question of work in consumption thus has wide implications for an analysis of concrete modes of life and the standard of living. It is a question which, incidentally, has a certain ideological appeal when constructed around theories of the 'leisure society'. It has been suggested that technological progress and the multiplication of domestic appliances has liberated man to such an extent that the major contemporary social phenomenon is the availability of leisure. It is worth noting in passing that these theories assume the character of work in our societies to be unavoidably tedious, and seek to make that 'doom' aceptable by holding up the glimmer of leisure as a compensation. Apart from this however, simply on the level of its relation to concrete social reality, this approach is completely contradicted by the results of analysis of ways of living. In our view it is necessary to distinguish between the concept of leisure, which refers to the idea of available free time, and the activity of consumption, which includes committed time. This distinction refers less to the nature of the activity or labour in question, than to the conditions in which it is carried out. One must in fact contrast (schematically and allusively here: this is one of the points where analysis needs to be developed) the activity or labour constrained by and committed to the most immediate needs of the reproduction of labour-power, and that which shares in a higher level of that reproduction and thus enable the workers to give free rein to their particular tastes and talents.

Some activities, by their very nature, can only belong to the second category: walks, cultural activities, film-going, theatre-going and so on. Others, depending on the conditions under which they are carried out, may belong to either category. The preparation of meals is a tiring, repetitive, tedious task for the mother of a family, particularly if she is also a wage-earner; on the other hand, cooking can be a very pleasant leisure activity for the gourmet. Car repairs can be a passion for the enthusiast, but they can represent a demanding and tiring form of extra work for the wage-earner forced to maintain the car he needs for travelling if his wage will not stretch to paying someone else to maintain it for him.

This difference between constrained activity and free or creative activity is crucial, since it points to the concrete relation between the labour of consumption and the level of reproduction of labour-power. All constrained labour represents, even within consumption, an extra expenditure of labour-power in addition to the labour-power used up during the working day, entailing an increase in tiredness and a greater need for rest, sleep and leisure. Whereas free and creative activities, though they can sometimes be more tiring than those carried out during working hours, represent, in the very expenditure of labour-power they entail and by the very nature of that expenditure, a positive contribution to the reproduction of labour-power.

But it is of course necessary to have first met the most pressing needs and to have responded correctly to the immediate demands for the reproduction of labour-power in order to have both the free time and the energy to make it possible, through sport, cultural activities, do-it-yourself, study or whatever, to express one's tastes and develop one's capacities, the development of the individual personality being a dimension of the development of the productive forces on the social scale.

Now we are very far from a situation where that kind of leisure is available to the majority of the population in our society. On the contrary, one could say that the workers, in the mass, are doubly cut off from it. Wage levels, which by and large limit consumption to the most immediately indispensable goods, and the very small amount of free time, available after spending the necessary time travelling, for rest and constrained acts of consumption, reflect and reinforce the exploitation in work through poverty and constraints on the way of life. The least favoured in this respect are married women workers who are mothers of several children, as time-expenditure studies clearly show.

This analysis also applies to the United States, despite its reputation as the 'affluent society', as recent studies have emphasised:

> Another unexpected result is the manner in which ways of spending one's time have developed over the years. John P. Robinson (Michigan, USA) has tried to compare various time-expenditure studies, a difficult undertaking in that the methods employed were not always the same, but which has nonetheless made it possible to draw the conclusions that there is no indication that the United States are in any real way moving towards a reduction in working time. Domestic work has increased rather than decreased, at the same time as there has been an increase in the time spent looking after the family. The picture which emerges from trends in the modern family is of woman being twice as busy, with work both inside and outside the home.[23]

This analysis of the significance of the labour of consumption extends the classic findings of Engels and Halbwachs: the higher a household's income, the smaller the proportion devoted to purely physical maintenance (and particularly food). Thus, in 1979, among the wage-earning classes, it was where the head of the household was an industrial worker that the smallest proportion of the budget was devoted to clothing, culture, leisure, holidays and transport, while the largest was spent on the cost of hygiene and health care.[24] If this fact about consumer spending already indicates the extent to which workers' consumption tends to be reduced to the most immediate aspects of the reproduction of labour-power, the significance of the labour of consumption, the proportion of constrained time within the time devoted to reproduction, are crucial factors in the concrete analysis of the way of life of different classes and social strata.

Thus, whatever certain ideologists may say, ours is not a leisure society. The real function of such a formula is revealed in the cynicism of the publicity concocted to promote 'temporary work', which presents it as a way of striking a 'balance' between work and leisure, whereas in actual fact it is one of the most shameful forms of overexploitation of labour ever engendered by the capitalist mode of production.

Consumption and female labour

Having set out some ideas on the nature of the work of consumption, we will now consider the social relations within which the processes of consumption function. These social relations are, on the one hand, the

---

[23] Jacqueline Feldman, summary of *Family issues of employed women in Europe and America*, ed. A. Michel (Leiden, E.-J., 1971), in *Cahiers Internationaux de Sociologie*, Vol. LVI, 1974, p. 188.

[24] See Table 4, p. 28, in Michel Glaude et Mireille Moutardier, 'Les budgets des ménages', *Economie et statistique*, No. 40, January 1982.

relations of ownership of the objects and means of consumption and, on the other, the relations of real appropriation of these objects and means.

The former can be seen first of all in the purchase of commodities, so far as goods consumed in the short term are concerned, and in a study of household estates, where durable goods are concerned. But this relates only to goods which are or become the private property of the household. It is also necessary to take into account 'collective goods', collective facilities, whose social ownership, as means of consumption, is highly varied, and which may or may not be, or may only in part be a support for market circulation.

The second relations define the concrete processes of consumption. We will deal here with those relations that concern the social unit of individual consumption, the household; more socialised forms of consumption will be considered later. The dominant form of the unit of reproduction of the labour force is the single family household.[25] The definition of a household is only an empirical one: a body of people living in the same dwelling. But insofar as the dwelling is a crucial means of consumption, it supports a number of consumption activities and is the place from which the family organises those activities which take place outside the home. This definition coincides in practical terms with the theoretical definition of the unit controlling the wage and organising the concrete processes of consumption.

The most important question concerning social relations within the individual processes of consumption is unquestionably the division of labour within the household, and in particular the role of the women, for this the point where the most significant objective transformations take place. In general terms, it is the question of female labour that comes to the fore here, both with regard to its social nature and from a quantitative point of view.

Some clarification is necessary here, since it is often said that more and more women are going out to work and, conversely, that they go out to work less than previously.

At first sight, it is the second statement which seems valid in the long term. Carré, Dubois and Malinvaud have put forward the following figures[26] for female participation rates, which, after various adjustments, provide a homogeneous series:

---

[25] The 'biological family' is defined by the INSEE as the couple, with their children if they have any; or the unmarried single parent or the single parent married but separated, and their children. In 1968, 72 per cent of ordinary households were made up of a family, and 25 per cent were made up of single persons.

[26] J.-J. Carré, P. Dubois, E. Malinvaud, *La croissance française, un essai d'analyse économique causale de l'après-guerre* (Seuil, 19XX), p. 69. M.-G. Michal, *L'emploi féminin en 1968*, Collections de INSEE, November 1973; Table 12, p. 22.

1901	1906	1911	1921	1926	1931	1936	1946	1954	1962	1968
36	36	35.5	35.5	33	33	31	32	30	27.5	28

This decline can be explained by a number of factors. On the one hand, a significant decrease among the lower age groups results from the effect of a higher legal school-leaving age and the expansion of further and higher education. On the other hand, the female population, like the rest of the population, has experienced profound social changes over the 1901–68 period, particularly a massive move away from agriculture, small shop-keeping and crafts towards other areas of employment. Now, for the two last categories and for agricultural work, female labour is often labour provided as family support, combining participation in the activity of the family economic unit and the labour of consumption. In 1968, 95 per cent of married women whose husbands were farmers, belonged to the same socio-economic category. Similarly, 69 per cent of women married to industrial and commercial entrepreneurs, categories mostly made up of shopkeepers and craftsmen, also belonged to the same socio-economic groups. It is still the case today that these categories have a higher female participation rate than that of wage-earners, and the decline in the agricultural population, small shopkeepers and craftsmen has been accompanied by a significant decrease in the general female participation rate.

If, on the other hand, one examines these rates according to social categories, and for a recent period where a comparable series is available, it is clear that there has been a continuous increase since 1954 in the employment rate for wives living with their husbands (see table 2).

TABLE 2 PERCENTAGE OF WOMEN WORKING ACCORDING TO HUSBANDS' EMPLOYMENT, 1954–81

	1954	*1962*	*1968*	*1981*
Professional	19.5	21.8	27.7	53
Upper management	17.8	23.0	29.4	
Middle management	31.9	37.2	43.6	67
Salaried employees	31.2	37.9	43.4	67
Workers	25.4	28.7	32.9	57
Service personnel	32.9	40.5	44.8	63

We have seen that these categories, particularly those of the employees and workers, are the largest categories today, in both relative and absolute terms.

Furthermore, during the period 1962–68 this increase has affected every age-group. It involves young married women without children just as much as young mothers, and even married women over 55 years of age, over the whole range of socio-economic categories shown in table 2.

In addition, the employment of the wives of wage earners is itself essentially wage employment. The distribution of the socio-economic categories of economically active married women in terms of the socio-economic categories of their husbands shown in table 3 was observed in 1968.[27]

TABLE 3   ECONOMIC ACTIVITY OF MARRIED WOMEN, 1968
(PERCENTAGES)

	Husband's socio-economic category		
	Middle management	*Employees*	*Workers*
Middle management	36	16.7	10.3
Employees	38.4	46	31.4
Workers	9.1	18.2	36.1
Service personnel	6.7	11.5	18.1
Total	90.2	92.4	95.9

The percentage for husbands in other categories is negligible except for middle management, 6.3 per cent of whom have wives in higher management or the liberal professions. In addition, 2.5 per cent, 4 per cent and 2.1 per cent respectively of the wives of middle managers, employees and workers belong to the category of industrial management and commercial entrepreneurs, most of them as small shopkeepers and craftswomen.

Thus the wives of wage-earners are also wage-earners themselves, employed in jobs outside the home and often, particularly in large towns, some distance from the home. This, in contrast to labour provided as family support, makes them unavailable during the day for domestic tasks and child care which are assigned to them by the traditional sexual division of labour.

It is therefore possible to assert that today the wives of workers are working in greater and greater numbers. This increase in labour, which brings in an extra wage to supplement the household budget, is only partially devoted to the purchase of means of consumption, made possible

[27]M.-G. Michal, *L'emploi feminin en 1968*, Collections de INSEE, November 1973, Table 12, p. 22.

by an increase in resources and a reduction in housework. Other aspects of the work of reproducing the labour force, such as the raising of children, in view of the lack of collective facilities, depend upon the work situation or geographical proximity of grandparents and can only be met with burdensome solutions which are highly unsatisfactory in emotional, education and health terms.

Overall, the work of consumption has decreased, but along with wage-earning participation, the total work has gone up. Thus behind the apparent rise in the 'standard of living', measured in monetary terms, there has been a decline in the way of life in terms of the significance of constrained, committed time. Moreover, it is women who suffer the most from this development, given on the one hand the devaluation of female labour by capital, which makes it more difficult for women to get interesting and well-paid work, and on the other the practical consumption ideologies which have meant that the division of labour within the household has not kept pace with other developments, so that the total amount of work done by women has increased.

Though female employment can be seen as potentially beneficial from the point of view of the general development of all the productive forces and the individual development of the social horizons open to women, it is not possible to speak of 'women's liberation' through work, as things stand at present. On the one hand, conditions of life within the household and the absence of collective facilities, has meant that the total burden of work, the amount of constrained time, has gone up. On the other hand, female labour in this mode of production is above all recruited for unskilled, repetitive work, which hardly fosters the development of the capacities of women as a full productive force.

Also, the functioning of the household as the social unit of consumption has been progressively disrupted and undermined. All members of a household, whether or not they go to work, have their own rhythm of activity, dictated by the timetables of work, school and travel. We are now witnessing a progressive desynchronisation of family life, which is most acute where shift-working is involved.

This desynchronisation of the individual's rhythms of work and rest has a number of serious social consequences since it disrupts a variety of consumption processes undertaken by the household collectively, which are not replaced by substitute social forms. There is thus a growing tendency for a disorganisation of family life to develop in a way which affects not only relations between the couple, but also parent–child relations, and the relations of the household as a whole to its 'social environment'.

NEEDS AND COLLECTIVE CONSUMPTION

The socialisation of consumption

The consumption practices we have just been looking at operate primarily through and within the social unit of consumption constituted by the household. This is to some extent the typical form in which the reproduction of labour-power within the capitalist mode of production occurs, and can be schematised by the cycle: labour-power → wages → commodities → labour-power. The worker exchanges his labour-power for wages, the labour being effectively consumed in the process of production. In exchange for his wages, he purchases commodities, the consumption of which makes possible the reproduction of labour-power. Consumption takes place in the form of individual consumption practices, characterised by, firstly, private ownership by the household of the objects and means of consumption, following their purchase through wages; and secondly, the real appropriation of those objects and means by members of the household in the process of consumption organised within the household.

This form only exists as a tendency of the mode of production, and is mixed with previously established forms or with forms expressing contradictory tendencies. First of all, certain elements necessary to the reproduction of labour power may be obtained without recourse to market exchange, as is the case of the self-supply of certain foodstuffs by farmers or by workers with their own gardens. More generally it is true of everything produced by the labour of consumption within the household, and which has not thus been purchased. The transformation of working and living conditions as a result of, among other things, the social forms of urbanisation, has entailed a reduction in the self-supply of certain products, and of foodstuffs in particular. When these elements of the reproduction of labour-power are then produced in the sphere of capitalist production that sphere is expanded and there follows an increase in the social and technical division of labour, socialisation in fact, but capitalist socialisation within production and not consumption.

In general, the pressure of constrained time resulting from the duration and intensity of work, from the time spent travelling, from exhaustion and the need to rest, and from the rapid growth of female wage labour impels a reduction in consumption labour which is partially replaced by the purchase of commodities: means of consumption such as electrical domestic appliances, or readymade meals, either preserved or deep-frozen. There is thus a widening of the field of social production in areas that previously derived from the labour of consumption, and certain types of domestic activity, for instance in the domain of food preparation, are abandoned.

Conversely, this transformation of consumption is strictly limited by household incomes, and as we have already seen, this constraint leads to the choice of cheaper modes of consumption which call for more work – within, however, the limits of the time available for that work, time which is considerably reduced. It is here that the whole problem of simultaneously managing the household's expenditure in time and money arises.

Individual consumption practices most often take place within more socialised practices, in the sense that the unit of consumption is not only the household-married-couple-family group, but in certain cases is widened to involve a larger social group, where various activities such as raising and looking after children, the preparation and consumption of meals and certain leisure activities may take place. These are most frequently socialised forms of consumption linked to social structures inherited from a precapitalist production, forms which have not (yet) been swept aside by the dominant mode.

They can sometimes even extend into the mode of capitalist production in the case of relatively homogeneous social groups, linked to fairly stable forms of production and reproducing themselves in a space adequate to their mode of appropriation: one can see this kind of socialised consumption persisting in some old working-class neighbourhoods, as Castells and Godard have shown in relation to dockers in Dunkirk,[28] and Maurice and Delomenie with regard to working-class districts in Marseilles.[29]

The more socialised character of consumption in these cases involves a different form of consumption relation, and above all a widening of the relations of the real appropriation of the objects and means of consumption to a larger social unit than that of the household-married-couple-family group, such as the extended family, and, often, the neighbourhood community. There is thus a lack of coincidence between relations of ownership – which usually remains private and individual – and the relations of real appropriation.

The mobility of capital, linked to the movement of profit, tends to undermine this kind of social organisation, and to stimulate the mobility of the work-force. Moreover, the processes of urbanisation break up the old working-class districts, and, with them, the old social structures, as Coing has clearly shown in relation to urban renewal in the XIIIe

[28] M. Castells and F. Godard, *Monopolville* (Mouton, 1974).
[29] M. Maurice and D. Delomenie, *Modes de vie et espaces sociaux* (Mouton, 1976).

arrondissement in Paris[30] or the GETUR team in relation to the 'rehabilitation' of the Très-Cloîtres area of Grenoble.[31] And the consequent changes in the way of life, in terms of committed time and the desynchronisation of the rhythms of life of the different members of the household, as well as the physical distances separating different households in the same family, make it difficult to rebuild that kind of structure of socialised consumption in the new urban areas, although mutual aid within the neighbourhood community still exists. But it is through class practices that one can best observe the emergence of new forms in response to this pressure on modes of socialisation.

To understand the nature and effects of the tendency towards the socialisation of consumption within a capitalist social formation, one must begin by looking at the conditions of the process of reproduction of labour-power. These conditions may, very generally, be characterised by a consistent tendency towards the limitation and constraint of the standard of living in the vast majority of working-class households, a constraint expressed both in purchasing power and in the constraints of committed time and consumption labour. Moreover, the workers' standard of living is not a static entity, but is constantly being undermined by the movement of accumulation of capital. That movement, slowed down by the downward trend of the average rate of profit, seeks to counteract that trend in various ways, which include increasing the rate of absolute surplus value or rate of exploitation. That increase may be carried out directly, through the wage policy of businesses, or indirectly, through inflation, for example. In fact, the workers' standard of living can only be defined as the outcome of a balance of power between conflicting forces. That is how one must see the determination of wages by the value of a labour-power: it is not the automatic effect of some mysterious self-regulating mechanism occurring outside the field of social relations themselves. It is through the class struggle that workers impose on capital wage-levels which make possible the reproduction of labour-power. In some historical periods, when the relation between forces was particularly unfavourable to the workers, capital raised the exploitation rate as far as possible, even going so far as to bring in from elsewhere (the countryside, foreign countries) the work-force lacking through insufficient reproduction.

Workers' demands relate not only to their pay, conditions of work and work rates — all of which are directly challenged by their immediate relation with capital — but also to the general social conditions in which

---

[30] H. Coing, *Renovation urbaine et changement social* (Editions ouvrières, 1966).
[31] J. Maglione et al., *Très-Cloîtres, analyse du processus d'insalubrisation d'un quartier* (GETUR, 1972).

they exist. In these struggles, in this social relation, one can see the tendency to the socialisation of the reproduction of labour-power arising as a class response to capital's tendency to increase the rate of exploitation, and to the inadequate living conditions produced by capitalist production.

The true reason for the chronic frustration of the workers' fundamental needs in relation to housing, health, and education is not the deficient effective demand of the population. The latter is itself the result of the limitation put on purchasing power by capital and its refusal to take these needs into account in the determination of the value of labour-power, whence the term 'fragmented needs' suggested by Patrice Grevet.[32]

Moreover, capitalist production does not and cannot respond to the requirements of the reproduction of the labour force, since the principal contradiction in the mode of production between the development of the productive forces and the relation of production also makes itself felt in the sphere of reproduction. Capitalist production only produces that which leads to profit, to an adequate profit. The law governing the movement of capital is accumulation, not response to social needs. And several elements necessary to the reproduction of the labour force, such as housing, health services, education and so on, are not produced if their production does not lead to a profit, or to a sufficient profit; to be more precise, they are not produced except within the strict limits of profitability, in profit-making forms which are inevitably market forms.

In other words, the contradiction in reproduction is revealed not only in the quantitative shortage of objects and means of consumption available to workers, but also in the qualitative inadequacy of the processes of consumption possible in relation to the demands of the reproduction of the labour force. This qualitative inadequacy relates as much to the social relations of consumption as to the physical nature and use value of the objects and means of consumption.

The relation of private ownership of the objects of consumption is questioned, not in an absolute way – according to the myth of wholesale collectivisation, down to the last toothbrush, that favourite bogeyman of bourgeois electioneering – but in its specific incapacity to satisfy social needs, which derives from the fact that the character of its social form is linked to the domination of commodity circulation, and, behind that, to the law of accumulation. To contest this relation of private ownership does not signify a need for its general abolition, but for its transcendence at the point where it becomes an obstacle to reproduction and the development of the productive forces. Nor does that transcendence

---

[32] Patrice Grevet, *Besoins populaires et financement public* (Editions sociales, 1976).

necessarily mean the 'collectivisation' of means currently in private ownership: rather, it means above all the development of new forms of social ownership.

Furthermore, the transcendence of the relation of private ownership is not necessarily linked to the transcendence of the relation of real individual appropriation. For instance, it can be argued that the development of privately owned second homes does not provide an appropriate response to social needs in terms of week-end and holiday leisure because of their excessively high cost, the negative consequences of private ownership of land, particularly in leisure areas, and a low rate of occupation. Obviously, the solution is not to 'collectivise' second homes, but neither does it lie in collective forms of leisure. Holiday villages run by works' committees, for instance, may provide a first step towards a social ownership of the means of consumption which, instead of hampering it, may make possible the development of individual appropriation of holiday places. And there are other forms of socialised ownership which could equally well contribute to a wide variety of solutions, such as cooperative societies, mutual aid societies and so on.

One may thus define the tendency towards a socialisation of consumption as a tendency towards the transcendence of individual commodity consumption, the transcendence of the twofold relation of private ownership and individual appropriation of the objects and means of consumption. It is a transcendence which operates either through the development of the social ownership of the objects and means of consumption, with the latter still being individually appropriated, or else through the simultaneous development of both social ownership and the collective appropriation of the objects and means of consumption, in concrete socialised processes of consumption where the labour of consumption is itself socialised.

This tendency is not the same as the tendency to replace individual consumption by collective consumption. It is rather the tendency towards the development of individual consumption (an individual process of real appropriation) through the production of the social conditions for that development, derived either from relations of ownership or from the socialisation of the labour of consumption. This last raises the productivity of that labour and saves on the individual labour involved, which is then available for an expansion of individual consumption. This movement therefore tends to reduce, where individual consumption is concerned, the amount of constrained time committed to the reproduction of labour-power, and to increase the amount of creative time available. Equally, socialism makes possible a qualitative transformation of consumption through the direct intervention of skilled living labour, which provides a wider range of possibilities than does the individual appropriation of commodities.

We should point out that this definition distinguishes the socialisation of consumption from other forms of socialised management of the conditions for the reproduction of labour-power, which are primarily concerned with wages and do not in themselves modify the social relations within which that reproduction is carried out, particularly the twofold market-private ownership relation. Many social benefits take the form of a supplement to wages or an indirect wage – travel allowances, housing grants, family allowances; these increase the purchasing power of the household that receives them but still remain within the framework of the forms of reproduction typical of the dominant mode of production. There are also forms of the 'socialisation of risk' (insurance and mutual aid societies) which may be related to forms of indirect wages (social security). These forms may constitute the prelude or the favourable preconditions for the development of other forms which transcend them in the direction of socialisation: thus, the social security system may make possible the development of a socialisation of 'health consumption' over and above the straightforward repayment of individual consumption of medical services produced in a private, money-making mode.

Socialisation and class struggle

The socialisation of consumption is no more an automatic process than the determination of wages by the value of labour-power; it exists only as a social relation, the effect of the primary contradiction. Nor is it a spontaneous movement contained within the processes of individual consumption. In fact, it only exists in and through the class practices which concretely produce that tendency.

The workers' struggle expresses this tendency in the work place, through demands for various social benefits, canteens and so on, through demands relating to housing and transport and to training, and through the action of workers' organisations such as the works committees, which organise and develop socialised forms of consumption. But this struggle goes beyond the relation to individual capitalist enterprises to make up a class relation at the level of the social formation, a political relation to capital as a whole, a relation to the state. It is through and within the state that the class relation within which the workers seek to impose the transformation of their conditions of existence is established. Thus class practices, as practices of an organised class, are crucial here as a fundamental element in establishing and defining the level of the political relation of classes condensed in the state.

For this reason, the concrete forms of socialisation of the reproduction of labour-power are in the main — though not exclusively — state forms, linked to the conduct of the state apparatus and to some extent internal to that apparatus. Equally the state forms of socialisation of consumption — the collective facilities [*équipements collectifs*] — and public services, are never purely relations and processes of consumption, but are always political and ideological relations and processes as well.

The tendency towards the socialisation of the conditions of reproduction of labour-power expresses the contradictions of that reproduction, and the transcendance of those contradictions within and through class practices: it is a tendency linked essentially to the workers' struggle. However, in certain circumstances and for limited periods of time, the concrete realisation of that tendency in state policies may produce effects favourable to an interest common to various capitalist undertakings. Thus an improvement in the general social conditions of reproduction of labour-power may appear beneficial to capital insofar as it provides a high-quality workforce; insofar as the direct cost of the reproduction of labour-power, and even occasionally wages, may be reduced because of the socialisation of some of the necessary elements which are thus taken out of the market cycle; and insofar as a perceptible increase in consumption, even in non-market consumption, usually stimulates economic activity. Some commentators have leapt to the conclusion that all this only helps the conduct of the capitalist economy, and that the demands for collective facilities and the achievements of working-class councils only contribute to a reformism that improves the situation for capital.

This is to overlook the fact that reformism is not the same as reforms, but consists in the negation, the political masking over of class contradictions and the need for their revolutionary transcendence.

It also overlooks the fact that while certain effects of the concrete realisation of this tendency in the 'social' policies for collective facilities are apparently favourable to capital, this realisation can only serve to deepen the principal contradiction of the mode of production. In the crisis of the mode of production in its state monopoly stage, this is revealed by the consistent countertendency of all monopolist policies towards a desocialisation of the conditions of reproduction of labour, and a systematic structuring of all sectors of social activity so that the points for the profitable insertion of monopoly capital emerge. The fact is that 'social peace' is a luxury which capital cannot afford because of the objective demands of the law of accumulation under conditions of intensified international competition, the lowering of the average rate of profit through the rapid increase in the organic composition of capital, and the contraction of the sphere of imperialist domination.

In every period one can see this contradiction at work, with every movement towards the socialisation of a sector of consumption being in direct contradiction to the interests of capital involved in that sector because it undermines the prospects for accumulation. Some sectors, due to the relation of political forces between classes and the relations of the internal forces of the dominant class, may find themselves more affected by the movement towards a socialisation of consumption: this was the case, for instance, in real estate and the building industry when social housing policies and rent restrictions were introduced. But the development of the crisis, as we have said, has driven capital and the state to undermine that socialisation so as to widen the field of monopolist accumulation.

For this reason, there cannot be, within this mode of production, any stable definition or continuous evolution of the sectors and forms in the direction of socialised consumption. On the contrary, there is on the one hand a tendency towards their development and expansion into new sectors through the influence of the workers' struggles and, on the other hand, a contrary tendency towards the reintroduction into the socialised sectors of new forms of domination by monopolist accumulation – and that is what is meant by the popular term 'privatisation'.

Collective facilities, needs and public finance

The socialisation of consumption can no more be assimilated into any linear movement towards progress than can the socialisation of production. Like productive forces, the processes of consumption reflect the dominant social relations, and are constantly shaped by them as they develop. Thus in order to understand their meaning and social consequences, one cannot rely on a straightforward opposition between two poles, that of socialisation, in the specific concrete form of publicly owned collective means and services, and that of private, individual ownership and use of commodities.

Traditional approaches to the study of collective facilities have always sought a criterion, or several criteria, which would enable them to make a clear distinction between the 'private' and the 'collective', and, having been unable to find one have resigned themselves to the idea of more or less 'pure' 'collective goods'. Current terminology expresses this lack of agreement: collective goods, collective services, collective functions, market or non-market consumption, divisible or non-divisible entities.

This is a real difficulty, which cannot be resolved so long as the search continues for criteria that can be used to classify different concrete processes of consumption so that each one may be unequivocally described as less or more collective. It seems to us, on the contrary, that what is needed is an analysis of the social relations characterising these processes, relations which can reveal themselves to be more or less complex and which always present a variety of aspects, making it impossible to reduce them to a single dimension.

Starting from the idea that all consumption is first of all labour, a form of production in which man reproduces himself, leads to considering labour power and means (of consumption), relations of ownership and the real appropriation of these means, a technical and social division of labour. The totality of these elements must be included in any definition of a particular social process, not any single criterion.

The socialisation of consumption can only involve the ownership relation of all, or one, of the means of consumption. Thus roads are publicly owned, but this allows 'private', individual appropriation by car drivers, road hauliers, and so on. There can also be collective appropriation of one means of consumption: for example, of a bus using those same roads. One can thus see that the 'collective' character is not one of a particular good in itself, but of the social mode of its utilisation.

Of course, while certain objects can be used equally well privately or collectively, the development of collective consumption implies the production of means of consumption whose use value is adapted to collective use.

In addition, a number of socialised processes imply the intervention of a specialised labour force other than that of consumers, whose characteristics – in terms of numbers, skills etc. – will carry decisive weight.

Their competence, the techniques employed and the ideologies reflecting and determining the processes of consumption should all be considered, as well as their development.

Finally, the question of mastering these processes is crucial, in terms of understanding both their internal workings and their wider political and economic dimensions.

There is no single exclusive form of the socialisation of consumption, the collective/public form – however vague and heterogeneous one might take that 'public' to be – but a variety of widely differing forms. These forms can be distinguished according to the different aspects of consumption relations, whose analytical framework we have just discussed. But this is not a question of an abstract 'neutral' or 'technical' combination, where the concepts make possible the classification of empirical objects. The forms of socialisation express political processes, relations of political and economic forces, which gave rise to them and shape their development. And though it may be true that the driving force behind their development is the class struggle, that development, particularly when underwritten by capital or by the state, cannot be treated as the natural response, point for point, to externally expressed needs. On the contrary, capitalist or state socialisation of consumption is characterised by an unending displacement of the terms and the site of response to the class struggle. That response is continually being worked out, shaped and directed in terms of the dominant political and economic interests. And its concrete forms – the collective facilities and the manner in which they are actually produced and function – have in turn an effect on the political processes and the politico-ideological formation of needs.

On the basis of these few remarks on the underlying principles involved,[33] we may now review the usual method of analysing collective facilities.

The most common method, in both economic analysis and political debate, consists in seeking to establish the extent of the financial backing of collective consumption, particularly the proportion of the state budget allocated to it.

Before proceding we should note the difficulties of such an exercise in France today, difficulties which can be ascribed to a variety of causes. The first is related to the fact that the presentation of accounts, whether in the Budget, Five-Year Plans or the budgetary reports put out by the public accounts department, are an inextricable mixture, under several different headings, of expenditure on collective facilities which are linked to working-class consumption, and collective facilities which are means of production and are often linked to monopoly investment.

The second difficulty concerns the multiplicity of sources of public finance: the state budget, local authorities, public organisations, and para-state bodies. The role played by local authorities is a very important one, though it varies widely from one sector to another,[34] and between towns and regions: on this subject, however, only very general data are available.

The third difficulty relates to the problem of calculating not only capital expenditure (construction of buildings, purchase of materials and so on), but also the current expenditure required for their functioning, e.g. on personnel.

To the extent that these difficulties can be at least partially overcome, the study of the public financing of collective consumption is likely to provide extremely interesting insights into the scope of public policies for

---

[33] Developed at greater length in my article, 'Equipements collectifs et consommation sociale', *International Journal of Urban and Regional Research*. No. 1, 1977, and in 'Collective consumption, the State and the crisis of capitalist society' in *City, Class and Capital*, ed. Michael Harloe and Elizabeth Lebas, Edward Arnold, 1981).

[34] See F. de Lavergne, *Economie politique des equipements collectifs* (Editions Economica, 1979).

the socialisation of consumption, their variations,[35] and the respective roles of different territorial levels of the state machine. From some points of view, this is an indispensable element in analysing such policies: the level of funding is a key criterion by which to judge the real meaning of a particular pronouncement, proposal or law, or the real nature of a local experience. For instance, the same meaning cannot be ascribed to the law on social housing passed in 1894, without financial backing, and to another law some 30 years later, hardly differing from the first in its stated aims but accompanied by significant sums allotted to it in the Budget. One of the major weaknesses in 'genealogical' studies of these policies is the obscuring of the historical discontinuities apparent in changes in funding levels (and thus the political conjunctures behind these fluctuations) in the search for an ideological and institutional continuity which would reveal the gradual historical realisation of the long-term strategies of the dominant power.

On the contrary, it could be argued that it is impossible to understand any aspect of state or capitalist policies relating to collective consumption without dealing with the dimension of effective expenditure. Let us concede what is to some extent true, that increased collective consumption – and individual market consumption too, since the argument holds equally true for theories of the 'consumer society' – by the workers ensures social peace and the bourgeois social order. How, then, is one to reconcile the recognition of this sort of 'benefit', which has been acknowledged at least from the early nineteenth century, with the fact that any possibility of applying that theory was overlooked until the very end of the nineteenth century, when there were the beginnings of a timid movement in that direction?

What is one to make of the fact that only a minority of workers have ever 'benefitted' from the 'efficient' company towns,[36] or even from social housing?

What is one to make of the fact that during the present crisis, in which power and capital must feel ever more intensely a desire for social control, there is nonetheless a continued retrenchment in the workers' individual and collective consumption?

The reason is precisely that the question of working class consumption, whether individual or collective, is primarily an economic question, lying at the very heart of the capitalist mode of production. Any allocation of

---

[35] Patrice Grevet's *Besoins populaires et financement public* (Editions sociales, 1975) is a useful example of the historical analysis of the long-term development of this type of financing.

[36] An orderliness and 'organisation' which fed the literary dreams of the employers, as is shown in L. Murard and P. Zylbermann's useful text, 'Le petit travailleur infatigable', *Recherches*, No. 25, Paris, 1976, an interesting study whose major weakness is precisely that pinpointed here.

some part of socially produced value for consumption purposes entails an equivalent reduction in the surplus value for capitalist accumulation. The growth of public financing of collective consumption, insofar as it is not merely state management and redistribution of one (socialised) part of the wage, is thus structurally contradictory to the expanded reproduction of capital. Close analysis of the development of public financing of collective consumption during the phase of state monopoly capitalism has yet to be carried out, at least in overall terms, although in some fields, such as health and housing, significant contributions are available. But the rapid increase in public spending on health, housing, education and transport in the 25 years following the Second World War does not seem to have been accompanied by any equivalent lowering in the workers' take home pay. In the last few years, however, this figure has had a tendency to stagnate or go down in real terms, as studies of various categories for the period 1975–80 have shown, parallel with a decrease in the public financing of collective consumption. This development is not the conjunctural effect of the austerity resulting from the 'oil crisis' but, as we have shown above, is structurally linked to the crisis of over-accumulation of capital. The crisis has forced monopoly capital to seek an increase in the overall rate of exploitation so as to maintain the profit rate; the transfer of public funds from collective consumption towards direct forms of financing accumulation is one form of this trend.

The justifiable criticism of economistic analyses of state policies which reduce them simply to an analysis of public finance should not, however, lead to the abandonment of all economic analysis, avoiding the decisive contradiction between workers' consumption and the accumulation of capital. To see in capital nothing but the quest for power and social control spreading its tentacles ever wider is to overlook the movement and concrete contradictions of the economy as well as social struggles. It entails all too frequently the reconstruction of a mythical history of the dominant power feeding on itself, by stressing the (selectively produced) continuity of its discourse.

On the contrary, we suggest that it is essential to take account of historical continuities as much as of the ruptures, fluctuations and reversals of tendencies. It is imperative that the analysis of the movement of accumulation and its contradictions be articulated, together with its appropriate periodisation and the analysis of social and political struggles, the relation between forces and their expression in the state and its policies. And an analysis of public finance must be included, but not only in terms of the volume of expenditure. In fact, even disregarding the accounting difficulties touched on previously, the analysis of the social effects of state intervention in the socialisation of consumption cannot stop at an appreciation of what some call the 'redistribution' effected through social policies. For with certain exceptions what is involved is something quite different from monetary redistribution.

Public finance is often linked to the forms of capitalist production of the means of consumption. Consequently what takes place is not redistribution but circulation of the means of consumption, ensured by public finance, in commodity or non-commodity forms. The social effect of the level of finance depends very much on the mode of allocation, which may vary, and on the relation to the intervention of capital in different sectors. Thus the social effects of loans advanced by the Crédit Foncier,[37] which act as devalorised capital underwriting capitalist profits in housing, are distinct from loans to social housing developers (HLM) producing subsidised rented accommodation.

Moreover, public finance makes possible certain forms of socialised consumption which can be seen to be, at least in part, qualitatively different from what they would have been under strictly capitalist production, as well as being less costly for the user. For the domination of capital selects the production of those goods most adequate for surplus-value formation and commodity circulation.

This contradictory involvement of public finance in collective consumption gives rise to a significant difficulty in the study of 'social policies', but it can also be seen as a characteristic of the contradictions of state monopoly capitalism and the ambiguity of its social policies, which express at one and the same time the tendency to develop socialisation in non-market forms and the contradictory tendency to re-establish all sectors of social life within the field of capitalist profit.

This contradiction has been noticeably aggravated during the crisis due to the increasing pressure of social needs and the intensification of social struggles on the one hand, and the tendency to directly support monopoly profit on the other. This tendency is expressed in two ways: a general reduction in public expenditure in sectors related to working-class consumption, with priority being given to the financing of sectors more directly dominated by capitalist accumulation; and the 'reorganisation' of collective consumption in order to create possibilities for a more profitable intervention by capital. An important aspect of this second trend is the systematic policy of increasing charges for public services and reinforcing the market circulation of collective services; this is clearly the necessary condition for realising the possibilities of profitable investment. Equally, however, one must not overlook the concomittant implication of

---

[37] Translator's note: The Crédit Foncier is a government-controlled credit institution which is the main source of loans for house purchase; the interest charged is slightly below market rates.

considerable waste and deterioration in the quality of collective facilities and their social unity.

The case of the motorway tolls is a particularly clear example. A government project concerning the A4 autoroute to the east of Paris which suffered a crushing defeat a few years ago because of popular opposition was a plan to install tolls not only on motorways running through the countryside, but also on urban motorways. This notwith-standing the fact that the cost of installation of toll collection points is extremely high and that they entail a slowing-down of traffic, which is precisely the reverse of the aims of building motorways.

The same tendencies can be seen at work in housing policy. As we remarked earlier, the last few years of the Giscard government saw a contraction in social house building, particularly with regard to sub-sidised rented accommodation, while simultaneously private housing, which had fallen more and more under the control of the big banks, took up an increasingly large share of total housing production. The crisis, expressed in overproduction relative to the effective demand of the population, which had, on the contrary, tended to decrease, has under-mined the profitability of housing at the same time as actual accom-modation needs remain increasingly unsatisfied. The 'solution' to the crisis, as advanced in reforms carried out on the basis of the Barre Report and under his government, consisted in emphasising the tendencies even further: cutting down on finance to subsidised rented accommodation (the most socialised form of public aid to meet needs, enabling a significant proportion of the construction of new accommodation to come under public control, and implying the possibility of regulating it) in favour of 'personalised housing allowances' confined to 'the most disadvantaged'. In this way, public control of the production and circulation of social housing is replaced by an attempt to increase the effective demand of one part of the population, and tends to leave capital in sole control of the production and circulation of housing, which thus enters more directly and significantly into the market cycle and into the accumulation of capital.

Apart from the fact that this revised and increased housing allowance is insufficient and the number of recipients far smaller than the number of potential recipients of subsidised rented accommodation (one of the avowed objectives of the reform being to reduce public finance in housing), it is important to emphasise that the private housing sector is highly inflationary because of speculation by building firms and the construction industry, and so the increased effective demand produced by the reform can only be marginal and temporary. All of this entails, at one and the same time, the imposition of an increase in household expenditure on accommodation – for several years now experts and residential developers have agreed that the proportion of their income that the French spent on housing is insufficient – and a considerable widening of the opportunity for the intervention of capital in housing development, with the redirection of finance towards 'personal housing allowances' making it possible for capital to benefit from the effects of funding which, when funding was restricted to the subsidised rented accommodation sector as in the past, was more or less entirely inaccessible to it.

A policy of this sort can only lead to a worsening of the living conditions of the population and contribute to inflation, as well as having the effect, through the displacement of control over most construction operations towards capital, of making the production of housing even more unstable, due to its direct dependence on the fluctuations of monopoly speculation. Finally, such a policy will entail a deterioration in the conditions of urban planning, making even more difficult the search for control over urban development and the necessary coordination between the production of housing and the production of the collective facilities which are indispensable elements of a residential environment.

From these two examples it is possible to see how the crisis policy operates so as to transfer socialised consumption to the cycle of capital accumulation through state intervention and, under the control of capital, undermines both quantitatively and qualitatively the conditions necessary for the reproduction of the labour force.

This desocialisation, as we emphasised earlier, is only one aspect of the reinforcement of exploitation on a general scale, and is justified by various pronouncements opposing a state-aided society, advocating the encouragement of individual initiative and responsibility. 'After all, why shouldn't people pay for things they think are indispensable and for which they're prepared to take responsibility?'[38]

Collective consumption and social distribution: selectivity or segregation?

This undermining of public services and facilities, which makes use of every argument it can lay its hands on to promote its case, also claims that collective consumption can only reproduce social inequalities, whereas it is possible to exercise greater control over a purely monetary redistribution, which would be less 'a prey' to the institutions. . .

---

[38] A remark by Michel Crozier, eminent sociologist and theoretician, supporter of the Giscard regime, during an international colloquium on 'The 80's: economic facts and choices' organised by the French Government at UNESCO on 3–4 June 1980.

This leads us to another dimension of the investigation of the social effects of the policies of collective facilities, the question of their social distribution. It is impossible to speak in a general way about social policies, as a whole, or even of state socialisation of the reproduction of the labour force, without seeking to specify which classes, or which sections of classes or social strata, have access to and effectively benefit from particular categories of collective facilities.

Most studies emphasise, from this point of view, the segregative nature of access to these services, but they emphasise it in different ways, depending on the types of consumption in question. The social selection highlighted by the research carried out by Bourdieu and Passeron,[39] and Baudelot and Establet[40] on the education system to some extent reproduces class differences, through the educational frustration and 'short cycle of studies' accorded to the working classes and the long cycle of studies and university or other higher education open to the 'inheritors'. Public hospitals have at present many more workers as long-stay patients, whereas the higher social categories are above all consumers of (private) medicine or of highly specialised hospital care.[41] Subsidised rented accommodation disproportionately favours the middle classes and the most skilled strata of the working class.[42] As for the most overt forms of welfare benefits and social services or of repression (approved schools and prisons), it is well known that they give priority 'welcome' to the poorest, most marginal strata of the working class.

This brief outline shows how difficult it is to use terms like 'redistribution' in talking about the concrete effects of the benefits of collective means of consumption, and also, from the opposite point of view, that it is too easy simply to see them as having a homogeneous segregative effect.

The social selectivity of such facilities is partially related to the institutional characteristics defining the 'beneficiaries' or users, as well as their mode of functioning, as determined by the institutional structure and by the systems of relations and practices tied into them, a subject we will return to later. It is sharply emphasised by inequalities in physical access to the facilities, resulting in social segregation, which pushes low-income workers away from the city centre towards the periphery, and in an unequal geographical distribution of facilities.[43]

---

[39] P. Bourdieu and J. C. Passeron, *Les héritiers* (Editions de minuit, 1964).
[40] C. Baudelot and R. Establet, *L'école capitaliste en France* (Maspero, 1971).
[41] See A. Chauvenet, *Médecine au choix, médecine de classe* (PUF, 1978).
[42] See Michel Pinçon, *Les HLM: Structure sociale de la population logée* (CSU, 1976).
[43] See our research conducted in association with Monique Pinçon and Paul Rendu, on the socio-geographical distribution of collective facilities in the Paris region; M. Pinçon, E. Preteceille and P. Rendu, *Classes sociales, equipements collectifs et structures urbaines* (forthcoming).

It is also related to the determination of the modes of life and needs of the different social classes and categories, which shape their relations to the facilities, whether they use them or not, the ways in which they use them, and so on.

Some of these determinants have fairly direct material effects. The level of income, for instance, since access to collective consumption often enough involves expenditure, either because of the pricing of certain services, or because there are associated costs such as transport, personal equipment and so on. Equally, the availability of spare time, resulting both from the length of the working day and so the degree of tiredness resulting, and from the timetable and place of work, which may or may not allow access to certain facilities near the work place and which, along with travelling time, may determine presence or absence in areas where services are available.

Other determinants, though more indirect in their effects, are no less significant. They may be termed cultural, so long as one uses culture in the widest sense of the term to include the whole body of understanding and images of daily life. On the one hand, in order to make use of a fair number of these facilities the user needs a certain range of knowledge, and the ability to move within a universe of norms and approaches and administrative regulations which relies on specific cultural elements deriving for the most part from 'educated culture'. The use of these facilities is both easier and more efficient (in terms of their mode of functioning, a point we will return to later) if the user has at his disposal this knowledge and these cultural elements. This has been demonstrated in a number of studies of educational institutions, but it seems that it should also be extended, in other forms, to a good many other fields, such as health, sport and so on.

But cultural determinations play a part at an even deeper level, in the formation of needs. These may be defined as the subjective forms of the objective determinations of the social practices that shape the repro-duction of the labour force, bearing in mind the contradictory nature of these objective determinations[44] and the extension of the social practices. Needs are not the mechanical reflection of the demands of production alone, but express or, rather, interpret these demands through a complex process. In this ideological and practical process, the modes of conditions of daily life, work as well as consumption in its widest sense, are involved as points of reference, as bases, and also provide the perspective for the social history of both individuals and groups. In this sense, then, culture

[44] See my article, 'Besoins sociaux et socialisation la de consommation', *La Pensée*, No. 180, 1975, and also 'Collective consumption, the State and the crisis of capitalist society' in *City, Class and Capital*.

includes these practical ideologies of everyday life, and is involved in a major way, as Pierre Bourdieu's researches have clearly shown.[45]

However, the internal dynamics of the practico-ideological cultural processes which go to make up needs still require substantial clarification. The concept of 'habitus', proposed by Bourdieu as a theoretical alternative to the concept of need in relation to this question, takes account of these preoccupations in the notion of 'the internalisation of conditions in practice' as the element structuring these practices. But because of an excessive anxiety to mark itself off from the strict economism attributed to the concept of the reproduction of labour-power[46] – which is present, it is true, in a number of its applications – the concept loses the fundamental wealth of the complexity of the concrete relations and processes of work, which cannot be reduced to income or 'status', and even more import-antly, loses their contradictory nature. If the determination of needs is a complex process, it is largely because their determination by economics – by their place in the production process – is itself contradictory. Capitalist production produces, for the worker, the need to reproduce his labour-power as a marketable commodity, and thus as a commodity adapted to the manpower needs of capital, but it also produces the need to transform and enrich his labour and to control it, both individually and collectively. It seems to us possible to suggest that it is an economistic reduction of economics which is used to justify the concept of 'habitus' and discard the concept of need, and that this reduction entails a consequent reduction of the concept of class to a classificatory category which makes no reference to the concept of production relations. Similarly, the concept of capital is reduced to something which one may have more or less of, i.e. whose volume can be measured,[47] as opposed to the definition, fundamental to a break with bourgeois economic ideology, of capital as social process and social relation. For Bourdieu, the worker is not defined as an exploited producer, he is an individual who is (substantially) deprived of capital (economic and cultural alike).

Paradoxically, this view tends to end by producing an economistic reduction of culture, with the introduction of the concept of 'cultural capital' constructed on the same model and supposed to represent one of the specific forms of capital in general.

It is unquestionable that class domination is also expressed in cultural domination, not so much in terms of the external domination of proletarian culture by bourgeois culture, as in the effect of domination in

---

[45] See for example P. Bourdieu, *La Distinction* (Editions de Minuit, 1978).
[46] This approach is applied and explained by Michel Pinçon, *'Besoins et Habitus'* (CSU, 1978).
[47] See Bourdieu, *La Distinction*, pp. 128 ff.

cultural practices. This effect, which tends to rank practices according to whether they are more or less 'legitimate', entails the passing over or exclusion of a number of (popular) practices from the domain of 'culture', and criticism and enslavement by the dominant practices (cultural as well as economic: as for instance show business and all the 'cultural' industries, the media, and so on).

This cultural domination is one of the mechanisms of hegemony, in Gramsci's sense of the active consent of the dominated classes, and entails the recognition of the dominant class as bearer of Knowledge, of Culture, for all society. It contributes to the formation of all needs, and not simply to that of 'cultural' needs in the narrow sense of the term.

But, here too, let us not overlook the fact that 'domination' is a contradictory process, a movement in the struggle between opposing forces. The effects of relations between classes on the formation of needs cannot be reduced to this sort of ranking, nor even to the impoverishment or deprivation (particularly in cultural terms) of the working classes. They too produce, on the same basis of production relations, contradictions in the economy such as we discussed earlier, and the formation of needs separate from domination and its reproduction. These, linked to the political struggles of the dominated classes, are expressed in consumption practices, both on an individual scale and collectively, practices which seek to undermine the domination in this domain and which rely on working-class capacity for autonomous organisation.

Thus it is not possible to pose the question of the social selectivity of consumption, and the social differentiation of needs, in terms of simple social inequalities — inequalities which would vary from the wealthiest and most cultivated to the most deprived within the homogeneous space of a series of continuous variables defining needs, modes of life, culture and consumption. In fact, the numerous inequalities and differences which can be brought out in the different domains of consumption have a cumulative effect. They fall into differentiated structures which express the situations of specific classes, in a way that has led certain researchers to put forward the notion of specialised 'channels' for consumption, and for the reproduction of labour-power.[48] There is still a lot that needs to be done, both in theoretical and empirical terms, in analysing these differentiated structures. The concrete study of the relation between the position in the production process and the mode of life outside work is certainly a crucially important approach in this field. It makes it possible to break away from the customary split between production and consump-

---

[48] See F. Godard, 'Classes sociales et modes de consommation', *La Pensée*, No. 180, April 1975, and Castells and Godard, *Monopolville*.

tion, and look at the fundamental determinants of practices, in their contradictory movement, in the reproduction of exploitation and domination as well as in the struggles which undermine it.[49] It also makes it possible to go beyond an over-generalised vision of the working class, and grasp, within the different positions in the work process the primary cause of the movement of division of that class by capital. This last aspect is particularly significant because of the way the transformation of the division of labour is linked to the process of accumulation. The working class is currently experiencing new modes of exploitation and reproduction, of fragmentation and social reorganisation, which are as yet insufficiently clearly recognised. Unemployment, temporary work, the crisis in the steel industry, or, in the Paris region, in printing, the de-industrialisation of major urban areas, the growing proportion of unskilled labour in industries previously using skilled labour, the growth of industries in semi-rural areas, and so on – all these developments result from new forms of the accumulation of capital in the current crisis; all have consequences not only for working-class conditions of life and work, but also, at a much deeper level, for the very constitution of the working class. As a result, they also have consequences for the needs, demands, class consciousness, capacity for organisation, for unification, and for alliance with other social strata of different categories of workers.

Let us add that the same approach is equally valid for the analysis of other classes, and especially of the 'new middle strata' whose rapid growth we mentioned earlier. It is as important as when dealing with categories of workers to define these strata on the basis of the positions they occupy in the different social processes of work, which are even more various. There is too great a tendency to lend them an artificial homogeneity, taking account only of the criteria related to distribution and the mode of life. Their needs and consumption practices are too easily seen simply in terms of a quest for social status and the imitation of higher social categories, whereas in fact, even bearing in mind the specific ideological conditions of the formation of their needs (the ambivalence of their relation to state authority or to the hierarchy within the place of work, for example), the question of the reproduction of their labour-power is still a key factor. And this labour-power is extremely heterogeneous, as are the social relations in which it is operating. It is heterogeneous in its degree of skill as much as in terms of the components of hierarchical or ideological domination.

It seems to us that there is no justification for treating these disparate

---

[49] See Castells and Godard, *Monopolville,* and D. Bleitrach and A. Chenu, *l'Usine et la vie* (Maspero, 1979).

strata as a new social class, the 'new petite bourgeoisie'. But it is even less justifiable to simply accord them the general status of salaried worker, and to see only the real movement which, through the change in working conditions and the standard of living, has drawn a number of these stata closer to the working class. The contradictory determinations of their needs cannot be reduced to an ambivalence between the two poles of bourgeoisie and proletariat. These needs express specific positions within the technical division of social labour, whether in the field of production, circulation, the reproduction of labour-power or state management.

As a result, their position within consumption practices, and particularly within socialised consumption practices, is something more than an intermediary stage. It is the expression of needs anchored in that division of labour, of which a significant aspect is undeniably the tendency to split apart manual and intellectual labour. The fact that some of the middle strata seem to benefit in fairly privileged ways from facilities such as schools or cultural organisations should thus be related in the first place to the positions these strata occupy within that division of labour.

Clearly these remarks only point the way to an area of research, as much concerned with the division of labour and its by no means direct and mechanical expression in needs, as with the reproduction of that division of labour through consumption processes, whether by individual market consumption or socialised consumption, which is by no means clear-cut and obvious. These observations aim to highlight the fact that the 'inequalities' observed in the sphere of consumption between the situation of these more privileged strata and that of the working class, inequalities resulting from, among other things, the 'social selectivity' of collective facilities, derive from more radical differences. They are not simply quantitative differences, which either are being or easily could be eroded. Nor are they simply relative 'advantages' conceded by capital and the state in order to obtain the support of these strata, as an excessively politicist interpretation tends to claim. They are primarily related to the reproduction of the social and technical division of labour and to the specialised reproduction of the labour force specified by that division. This is a concept which we will develop further a little later, particularly in relation to its ideological and political consequences.

Needs, collective consumption and power

An analysis of the social effects of collective facilities entails a consideration of the social structure of the population of 'users' and the general determinants of their needs and consumption practices, but it also implies an analysis of the social practices which organise collective consumption.

What is involved here is the management of collective facilities, the concrete content of the work of consumption produced in them, and the practices and ideological relations involved, which cannot be reduced to a simple functional process of reproduction of the labour force.

Every consumption process is linked to class relations, and socialised processes of consumption are linked to the class relations determining the forms of that socialisation. This, in our society, is primarily a state socialisation, and is the direct or indirect effect of the workers' struggles to improve and extend the reproduction of the labour force.

These forms of collective consumption, financed, organised, managed, even controlled by the state, cannot then be considered simply as gains won from the opponent once and for all, as islands of socialisation to be relied on just as they are. Like municipalities and public services, the majority of collective facilities are state institutions, and, as such, are embroiled in the class struggle and stamped with the domination of the capitalist class, a domination affecting not only the material conditions of the workers who ensure that these facilities function, but also that very functioning itself.

Does that mean, as 'radical' commentators maintain, that collective facilities can only be correctly analysed as ideological state apparatuses – a position which echoes that put forward by Althusser in his discussion of educational institutions?[50]

Though an approach of this kind has the merit of bringing out real functions of repression, integration and political and ideological domination, functions which have been hidden for too long behind the reformist ideologies of local institutions and public services, it nonetheless fails in its object since it deals with the problem in such a one-sided way. It serves no purpose to stamp all collective facilities indiscriminately and in a general way as ideological state apparatuses, and see them as simply determined by the political and ideological interests of the dominant class.

The one-sided nature of this point of view goes with a one-sided analysis of the state and class domination which excludes the fundamental concepts of class relations, contradictions and the class struggle, from an analysis of state machinery and the collective facilities themselves, as if the state, in all its ramifications, were just one monolithic block.

This one-sided position is incidentally linked to the *a priori* disqualification of concrete struggles, particularly if they are organised as revolutionary struggles, by those who adopt the hypercritical approach

---

[50] L. Althusser, 'Ideologies and the state ideological apparatus, notes for research', *Lenin and Philosophy and Other Essays* (NLB, 1971).

inspired by the work of Michel Foucault.[51] From this point of view, any form of organisation of the workers is seen as placing them by that very fact within the grip of the trap of Power. Only marginals, perhaps only the mad, escape the trap. Apart from them, domination is total, everything is recovered or recoverable, and all that is left is the lonely dream of a subversive utopia. This failure to take into account class relations in the determination of collective means of consumption, or the contradictory complexity of their position in the movement of reproduction of the social body, makes it impossible to understand the concrete conditions and forms shaping the historical development of collective facilities or their growth, with their present differences and contradictory aspects. Thus the crucial question, the question of the social production of conditions for the reproduction of the labour force and its relation to the accumulation of capital, is simply obliterated. Collective facilities are seen to exist only as effects and forms of the extension of domination. It does not matter if historical analysis of state intervention in this area shows that public finance devoted to social needs is always the result of the class struggle imposing, whether directly or indirectly, a recognition of developed needs – what Patrice Grevet calls fragmented needs, since capital excludes them from the determination of the value of labour-power. It does not matter if a major brake on the development of socialised consumption is nothing other than the structural tendency of capital to maintain and reinforce exploitation, including cutting down the 'indirect wage' which they represent. The over-politicisation of analyses of domination which leave out the class content, i.e. the reproduction of the relation of exploitation, overlooks the whole social nature of capital, the relation of exploitation and the movement of accumulation, so as to make of it a pure historical subject of domination.

Having postulated that the only significant element is the relation of domination which is *a priori* a constituent part of any collective facility, there is no need to look further into the concrete modes of social consumption and whatever diversity and contradictions they may show. But is it really possible to treat such an approach as an adequate analysis, lumping together as it does roads, public transport, the health service, the electricity service, telecommunications, nurseries, social security, canteens, clinics, swimming-pools and so on? This leads to a total historical misunderstanding, emphasised by the difficult struggles carried out by the workers at different times in order to impose the establishment of the collective facilities necessary for their survival: campaigns carried out by the inhabitants of jerry-built housing estates between the wars, campaigns

[51] F. Fourquet and L. Murard, *Les Equipements du Pouvoir* (C. Bourgois, 1977).

carried out against the lack of facilities in the new towns, campaigns being conducted currently on a local as well as on a national scale to impose on the state the establishment of collective facilities in the face of the Malthusianism of monopolist policy, which aims rather at cutting down as much as possible on the production of the means of collective consumption in order to favour 'industrial policies' and 'redeployment', that is to say, in order to favour accumulation.

The identification of collective facilities as being purely instruments of power, and of needs as the ideological products of authority, leads in the vast majority of cases to lack of interest in the concrete study of consumption practices and the effects of the policies being carried out, and a tendency to confine comment to illustrating the thesis of domination, on the basis of what the authorities themselves say about their policies.[52]

How is it possible to avoid such a one-sided approach, particularly if one cannot get any satisfaction from reformist positions (which defend public facilities and services as they stand as being so many gains to protect and augment) or from technocratic commentaries? Even within some ways of thinking which call themselves Marxist there is a strong tendency towards a 'dualist' analysis of the state, in which the state is conceived as having a double nature. It is seen on the one hand as the reinforcement, the concretisation of 'inevitable' processes of socialisation, linked to the development of productive forces: economic planning, public services and nationalised enterprises for the socialisation of productive forces; collective facilities and services for the subsequent socialisation of consumption. On the other hand, the government and the organs of repression, the army, the police, the judiciary and so on, are seen as making up the capitalist, even the monopolist core, controlling and directing the whole in favour of the interests of the upper bourgeoisie. This dualist vision recognises the exercise of class domination through the whole apparatus, but, where aspects relating to the processes of socialisation are concerned, sees it above all in the use, control, direction, even restraint, put on these sectors by the central power, so that domination is seen as being exercised from the outside.

The socialisation of consumption, like that of production, is neither the neutral product of the autonomous and inevitable development of the productive forces and the needs resulting from it, nor purely as the product of a strategy of domination. It is, as we have said, the contradictory response, continually displaced and reshaped by the politi-

---

[52] A typical example of this reductivist approach is provided by the work already referred to, Murard and Zylberman, *Le petit travailleur infatigable.*

cal relations which produce it, to the contradictions in social reproduction as they are expressed in needs and in social struggles.

But such a statement of principle is really no more than a pointer to the approach to be followed. The whole point, the crux of the whole theoretical and political problem, is precisely that one must not rely on dogmatic assertions of one kind or another, that one must not obscure the problem by opportunistically manipulating contradictions but proceed to the concrete analysis of these contradictory processes.

Without claiming to be able to anticipate the results of the numerous studies being undertaken from this point of view, we would like to draw attention to some of the investigations which seem to be the most promising.

It is above all essential not to stop short at the discourses and representations put forward by the institutions managing the collective facilities, but to examine, in all their diversity, the practices of socialised consumption. Contrary to the view presented by the dualist vision discussed above, it is in the practices themselves, in the concrete organisation of the processes of consumption, in the techniques being used and in the forms of division of the labour of consumption, that state domination is constantly present, and it is undoubtedly through these channels that it is most effective.

In this way, the tendency for class relations to be reproduced in schools is not only the effect of decrees or circulars, or the result of the orientation of the overt contents of subjects decided on centrally, but is present in the very teaching methods carried out spontaneously by the teachers – a spontaneity which is itself the product of ideological and practical training. Whence the constantly renewed obsession with grading, with the constant individualisation of work linked solely to the criteria of individual marks, an implicit exaltation of competition between individuals as distinct from collective practices of cooperation. The inculcation of discipline (strictly kept timetables, limited space, silence, the unquestioning acceptance of the authority of the teacher and so on) has an effect in a similar way.

But consumption (the work of reproduction of the individuals themselves) within these techniques and this division of labour is something more than simply working out political relations; through the reproduction of individuals which it brings about, a reproduction which is also always a transformation, it creates new social potentialities (productive forces, but also the totality of the social capacities of individuals in practices outside production). And these, in their turn, may have an effect on political relations.

To continue in terms of the same example, a good many other things occur in schools, and happened in the past quite as much as now. Today there is an increasing number of attempts, whether on a collective or on an individual scale, to transform teaching methods by involving parents in discussion, opening classrooms for visits, establishing school councils, bringing in parent–teacher associations, the demystification of the teachers' authority for (and by) the pupils and so on. And, with all its limitations and its faults and its social selectivity, the training carried out in schools may potentially have effects which should be looked at closely. Training in reading, in mathematics, in history, is always more than mere discipline, and may well open other doors than a simple docility before capital.

One must always pay attention to the complexity and diversity of the concrete processes, which cannot be reduced to the ploys of the dominant power or to the reformist ideology of the public services. Knowledge must not be reduced to power, nor science and technology to the ideology of domination.

The analysis of these contradictory aspects should not only concern the concrete practices revealing the way these facilities function in terms of their users, nor the more general social determinations touched on earlier which relate to the users, but should also deal with the direction and control over these processes of socialised consumption. There are three forms of such control: immediate control over the processes themselves, linked to the division of labour; control of the way in which these institutions function; and an even more general control exercised over their definition and establishment.

The forms in which this control is expressed are in fact very various, as is their relation to the central state power, to the groups of workers in the collective services, to the users, and to the different social classes or strata. The facilities are not uniformly manipulated by an all-powerful dominant power. Different types of politico-technico-ideological relations define the way in which they are controlled, reflecting the institutional forms (central administration, local authorities, public organisations, privately established associations and so on) and the political relations expressed in them. One must not, of course, fall into the dualism criticised earlier. For instance a local authority, even if administered by left-wing delegates, still remains a territorial segment of the state machine. But left-wing local councils, partly through the way they behave but also through the orientation of the management and conduct of the facilities, have been able to change the direction given them by the central power. The workers or the users may be able to have a greater influence. Even here, however, a concrete analysis that bears in mind the diversity of prevailing situations is indispensable, since the 'political' variable (the parties represented on the local councils) is not absolutely homogeneous in this respect.[53]

This question of control is very important for the study of the historical development of collective consumption. The general movement has been towards the state control of collective consumption, either through the state taking over particular practices of 'paternalistic' capitalism, or through absorption into the state of workers' collective practices. But the movement itself is not homogeneous. It is necessary, for instance, to take account of the specific nature of the politics in periods such as that of the Popular Front or of the Liberation, times when there was an intense development of public (state, but with a politically specific type of state power) forms of collective consumption. It was a development which can be linked directly to popular struggles, to a relation of political forces working more in favour of the working classes, which was expressed in political institutions and state structures: let us cite, for example, the system of social security set up in 1945, at that time under the control of the workers' unions. Through successive reforms, the movement towards state control has subsequently taken on the form of an ever more direct control by the government and the employers.

This general movement is related to the twofold stake involved in the socialisation of consumption. Firstly, there is the economic stake: financial control, but also adaptation to capitalist demands for increase, or for the reproduction of certain elements of the labour force. Secondly, there is the political stake: the constant search for the integration of institutions supporting collective consumption into the apparatus of the bourgeois hegemony. Both aspects, economic and political, contain contradictions. For state provision of collective consumption unquestionably contributes to bourgeois hegemony through the recognition that the 'welfare state' is capable of controlling the whole process of social reproduction and smoothing over any difficulties in its way, in periods when the rapid growth of capitalist production makes any concessions in this area more tolerable. But, and this is a point we will return to, it also tends to make the satisfaction of popular needs an overtly political question, directed to the state. Consumption, its level and the forms it takes, ceases to be simply a purely private affair, based on relations between the wage-earner and his employer, and on the individual's management of his income for his own consumption. And, with the crisis and policies of austerity, the state tends to appear as collective exploiter,

[53] See my paper, 'Left-wing local government and services policy in France', *International Journal of Urban and Regional Research*, 5/3, 1981, pp. 411–25.

while the question of the standard of living and living conditions comes to be linked with that of political and economic power.

It seems possible to distinguish in the development of state monopoly capitalism in France two phases in this movement towards state centralisation of the means of controlling socialised consumption. The first phase, which took place during the sixties, a period of rapid accumulation was that of direct state centralisation. It corresponded, in our hypothesis, with the period of constructing the apparatus for the hegemony of monopoly capital, reorganising and centralising the more diffuse network of the non-monopolist bourgeoisie, or breaking down gains previously made by the workers. It was the central state apparatus which tended to codify needs, to define, normalise, establish and even run the collective facilities by limiting the responsibility and involvement of local authorities or non-state bodies (the cooperative movement, works committees and so on).

This direct control has the effect of making it possible to adapt the way these institutions function to the major directions of the policy of state monopoly capitalism – in, among other areas, the domain of the allocation of public finance. But it also aims to attempt to control and direct their ideological conduct, which is not merely a question of pronouncements but also of consumption practices. This is expressed in a hierarchisation, in an authoritarianism and an enforced bureaucratisation, which entail a wastage and deterioration in the quality of consumption and at the same time a strengthening of the oppressive nature of state institutions and a tendency to eliminate opportunities for democratic involvement of the workers and users of the collective services.

The second phase corresponds to the crisis, from the beginning of the 1970s. The movement towards state centralisation continued, but in more complex and less direct ways. The strengthening of the centralisation of power has been accompanied by a certain decentralisation of immediate management, and of the formal responsibilities exercised under central control, to the 'benefit', for instance, of local authorities.

This development has been possible to the extent that the apparatus of monopoly hegemony is already established. It has become necessary to put a distance between the central state and the political consequences of the policies of austerity. To set up a distance, but also at the same time to integrate more closely the local relays (local authorities, cooperatives, housing associations and so on) into the apparatus of hegemony by drawing them in actively into the capitalist management of the crisis; that is to say, from the point of view of individual and collective consumption, into the management of austerity.

The policy of austerity means the crisis of the welfare state, and thus of a large part of the material base of the monopolist hegemony. Hence the need to reorganise its concerns, through an intensification and diversification of both ideological practices and repressive practices, as seen, for example, in the extension of anti-union measures. The involvement of the local authorities, cooperatives and so on, in the management of austerity also contributes to the organisation of the disorganisation of the exploited classes, and serves to prevent any political alliance between the working class, the new strata of wage-earners, and the traditional petty bourgeoisie by setting up material and ideological conditions capable of stimulating political competition between them, and competition for collective consumption, at the local level.

To develop this last point in parallel to the two aspects of the question we have already considered – the concrete organisation of consumption practices, and the techniques and division of labour on the one hand, and political and institutional control over these processes on the other – we must conclude by examining a third aspect, that of the role of the state in the ideological construction of needs. It is not, in fact, a separate question from those we have already examined, since ideology is not a process which exists in a vacuum. It is rather a specific aspect of the same questions, though with a difference. Although the state character of the socialisation of consumption is conducted through control over the concrete processes, and is expressed in the very techniques of consumption, in the division of labour and thus in the totality of ideological practices which shape its representation and reproduction day by day, the ideological consequences of that socialisation reach beyond the framework of state institutions and state practices. Through the concrete response it makes to needs, and the representation, the codification of those needs in its pronouncements and its practices (laws, rules and so on), the state contributes to the construction of practical ideologies of consumption, and, hence, finds itself involved in 'civil society', shaping the expression of needs outside the sphere of any institutional practice.[54]

The way in which the state influences civil society is all the more marked the more highly developed its material involvement in consumption, as is particularly the case in the phase of state monopoly capitalism. This, let us emphasise, is something quite different from the process of inculcating needs which have been invented wholesale by the state and by capital, proposed by Baudrillard and Foucault. It is also something quite other than a discourse by the state. The state does not invent needs but, through its practices and the material response which it makes, it shapes

[54] A number of stimulating observations on this point are to be found in F. Godard and J.R. Pendaries, *Les modes de vie dans le discours de la représentation* (Laboratoire de Sociologie de l'Université de Nice, 1978).

needs, moulds them and codifies them. In this ideological process the state relies on the contradictory nature, which we have emphasised earlier, of the economic determination of needs.

The spontaneous expression of needs by individuals or social groups is thus from the outset a political process, in which the state already maintains an invisible presence. It would thus be misleading to see in it the transparent consciousness and direct expression of exploitation, the pure source of revolutionary demands. There is, in the determination of needs felt 'spontaneously', an element of acceptance of capitalist economic domination and of the state organisation of collective consumption. But there is also a contradictory movement, based in the experienced contradiction of exploited labour, just as there is that born of the insupportable weight of the state bearing down on ways of life. Cutbacks, deterioration, and the increasingly bureaucratic, even oppressive, nature of collective consumption in the face of the growth of social needs and the expansion of opportunities opened up by scientific and technical developments, have produced of growing sense of dissatisfaction, of criticism, and demands directed at both the quantitative insufficiency of facilities and their content and conduct. It is a movement felt both by the users and by the specialised workers who ensure the organisation of the process of consumption, and who are not simply cogs in the state machine, but workers who themselves, given the increasing monopolistic concentration and its consequences for the state, are ever more actively involved in building up the balance of class forces side by side with the working class.

But though this dissatisfaction may be felt, it is not a spontaneous source of revolutionary needs or of movements towards struggle. There is also a need for collective political processes to work out the needs – and not only the collective demands – which reveal and transcend the ideological effects of domination. These processes are at the very heart of the struggles of the exploited classes. As transformations of the consciousness of their objective situation, and a major element in the formation of 'class consciousness', they are at one and the same time the result of and the driving force behind these struggles, and the bearers of social changes capable of responding to the fundamental need for an end to exploitation.

4

Needs, social struggles and socialist perspectives

SOCIAL STRUGGLES AND THE EXPLICIT FORMULATION OF NEEDS

The crisis in capitalist society not only produces an increasing non-fulfillment of needs, but develops needs and intensifies their expression; it emphasises their diversity and complexity, and reinforces the pressures on their ideological and political formation. We can no longer define the questions arising from social struggles and the political plans and efforts that aim at the transformation of society only on the basis of assumed needs, or those presumed to be self-evident. The reality of needs, the legitimacy of their expression and the nature of the modes of consumption engage social movements and political practice more and more explicitly. These questions are at the heart of contemporary political and theoretical debates.

One may well say that there is nothing really new here. Working-class struggles, whether directed towards demands concerning wages, working conditions or hours of work, have always expressed the needs of the working class: needs concerned with the reproduction of labour-power, freedom from exploitation, and control by the workers over their work and their own lives. Capitalist tendencies towards control of working-class consumption and living conditions are hardly recent phenomena.

From Marx and Engels . . .

However, there have been developments in the fundamental structures of the economy, in production and consumption, and in their ideological and theoretical consequences, which cannot be ignored. In the nineteenth century, the essentials of working-class consumption were taken care of by wages in terms of market relations. The question of needs, their expression, recognition and satisfaction, was raised principally in the private, individual terms of the worker's management of his income, and in terms of demands to the bosses. The positions taken up by the organised working-class movement in this regard were confined – apart from support for the workers' demands – to a statement of certain principles, though principles of great importance. In the same way, only a general theoretical view is to be found in the works of Marx, and he barely elaborates on the definition and specific content of needs. Marx's position indicates a decisive way forward, a way forward we have tried to clarify and elaborate in previous chapters, but it contains practically no concrete analysis and is limited to a few allusions, which, moreover, are not without their ambiguities:

> His natural wants, such as food, clothing, fuel, and housing, vary according to the climatic and other physical conditions of his country. On the other hand, the number and extent of his so-called necessary wants, as also the modes of satisfying them, are themselves the product of historical development, and depend to a great extent on the degree of civilisation of a country, more particularly on the conditions in which, and consequently on the habits and degree of comfort in which, the class of free labourers has been formed. In contradistinction therefore to the case of other commodities, there enters into the determination of the value of labour-power a historical and moral element. Nevertheless, in a given country, at a given period, the average quantity of the means of subsistence necessary for the labourer is practically known.[1]

This passage, which occurs in the midst of Marx's remarks on the necessities of the reproduction of labour-power, is notable for suggesting the need to also take into consideration certain specific determining factors in the modes of consumption, and not simply reduce them to the mechanical consequences of the mode of production. But, because of its ambiguity when removed from its context, this passage can be used to support all kinds of culturalist interpretations, interpretations of which there has been no shortage.

If Marx is more precise on the question of the duration of work, both in terms of his theoretical conceptualisation and his concrete examples, then it is no doubt because this question, along with that of wages, is central to class conflict. As for the specific content of needs and their relation to consumption, Marx only elaborates on a few points, which again are those most directly linked to social struggles: for example, his remarks concerning the denaturing or poor quality of certain foodstuffs. However, this relative silence may also be interpreted as an implicit stand

[1] Karl Marx, *Capital* (Lawrence & Wishart, 1954), Vol. I, Part II, Chapter VI, p. 171.

on two related points. By thus noting the individual-private character of wage use, is not Marx opposing the numerous ideologists so concerned with rationalising and moralising about working-class consumption, seeking to control the content and rhythm of working-class consumption so as to increase its efficiency from the point of view of capital by promoting a healthy reproduction of the labour force, and so tending to diminish its cost, and also to reorientate it towards particular consumption patterns that could expand profitable markets, particularly for durable goods such as housing? Is he not opposing those who seek to moralise working-class consumption within the framework of bourgeois values, centring it on the close-knit family away from those dens of moral and political iniquity, the street and the bar? The work of Maurice Halbwachs provides a good example of this moralistic and condescending point of view which, in the final analysis, is blind to the social reality which it claims, with all academic caution, to be analysing in detail. If the worker wastes too much time in the street, is not sufficiently disposed towards family life, does not organise his budget with sufficient forethought, then this, of course, has to do with

> the fundamental nature of wage labour, that it is necessarily undertaken 'outside' society . . . the habits acquired in the factory are clearly too deeply embedded, and it has proved too difficult for the worker to awaken in himself the 'social man', that might allow him to establish his family life on solid foundations, to feel within himself the intense need to do this. . . . He remains in that superficial area of social life where he still survives to too great an extent on passivity and inertia. . .[2]

In fact, the improvidence and immorality of the workers indicate their refusal to submit to the bourgeois order of exploitation in all those areas where some freedom may be preserved or won. The determination of consumption patterns is an element in this, as is 'derision for the power of the bosses', to use Alain Cottereau's phrase. Cottereau has clearly shown[3] the importance and social significance of working-class resistance to the exploitation of their everyday practices, a resistance which has been much denounced by bourgeois moralists.

To refrain from denouncing needs from the outside, to see practice as defining necessity, and to exclude nothing in the name of a moral concept of 'correct' consumption ('it matters not at all whether such and such a product, tobacco for example, is or is not an indispensable means of

[2] M. Halbwachs, *La classe ouvrière et les niveaux de vie* (Alcan, 1912), p. 450.
[3] In his excellent introduction, 'Vie quotidienne et resistance ouvrière à Paris en 1870', to the new edition of Denis Poulot, *Le Sublime* (Maspero, 1980).

consumption from a physiological point of view, what matters is that it has become indispensable to us through habit'[4]), is this not also to recognise that 'necessary needs' cannot be decreed without consulting those who feel those needs? We will come back to this point later, in connection with the political working-out of needs: for the moment, let us simply bear in mind the position stated in the Communist Manifesto and found in the programmes of working-class parties,[5] stating the principles of the struggle against capitalist exploitation and oppression, and rejecting detailed programmes, which are described as 'utopian'.

Certainly, when Engels wrote, 'I will be satisfied if I have been able to show that production in our modern society is sufficient to provide enough to eat for all its members and that there exists enough housing to provide the labouring masses provisionally with spacious and sanitary shelter. But speculation on the manner in which future society will regulate the allocation of food and housing would lead us directly to utopia,' he added immediately afterwards:

> At the very most, all we can establish through our knowledge of the fundamental conditions of all pre-existing modes of production is that with the fall of capitalist production, certain forms of appropriation in contemporary society will become impossible. The transitory measures should everywhere be adapted to the conditions which will then exist: they will be fundamentally different in countries with small property-holders and in countries with large landowners.[6]

This is a polemical position, in opposition to the 'pseudo-socialists' who propose, under the pretext of their being practical and concrete, isolated solutions which are more or less universal to sector-based problems such as housing. And Engels rightly criticises them for their failure to take into account the general dynamic of the relations of production in which these problems arise. But it is uncertain whether, even then, existing frameworks would have been able to respond even provisionally to the needs created by the capitalist urbanisation which Engels himself described so well.[7]

Since that time, the theoretical and political debates and the demands of the workers' movement have changed considerably. And today, nobody would defend Engels' position on this point. The immediate demands

---

[4] Mark, *Capital*, Vol. I. Part II, Chapter VI, p. 171.
[5] See for instance, Marx and Engels, *The Critique of the Gotha Programme* (Moscow, Foreign Language Publishing House, 1960).
[6] Frederick Engels, *the Housing Question* (Progress Publishers, 1969).
[7] Frederick Engels, *The Condition of the Working Class in England* (Basil Blackwell, 1958).

regarding living conditions, rents and utility payments, and the building of subsidised housing, and – on a more general scale – proposals and policies for the positive transformation of the present situation with regard to these particular areas, by linking them with the abolition of capitalist domination: these are crucial political questions at stake.

. . . to the diversified expression of needs in current campaigns

The relation between sector-based struggles and policies, and the transformation of production relations remains a major question, a point of division and conflict. But this division, traditionally expressed as being between revolutionary and reformist practice, has become all the more difficult to define and analyse concretely since what is involved is seen to be the more complex and diverse the more specific one becomes.

The recognition of needs satisfied by market consumption through wages remains essentially general and implicit. But it is interesting to note a certain clarifying tendency linked to the demands for the definition of a basic minimum wage. Thus the discussions on the fixing of a guaranteed minimum cross-sector wage (*salaire minimum interprofessionel garanti,* SMIG, renamed SMIC, *de croissance,* in a growth period) which were held in 1951 in the context of the Commission Supérieure des Conventions Collectives, focused on drawing-up a model household budget 'such that the satisfaction of at least those social and individual needs, considered basic and irreducible, should be ensured, whatever the circumstances'.[8] The stand taken by management in these discussions is most instructive. The views of the representatives of the Conseil National du Patronat Français and of small and medium-sized businesses are nothing less than savage. Those who consider themselves critics of the theory of the consumer society, of the constant stimulation of new needs in order to artificially boost consumption, should reflect on the contents of this minimum budget, as on those millions of workers who still today do not earn even the minimum wage. In short, for management, 'it is important to maintain some degree of poverty in the minimum wage, so as to prevent the workers from sinking into idleness':[9] living accommodation should not be provided with anything more than running water on the landing – it should, in other words, be in the slum category – there should be no scope for a new suit more often than every five years, there should be no allowances for laundry, holidays or leisure activities, there

[8] See H. Nolleau, 'La conception patronale des besoins des travailleurs', in 'Réflexions sur la notion de besoins', *Economie et Politique,* Nos. 153–5, April–June 1967, p. 119.
[9] Ibid., p. 121.

should be 2400 calories per day for a man, 2200 for a woman, and 'cheap' calories at that – margarine, cheap cuts of meat, potatoes, no butter, steak or green vegetables.

In parallel with wage campaigns, the movement for the socialisation of consumption has been marked by a considerable expansion of demands in a variety of areas: housing, health, education, leisure and culture etc. Specific campaigns have been undertaken, numerous needs have been explicitly recognised by the state – in its own way, of course – in its 'social legislation', and in the setting up and running of a number of public services. There is scarcely any political programme aimed at the transformation of society – however radical – which has not tried to work out some kind of measures, whether economic, institutional or whatever, in response to those needs.

Without wishing to embark on a detailed historical analysis, one may stress the considerable growth and diversification of the explicit awareness of needs expressed in the various political stages which mark the history of the working-class movement. In France, the Popular Front of 1936, the policies of the Liberation government in which the Communists participated (1945–7), and, more recently, the Common Programme for government which was adopted in 1972 by the left-wing parties, show in the measures they proposed and, in a number of cases, put into practice, a progressive widening of the scope and aims of political intervention.

And today there is scarcely any aspect of social life which is not the subject of a debate where needs and demands are expressed, which is not affected either directly or indirectly by social movements which are themselves diverse. In addition to the questions of purchasing power and wages, demands have emerged concerning the various areas of collective consumption, but also ecological and environmental issues, the protection of beauty-spots and the fight against pollution and noise. Consumer groups seek to keep a check on the price and quality of products, while other movements aim for the transformation of social relations in a way that goes well beyond what could strictly be called consumption – relations such as those between men and women, attitudes towards homosexuals, the place and status of the disabled in our society, of the 'mad', the social management of death – to such an extent that it is impossible to make an exhaustive list. Numerous questions which used to be of concern only to philosophers, writers and artists are now becoming the object of collective thought and practice on a political level, and are thus challenging the dominant social relations.

This development has been paralleled in production, and generally in a number of areas affecting wage-labour. Over and above demands for wage settlements, problems no less fundamental for being chronic, campaigns have developed which are concerned with the conditions and duration of work, with work rates, skills and safety. Beyond such campaigns, which one might characterise as being a defence against exploitation, others of a more offensive nature are beginning to develop. These concern trades union and political freedoms within the work place and in addition due to the preoccupation with the defence of jobs, they are concerned with the organisation of production, management, investment policies and so on.

Of course, as we shall see in greater detail later, this expansion has not occurred at an even rate, and there are many areas which are as yet untouched. It has been accompanied by numerous ambiguities, and by splits in the social movements which make their political convergence problematic. But for all these reservations and ambiguities, it is, in our view, a major phenomenon which is having a profound effect on the status of the question of needs. Hence the crucial importance of debate and the necessity for further investigation.

But it is not enough simply to record this development, this diversification, as the mere end product of a build-up of unsatisfied needs. It is important to guard against too linear a conception here. Such a conception, starting from the development of productive forces, mechanically deduces from this the expansion of needs, which in its turn produces social conflict, and this then demands some kind of response from the state and from capital, and such responses, inevitably inadequate, then restrict development, necessitating new production relations permitting the resumption of this development and the even greater satisfaction of needs. Two million unemployed, millions of workers on the minimum wage or below it, millions poorly housed, hundreds of thousands of young people debarred from access to proper vocational education and cultural opportunities. . . . All these aspects of our society, aggravated by the current crisis, clearly make the provision of greater resources with which to respond to needs indispensable. But the evolution of these needs also reveals the concomittant necessity for a simultaneous transformation of the ways in which those needs are responded to. Today, these needs and campaigns seek something other than the continuation of the developments brought about by the evolution of the capitalist mode of production. They challenge once again the traditional conceptions of progress and the linear view of society's development in terms of quantitative accumulation. And this questioning concerns both production and consumption.

Though Marx saw the goods entering contemporary working class consumption as *de facto* necessities, and although the development of capitalism has been able for a long time to persuade us that it would ensure an ever greater abundance of consumer goods, to such a degree as to appear to some, in countries seeking a socialist path of development, as a model to catch up with and overtake – nonetheless, the mode of consumption in capitalist societies is today strongly under attack.

Social inequalities, poverty and even destitution, which are still the dominant features of income distribution in even the most developed countries, cannot be eliminated without a substantial increase in the volume of consumption of millions of households and individuals. However, the historical inability of the capitalist system to resolve this problem calls into question the nature of the production relations which determine this pattern of income distribution as well as the mode of consumption itself.

A *critique of commodity consumption*

The response to needs provided by commodity consumption is ever more frequently challenged today, first and foremost because of the change in the quality of products. This is contradictory in a number of ways. On the one hand, the latest technology is employed in order to produce more sophisticated products, the usefulness of which has undeniably been improved in many respects – performance, efficiency, comfort etc. But at the same time, this growing sophistication masks a tendency towards the standardisation of products resulting from the concentration of industry (e.g. cars, electrical goods), variety being only superficial. In a number of cases, a reduction in quality in certain respects may be observed, particularly in durability and resistance. An article will be designed in such a way that it will last only a certain time, thus making necessary regular replacement. The pharmaceutical industry is constantly putting out a variety of new products, while a particular vaccine or antibiotic which has proved its usefulness may no longer be produced because it did not make enough profit.

The same contradictory development can be seen in the case of food products. Thus, in large towns, all kinds of fruit and vegetables are available at almost all times of the year, thanks to the development of transportation and storage techniques. But, more and more, these foods lack real flavour, since they have been harvested too early, and are crammed with insecticides and a variety of chemicals. And let us not forget the case of hormone-fed veal which, for the first time in France, provoked a boycott which brought about a change in the regulations, and decisions which should entail substantial changes in animal husbandry. This last example also demonstrates the growing impact of consumer groups.

This highlights the contradictory nature of the commodity in capitalist society, where use-value is the support of value, and its characteristics are determined by the conditions of the realisation of surplus value. And not only its immediate realisation but, and this is something new, the realisation of value in the long term and the development of the process of accumulation over time. Also new is the growing political impact of this contradiction. Even if the political significance of these movements and their effect on consumption is limited and uncertain, they demonstrate the gap between needs and the goods offered for their satisfaction, thus emphasising the contrary point, that needs cannot be reduced to the direct reflection of capitalist requirements regarding the realisation of value and the expansion of markets.

However, considered in themselves, the demands of consumer groups do not necessarily challenge either the market relations which dominate consumption, nor the capitalist character of production. But these latter do tend to be disputed in certain areas by the movement for the socialisation of consumption. We will not discuss again this movement, its contradictory nature, the driving force of class struggle, the dominant nature of state socialisation and the social inequalities which are both present in and reproduced by the distribution and functioning of collective undertakings. The more directly political nature of the expression of needs in this area emerges quite clearly.

But the political effect of state socialisation of consumption is ambivalent. On the one hand, the response by the state to particular needs, and the formulation and control of this response by the state, contributes to the extension of the hegemony of the dominant class. On the other hand, this response tends to direct demands towards the state and to accentuate the social and political nature of questions of consumption, and so links them more directly with questions about the nature and exercise of political power.

The necessity for the development of collective consumption

The crisis in the welfare state has changed the conditions of the debate but has not eliminated this ambivalence for, as we have stressed, austerity policies are accompanied by a reinforcement of state control and/or control by capital. Such policies have clearly provoked some more or less significant protest movements against the reduction in public spending on collective consumption. And, as with wage-determined commodity consumption, the question of the level of resources allocated to popular consumption cannot be shelved, indivisibly linked as it is to the question of exploitation on a general scale. But as with market consumption, and perhaps to an even greater extent, the increase in the allocation of resources is a necessary but not sufficient condition for a correct response to needs.

To content oneself with demanding more and more amenities means allowing oneself to be taken in by the mirage of the Welfare State, or even to fall victim to the illusion of the progressively socialist nature of state socialisation, while in fact the transformation of the modes of collective consumption themselves is just as necessary, as we shall try to show below. Moreover, right from the very first proposals, campaigns and, especially, the collective practices of autonomous socialisation by the working-class movement, the stress has always been put on the requirements of collective consumption in terms of content and social relations. The socialist utopias are the clearest examples of this, but one might also recall nineteenth-century debates on education, attempts at cooperatives, friendly societies, and so on.

With the development of collective consumption and the intervention of the state, there is more at stake. It is clear, as may be seen from the numerous movements already mentioned, which carry out the struggle and formulate demands in every area, that today the satisfaction of the needs of the population as a whole can only be undertaken at a higher level and through new forms of the socialisation of consumption. On a general scale, collective consumption means that the limits and constraints of market consumption may be transcended, and new patterns of consumption created, patterns which are impossible within market relations, and even more so within the capitalist process of the realisation of value. These new patterns are conducive both to the reduction of inflation and to the development of what one might call the social productivity of consumption. The social efficiency of that development is a necessary corollary to the fight against waste in production and distribution, and the creation of productivity, not in terms of profit, but in terms of real social utility, in terms of a better utilisation of the means of consumption, conscious of their indirect social and economic effects.

Such an extension of socialised consumption has nothing to do with the 'collectivisation' or 'barrack socialism' to which some would like to reduce it. This is because of the effects of democratisation, the reduction of state control, and the political conditions which are today the necessary components of this extension — all points we will return to later. It is also because the socialisation of consumption is not in opposition to individual consumption, and is not an alternative solution to be developed at the expense of the latter. Rather it is a complementary solution which widens the range of possible choices, a way of encouraging, stimulating and enriching individual consumption, and often of improving its conditions. In this way, the improvement in the conditions of use of the motor car as an individual means of transport in towns necessarily involves improvements in public transport, with the provision of a fast and comfortable service at a low individual and social cost on an increased number of routes, in particular those between home and work. At present motorists, deterred by the condition of public transport, are more or less constrained to use their cars, and it is only if this superior social solution is available that freedom and flexibility – particularly important for leisure outings, for example – will be restored to the car. Neither the systematic destruction of towns to make way for motorways and car parks, nor the suppression of the car, nor forcing workers to use expensive, overcrowded, uncomfortable and inadequate means of public transport can offer any real solution. There are many other areas, such as cultural activities and recreation, where collective and individual forms of practice complement and stimulate each other.

The transformation of collective facilities: the reduction of state control and the growth of self-management

A certain number of 'gains' made during particular periods such as the Popular Front and the Liberation, for example in social legislation, social security, the status of civil servants, nationalised enterprises and through the existence of left-wing town councils with control over various services (local administration of subsidised rented accommodation, promoting and managing social housing, crèches, cultural and recreational amenities etc.) have helped to develop a widespread 'public services' ideology. This ideology which is not without its positive side – far from it – has, however, masked numerous segregative effects; it has hidden the state domination in public services, and has too often limited the demands of working-class organisations to a position of defending 'gains' and seeking an increase in resources and staffing. This is particularly the case because of the way in which the weight of public service workers in the trade union movement has increased significantly, and because campaigns concerning one sector or another of collective consumption mobilise, in the first place, the workers in that sector. This has had positive effects in terms of an alliance between these workers and the working class as a whole, but it has also tended to give too great an importance to their corporate interests, in the political elaboration of needs and demands concerning health, education, and so forth.

Paradoxically, the brutal acceleration in the dismantling of 'democratic gains' (subsidised housing and social security among all too many other areas) has brought about a significant extension of the movement of critical revaluation of the public services not only among their users, but also among those working in them. Clearly their interests converge in the fight against wastage and deterioration of services resulting from reduced budgets, from insufficient manpower, from enforced forms of the organisation of work, and in the battle against the 'parasitic' activity of private capital in the areas most likely to provide a profit. Their interests also converge in the denunciation of authoritarian control, centralisation and increased hierarchisation, in the wish to fight for the democratisation of all public services and amenities.

However, the development of needs makes this convergence problematic in certain respects. We have already seen how collective consumption has tended to reproduce social inequalities. Now the democratisation and decentralisation of the management of institutions are necessary but not sufficient conditions for the elimination of the mechanisms in question, since the latter are to quite a significant extent embodied in the knowledge, skills, techniques and professional ideologies of specialised staff.

For example, this is true of many teachers who have internalised educational concepts, criteria for judgement, conceptualisations of authority, intelligence, competition and individual achievement, which to a large extent conform to the dominant class relations. These concepts and criteria are all the more effective because they are not perceived as an ideology imposed from the outside, but are seen to be borne out in everyday practice, in the 'neutrality' and importance of professional skills. It is clear, in fact, that one cannot hope to transform the education system so radically as to eliminate the segregative mechanisms which make it a machine which rejects working-class children, unless one can also transform the practices and concepts of the teachers, opening them up to debate and criticism, to the involvement of and suggestions made by the users (parents and children) in a way that is not at present considered acceptable.

The same is true of many doctors. It is difficult to obtain from them any precise explanation of the ailment from which one might be suffering, or any further information on the prescribed treatment and the prognosis – particularly if one comes from a working-class background – and this exacerbates the social distance separating doctor and patient.

In a more general way, collective facilities today tend to function too much in the mode of 'taking care of', of dispossessing the individual in the interests of the institution and its specialists. The demands for self-management which have been put forward in various forms by users' movements go further than a demand for democratic participation in their administration. They open a perspective for the transformation of practices which would restore to the user an active and creative role – a transformation already visible in embryonic form in a number of 'alternative' institutions. They are moving towards the reduction of state control, the abolition of the rigid and constricting state codification which standardises needs, towards a better adaptation of the institutions to reality and to the diversity and development of needs. They are thus moving towards a recognition of the unity of the individuals concerned, in the face of the fragmentation of the social body and the individual's life, into as many 'users' as there are 'services', and with the links with the social environment and with working life being denied.

Responses other than the multiplication of facilities

This last point is all the more important because any real improvement in responding to needs presupposes, in many areas, something more than the mere multiplication of amenities and organisations. The most striking example is probably that of health. Experts and ministers justify austerity measures by referring to 'medical overconsumption', which must be limited urgently, since if health spending were allowed to increase at the present rate, it would swallow up the whole state budget in a few years time.

This statement, taken in isolation, is perfectly true. But one cannot derive the proposed – and imposed – conclusion that excessive consumption must be reduced, without cutting out the causes of this overconsumption, and refusing to consider the enormous social inequalities in terms of illness and accidents. Apart from occupational diseases, whether recognised as such or not, many ailments result more or less directly from the rate of work, from its intensity, from excessive hours, from the work schedule and working conditions (noise, vibration etc.),[10] often coupled with poor conditions outside the work place (long and tiring journeys, cramped and noisy housing). A large part of the increase in medical consumption therefore corresponds to restorative work, treating the effects without intervening to rectify the causes. Thus improved standards of health care will not really be achieved by forever increasing this kind of restorative expenditure, still less by summarily reducing this expenditure

[10] See among others, A. Chauvenet, *Médecines au choix, médecines de classe* (PUF, 1978), pp. 176 ff.

without changing anything else, or even aggravating the exploitation of the labour force.

A similar analysis may be made in many other areas. Thus the best response to the needs of the elderly is probably not by multiplying the number of old people's homes, even if these are improved from the point of view of material conditions or the number of staff available, but rather through a search for solutions which would allow them both a quiet life and integration into the social life of the community.

In the same way, the response to those all too easily labelled 'mentally ill' should seek alternatives to the multiplication of psychiatric hospitals. From the point of view of cure, the efficacy of these hospitals has been seriously questioned and many are experimenting with alternative solutions. The Italians have performed very important experiments in this regard, and in France certain branches of psychiatry are following the same lines. But it is not enough to announce brutally the immediate withdrawal of thousands of beds from psychiatric hospitals as was done in proposals made in a report put out by the Ministry of Health under the Giscard government, without first setting up new facilities necessary to provide the requisite treatment without totally removing the patient from society (day centres, therapeutic communities). Neither is it sufficient to fight for a better society, on the off chance that this will eliminate disease and mental illness. We must respond immediately to the needs of those afflicted, as well as we can. But it is important that we also try to change the social relations which are known to provoke, encourage and aggravate many of the psychological disturbances leading to mental illness.

Finally, criticism of wastage and of the dead-end solution of multiplying restorative facilities must include the major trends in capitalist policy in this area, that is, the growing importance of social amenities and services of containment and repression. Even though it is necessary to help the unemployed, the problem of unemployment will not be resolved by social work, any more than the problem of poverty can be resolved by putting families in the care of the social workers, who manage their inadequate resources for them. And while the increased police presence in some suburban areas where police were once scarce may in the short term limit acts of aggression, and though this is less pernicious than the organisation of vigilante groups, it will still not solve the problems of delinquency and attacks on persons and property. In such a case, moreover, care would have to be taken that the police presence did not itself lead to a breakdown in security through intimidation, racist attacks and 'unfortunate mistakes' — the surveillance of the population by a repressive machine. Vandalism, acts of aggression and theft will not be reduced, let alone eliminated, by an infinite multiplication of police stations, patrols, special detention centres, prisons, and all the rest. To take only one example, that of juvenile delinquency, more satisfactory living conditions and a more accessible educational system which was more attentive to the needs of young people, and particularly of young people from working-class backgrounds, a system which opened up cultural and recreational opportunities and the possibility of interesting and well-paid jobs, would certainly be more effective. We note in passing, moreover, that none of the amenities – from the social services to the machinery of repression – can be seen as responding to the needs expressed by the 'users'. They are clearly state initiatives, supplying solutions of a capitalist nature to serious social problems, but resolving nothing. Rather, by containing and sealing off the working class, they contribute to the maintenance of a social order based on relations of exploitation.

To summarise, it thus seems that three principal ideas emerge from the development of needs and social movements. The first is the necessity for an increase in consumption for the working class and for the most underprivileged social groups, through an increase in individual market consumption and improved access to collective consumption. The second is the necessity for a qualitative transformation of the use-value of consumer goods and of the modes, techniques, organisation, and division of labour of consumption. This transformation affects both the relations between men and women within the household and the relations between these household or individual users, and institutions. The third concerns the search for an end to the vicious circle of cumulative waste constituted by compensatory and restorative consumption, by the institutions of social supervision which aim to treat, through consumption, the consequences of problems which have originated elsewhere, particularly in production. This now leads on to the question of the relation between the expression of needs, social movements and the developments of the process of production.

Producing more, something different, in a different way

This discussion of the development of commodity consumption has clear implications for production. If the satisfaction of needs, particularly those of the majority of workers, presupposes that more consumer goods should be made available to them and that they should be goods of better quality, then clearly such goods need to be produced. Thus an alternative logic to that of the profit motive must determine the criteria which shape the volume and the content of production. But, once again, this remains a demand external to the process of production and it can be made to fit in with an instrumental conception of that process, taking over wholesale the machinery, the technology, the division of labour and its organisation, while only altering certain requirements, certain criteria for defining the product and the evaluation of the results, so as to gauge in a different way an article whose obsolescence is today meticulously programmed. And after all, the capitalist organisation of production might itself proceed to some degree towards such qualitative modifications. It is after all responsible for producing the greatest quantity and the highest quality in the majority of areas today. If one looks no further, this justifies the social democratic position which aims only to impose certain ground rules on capitalism's 'admirable machinery of production', and to arrange for the negative consequences of the inevitable exploitation of wage labour to be compensated for outside the work place.

However, if one wishes to attack social inequality at its source, to break down the logic of recovery and compensation, to stop confining the expression and satisfaction of needs to the area of consumption, one is led to a deeper critical revaluation of the social organisation of production, and, on a more general scale, of wage labour as a whole.

The work place is potentially a fundamental locus for the expression of workers' needs. It fulfills this role in a concrete and strictly limited way through struggles concerning wages and working conditions, and also through a certain socialisation of consumption practices undertaken by the firm or, more often, by trade union organisations through the works committees: e.g., canteens, crèches in some instances, cultural activities, sports, summer camps, holiday villages and so on. These activities, which mainly apply to workers in large firms, are nevertheless centred on the maintenance and reproduction of the labour force through consumption, even if they are more than that. As for the training of the work force, this only affects a very limited number of workers and is tightly regulated to suit the technical and ideological requirements of capitalism.[11]

Dictatorship by the firm's management leaves a lot less room for the free and autonomous expression of needs linked to the process of production itself. However, as we have already stressed, the aspects of this process which give rise most directly to significant needs for the protection and recovery of the labour force in the short term, particularly when the workers' physical capacity and even their lives are under threat, were included very early on in the demands concerning conditions and rates of work, industrial safety, and the recognition of and compensation for occupational diseases. Thus certain particularly obvious or spectacular hazards have been reduced or eliminated: work space excessively open to

[11] See C. Dubar, *Formation permanente et contradictions sociales* (Editions sociales, 1980).

accidents is altered, certain production processes giving rise to serious illnesses have been abandoned. But at the same time, whole occupational sectors continue almost inexorably to pay a heavy toll, such as the miners with silicosis. The struggle for safety and accident prevention is a constant one, but workers have constantly to accept risks, sometimes rising to certainties, in order to earn a living. This is the effect of an insufficiently favourable balance of forces, which makes it impossible to enforce greater safety. It is also a compromise, a fatalism accepted to some degree because there is no choice.

Campaigns concerning job status are also of a defensive nature. They deal particularly with the recognition of the skilled nature of the job done and its reflection in the wage. They also deal with the rejection of reductions in skilled work, and downgrading. The technological changes sought by capital aim to increase productivity by the reduction of living labour and particularly of skilled labour. Capitalist technological 'progress' means a continual fight for the relative reduction in skill of all categories of manpower. It implies the reduction of autonomous initiatives by wage-earners, the constant attempt to separate intellectual work (design, organisation, programming) from manual work (actual production). This 'progress' involves a selection of technological innovations and investments according to very precise criteria which, even according to the principle on which they are based, run contrary to the workers' interests. The workers try to limit the negative consequences which the changes forced up on them are bound to have. This appears to some observers to be a conservative move, opposed to progress, whereas a more favourable balance of forces in certain sectors has enabled workers to better defend themselves, as in the case of the press and printing industry in France. Where this has happened, workers are accused of refusing the necessary changes, an accusation which carefully obscures the idea that these changes are only necessary from the point of view of profit, and that alternative changes are possible, 'forgetting' or masking, for instance, the proposal put forward by the CGT union for the printing industry, to fit technological change to the workers' interests.

In general, one can say that capitalist relations of production only allow workers to express their work-related needs defensively, whether it be a matter of work conditions or the nature and interest of a job. It is necessary to point out however that we are talking here of the dominant tendency, and not of a totally static situation. There are still quite a number of areas where workers or wage-earners are able to express some degree of creativity and to exercise initiative in their work. It is in sectors where the division of labour has been greatest, with a total fragmentation and categorisation of tasks (assembly line work, for example), or in certain completely unskilled occupations (cleaning and stock handling) that all initiative is excluded. From this, paradoxically (for capital), there has resulted a crisis in labour productivity. Absenteeism, and manpower turnover are growing considerably, as is the percentage of 'rejects', defective items which have to be discarded. The frenetic quest for increased productivity has thus led to the opposite result. And management is starting to be seriously worried by this crisis, to the degree of seeking and experimenting with means of restoring a minimum of interest to the work in order to be able to profit from the creative investiveness of the workers by abandoning the production line, setting up small mixed groups responsible for the organisation of their individual and collective work in order to achieve a production objective, an objective which is, of course, imposed from outside. Such interventions have proved necessary but dangerous, for the workers have developed a taste for this limited amount of autonomy and initiative, and have been quick to ask for more. There is thus the risk of factory discipline being challenged if the process is allowed to develop, and the alternative risk of a return to the earlier crisis in productivity if it is suppressed.

In reaction to this movement towards increased discipline, workers' struggles tend to give more attention to the possibility of expressing their needs within the firm, at work. The progress of the idea of self-management is the political demonstration of this on a general scale. But in a growing number of firms, workers are also asking for the right to be involved in the concrete organisation of work. The demand for office or shop-floor councils is today a concrete objective, even a campaign, leading to the creation of a more permanent means of involvement with direct democracy and initiative, consolidating and widening trade union action.

The overall defensive character of the expression of workers' needs related to the labour process is true of the majority of the working class. But it is important to underline how much capitalist pressure also stimulates the counter tendency. In the same way that intensified factory discipline creates conditions which favour a growing need for self-management, the fragmentation and deskilling of labour are objective bases for an offensive mobilisation of the working-class movement on the issues of the goals and manner of production, the technological division of labour. So much so that it may be argued that the efficient defence of workers' interests today depends more and more on their capacity to take the offensive on economic and technological issues. This is of major importance for the working-class movement. But in order to really exist as a large-scale social movement, the need for such a mobilisation must be developed and conquered. The development of its 'objective bases' alone is not sufficient and will not automatically generate a capacity in the working class to take the offensive. There are too many examples of this, whether in Great Britain, the USA, Japan or West Germany. There are political conditions for the transformation of objective conditions into widely experienced needs and workers initiatives regarding the division of labour and technology, and we will discuss them later on.

'. . . living and working on your home ground'

Another major form in which workers' needs find current expression are the intense struggles against the closure of firms, even of complete sectors of industrial production such as printing, the steel industry, coalmining, shipbuilding, machine tool manufacture. . . . Superficially these are all defensive struggles against unemployment. But in fact they have a much greater impact. During these struggles, workers defend not only their wages but also their social existence as producers, the social use-value of their labour-power with all their experience, skill and know-how, not to mention that of the machines and the various means of production. In the face of those who invoke the inevitability of the crisis and the need for restructuring and redeployment, these workers are put in a position which shows up the growing split between the social utility of their work and its products on the one hand, and the criteria of capitalist profitability on the other, a split developing not only at an individual or shop-floor level, but also at the collective level of the work of a whole firm, even of an industrial sector. In defending their needs and their existence as producers, they are led to denounce the incredible waste of time, energy, raw materials and work brought about by the economic domination of the multinationals and their profit-based criteria: modern steelworks and working mines are being closed down, while sheet steel is imported from Japan and coal from the United States. The ultraspecialisation and the regrouping of production into huge units, and the consequent redeployment, destroy the industrial fabric and result in an expansion of freight transport and a tremendous growth in infrastructure.

The regional dimension of these struggles is also very important. This reveals not only the economic solidarity that exists at this level, but also the concrete unity of geographical situation and conditions of work and consumption, the economic, social and cultural wealth that the existing urban and regional frameworks represent. The slogan, growing in popularity in France, *'vivre et travailler au pays'*, living and working on your home ground, voices this growing awareness of the links between the needs of working life and the needs of life outside work, between the conditions for the satisfaction of these needs within the firm and outside it, in the town and in the region as a whole. The way in which these campaigns are organised, mobilising the population around the employees of a firm, emphasises the growing awareness of the solidarity and convergence of the economic interest, needs and living conditions of more and more social strata.

Finally, one must not neglect the links that have been established between the needs and demands of workers in their immedite confrontation with this restructuring, and questions on a national scale, such as that of economic independence. For the systematic restructuring of production in what are thought to be more viable units takes place within the framework of a hierarchisation of the international division of labour, controlled by the multinationals. The latter tend to give control of production processes and technological power to the most secure imperialist countries (USA, West Germany, Japan). This international division of labour is increasingly moving away from the development of economic cooperation to the establishment, through the geographical and functional specialisation of units, of increased dependency, reinforcing the control over less 'safe' countries.

Needs to be conquered

While these new aspects of the evolution of needs and demands are of considerable importance, they are far from applicable to all firms and all workers. However, they represent a strong tendency of the social movement, curbed and resisted by every apparatus of the existing hegemony, which attempts to induce acceptance of class domination and, more specifically, of the inevitability of the crisis, of austerity and economic redeployment, under the aegis of the multinationals.

Furthermore, it must be added that certain questions concerning the relation between needs and production have been raised to only a very limited extent by the workers' struggles. The question of use-value, of social utility, and of the quality and durability of products in relation to the needs of the consumers, is one example of this. Whether foodstuffs or manufactured goods are concerned, the workers in a firm are rarely seen to criticise the poor quality of the products they have to produce. The technological division of labour and the extreme fragmentation of tasks are obstacles to such an awareness, in the sense that the finished product is never seen by the assembly-line producer. Indeed, fewer and fewer workers even know what they produce, or what it is used for. Only a collective campaign can bring about the reappropriation of the meaning of work. But this subject still appears to be taboo, as if the criticism of products might produce a backlash against the workers themselves. The convergence of the two campaigns, of the questions being asked by direct producers and consumers could only be of benefit. And, in the longer term, does not the development of a truly socialist and self-governing society imply the ability of interested social groups to engage in face to face debate – not mediated by the market or by administrative rules – in order to analyse, define and change products, in a deeper awareness of the concrete needs of the consumer?

Another question still rarely raised is that of pollution and environmental hazards. Of course, the workers are the first to be concerned – 'a polluting factory is a polluted factory' – but we have already pointed to some of the limits of the campaigns regarding working conditions. And so far as pollution is concerned, it seems once again that the workers hesitate to take on themselves the justified demands of the ecological movements and of movements for the protection of the environment, because of the negative consequences for their jobs that might result. Many managers whose factories have been criticised and threatened with heavy fines because of the pollution they cause have cynically blackmailed their workers by threatening to close the factory if they have to pay the fines or meet the cost of anti-pollution measures. The most significant developments have probably been in the nuclear industry. There have already been several major incidents of radioactive leakage in France, as well as faults in the construction of nuclear equipment and incidents concerning the transportation of radioactive material. These have been made public and have been severely criticised by the trade unions of the production unit directly concerned. This development is certainly linked to the novelty and increased risks involved, while in many earlier instances, more usual, less spectacular and less sensitive to public opinion, the pollution or destruction of areas of natural beauty has continued without any particular mobilisation of the workers.

The fight against pollution should moreover be seen in an entirely different perspective from the production of anti-pollution equipment, which only deals with the results after the event. Such a practice, which is on the increase at present, puts the finishing touches to the wastage of natural and human resources, and without offering any real remedy closes the circle of environmental destruction, while at the same time opening up new opportunities for profit-making. These are often taken up by the very firms which were responsible for the pollution. In order to protect nature and mankind in any real way, the true fight against pollution must be conducted at the source, by the immediate installation of anti-pollution equipment in units of production, by research, and the introduction of new non-polluting processes of production. Technological research, production choices and investment must make these primary considerations. We might point out in passing the close parallel between this question and the use-destruction-restoration cycle of the labour force, which we discussed earlier with regard to problems of health. The search for a qualitatively superior mode of responding to needs presupposes that these needs be taken into consideration at the very heart of the production process, in the organisation of the work process, in the technological choices which concern both men and machines, which crystallise the division of labour, and which, while being technological, are nonetheless the expression of dominant social relations.

Such a direction is currently impossible because it would prejudice the immediate profitability of each production unit. It would imply a complete redefinition of profitability. But profitability, defined strictly by the profit made by each production unit taken in isolation, must be questioned, forcing back as it does on to 'competition' and in particular on to the workers, consumers, public services and public financing, the extensive wastage and social cost connected with the concrete mode of production, with the overaccumulation of capital, with the nature of products and with the external effects of production on the environment, towns, regions and so on. It is becoming necessary to envisage social productivity and profitability in a far broader sense, taking into consideration all these effects, and giving particular attention to the quality of the response to needs. The struggles that are developing to defend the economic potential of towns or of whole regions follow the same direction.

There remains, however, one area which has been overlooked by these struggles and in regard to which they maintain an essentially defensive position: that of opening up concrete alternatives regarding the division of labour itself. Of course, the principal political and trade union organisations of the working class reaffirm in their theory and their political programmes the necessity of developing scientific research in order to discover the means for a new development of productive forces which would respond to needs, both in terms of production and in terms of consumption and culture. But little has been done, it seems, to translate these theoretical possibilities into concrete practice in the field of production. It is true that here we are touching the very heart of the process of accumulation and thus of the dictatorship of capital, and that any far-reaching change at this level implies the previous transformation of general relations of production. The proposal would break with that dictatorship, and set up forms of social ownership of the means of production and exchange which would allow workers a greater say in the organisation of production in all its aspects. But to set in motion the process of severance from the hegemony of the capitalist class, is it not necessary to show concretely, in the course of struggles, demands and political proposals, that another way of production is possible, one which would gradually eliminate work which is slavish, fragmented, repetitive, without meaning and without status? Is it not necessary, from this moment on, that in order to build the counter-hegemony of the working class, it should take up the fight for an alternative division of labour, an alternative technology, alternative investments? The idea most frequently put forward, that the advances made by science and technology can provide the means for this change, does not go far enough. For these advances themselves are oriented to some extent by the relations of production, and even more so by the uses to which they are put. For example, it is often said that automation is the technological solution which will allow the elimination of repetitive and unskilled labour. In fact, automation has begun to be introduced into capitalist production, but it is automation directed to the same ends as the previous techno-logical changes; in other words, towards the elimination of skilled living labour. [12] And if Japan has the reputation for being the country where the use of robots is most advanced, it also has the reputation of having reached new levels of intensity in its exploitation of the working class.

Only the ability to make this concrete criticism of the productive forces of capitalism and, through struggles, to open up alternatives in terms of technological change, work status and work methods will allow the major element of the hegemony of the capitalist class to be challenged in its mastery over development within the place of work. It will also counter the parallel trap of the wholesale rejection of science and technology, particularly fashionable at present, which regards these as the ultimate incarnation of all the evils of our society and thus advocates a return to pre-mechanised forms of production and the small craftsman – a position which, in another way, protects the capitalist class hegemony.

For this reason, it is clearly indispensable to form an alliance between the working class and other categories of labour, particularly those involved in research, planning and organisation – managerial staff, engineers, technicians, research workers – an alliance which would not just be a political tactic, but would be based on the work place and represent an effective cooperation aimed at challenging present forms of authority, hierarchy and the division of labour, and at collectively inventing new forms which would bring manual and intellectual labour closer together and allow their mutual enhancement. Without such a formulation and the implementation within the struggle of a common plan for the transformation of the division and organisation of labour, one might well question whether any kind of lasting alliance would be

[12] See M. Freyssenet, *La division capitaliste du travail* (Savelli, 1977), and J.C. Poulain, *Décider au travail* (Editions sociales, 1979).

possible. In order to abandon their relative privileges – however fragile they may be, since they are eroded day after day by the extension of unskilled work and the centralisation of the crucial design and organisation tasks – managerial staff, engineers and others must see concretely what they have to gain, in both their work and their social position, from an alliance aimed at introducing a new economic and political order in which the working class would be dominant. Equally, it is necessary for the working class to perceive them as other than the instrument of its exploitation and deskilling.

Let us conclude by stressing the profound transformation of attitude which these struggles and questions – be they highly developed or barely articulate – reveal in relation to the productive forces and their development. The working-class movement has long been marked – it continues to be so, although to a more limited extent – by a linear conception of scientific and technical progress as a cumulative progression of productive forces, with its own dynamic first stimulated and then hampered by relations of production which had become too 'narrow'. Stalin gave this conception its most rigid caricature with his universal theory of the succession of modes of production,[13] but it is a view which has been – and still is – commonly held even beyond his political followers, particularly because it does, after all, conform to the dominant ideology of the inevitability, the necessity and the superiority of the forms of organisation and division of labour which have been enforced by capital. The critical analysis of the productive forces shaped by capitalism is gaining a larger audience just when the struggles which develop this critique in practice, in the place of production itself, must seek to establish a vision of a new type of development. More must be produced, but of a different kind, and in a different way. More must be consumed, but of a different kind, and in a different way. And the strongest link between these two aspects is the unity of the workers' lives, the tight interdependence of their needs, the satisfaction of which involves expanding their responsibilities, their initiative and their creativity in all areas of their existence.

NEEDS, POLITICAL PRACTICE AND DEMOCRACY

The considerable expansion of needs and of their expression in trade union and political demands, which we have just described, involves a significant number of workers. However, some are only dealt with by an

[13] Joseph Stalin, *Dialectical and historical materialism* (1938); repr. British and Irish Communist Organisation, 1984).

extreme political and trade union 'avant garde'. There are other workers who are only really mobilised by a few of the questions we have touched on. Above all, a large part of the population (in France a fairly narrow majority for a number of years; since May 1981, a narrow minority) remains reluctant to get involved, electorally or in terms of social struggles in a process of political and economic change which the parties of the left, and in particular the Communist Party, assert to be necessary for their unsatisfied needs to be met. And the working class itself, though the group most directly concerned in this change, is far from being totally committed to it.

Whence the age-old question posed by revolutionary movements: what is the obstacle, how can it be shifted? How can one spread 'class consciousness', the 'raised consciousness' of the necessity for a radical transformation of society, and, most of all, relations of production?

The weight of capital on popular needs

The political pronouncements made by the left often tend to oversimplify the problem by assuming, explicitly or implicitly, that all the needs which we have described exist for, and are therefore felt by, all workers. This suggests that the obstacle to 'consciousness' is essentially 'ideological', ideology being here thought of as a system of false notions imposed wholesale by the dominant class. What is involved here is a 'spontaneous awareness' of needs, much more widespread than the strict political spontaneity which postulates the already established existence of revolutionary political needs, but which is not essentially different in terms of the assumptions made about needs, though obviously its consequences are different. This is expressed in a certain idealisation of workers' consciousness and culture, as well as in a vision of the political process in which the registering and expression of these needs through political and trade union organisations is a more or less straightforward process once the working class is correctly represented in those organisations. The objective nature of social needs having been established, the worker-militants, their 'class consciousness' supported by an appropriate theoretical framework, have no trouble in perceiving those needs, registering and expressing them.

The analysis of needs as subjective forms of the objective determination of the social practices shaping the reproduction of labour-power has nonetheless led us to emphasise the substantial role played by capital and the state in their definition. [14] This is a point we wish to return to in order

---

[14] See my article, 'Besoins sociaux et socialisation de la consommation' in *La Pensée*, 1975, and the preceding chapter.

to spell out some of its consequences, but we would first like to emphasise that what is involved here is simply one aspect, one tendency, which stands in contradiction to others in the determination of needs: an aspect which should neither be overlooked, nor overemphasised, so as to make it, as several of the authors we will be looking at tend to do, the dominant or even the only element in 'working-class culture'.

To a great extent, the workers' needs are stamped by capital through the organisation of the work process, the use made of the productive forces and the way in which they are developed and changed, the commodities they produce and circulate, and the organisation of consumption. They are stamped in a positive way – through the type and skill of the labour-power required, and thus through the need for the labour force to reproduce itself in an appropriate and marketable way, as well as via the modes and practices of market consumption; but they are also stamped in a negative way. Various writers have emphasised, in relation to a number of working-class sectors, that 'deprivation of needs' mentioned by Pierre Bourdieu. This deprivation can be the direct consequence of the nature and conditions of the work process, and the exhaustion and lack of any spare time it imposes, so that any desire is crushed by the overwhelming search for rest. [15] But it is also due to the more complex processes which go to make up a dominated class, through the internalisation of a restricted range of opportunities and the construction of an identity through refusing to 'leave one's station', which may even go as far as the 'autorepression of desire'. [16] The low attendance by workers in theatres in suburban municipalities which make substantial efforts to inform and diffuse culture is not only because of tiredness and lack of time, but is also the outcome of a lack of interest, of cultural distance, of a profound feeling that this is something for 'them', not 'us'. The same statement can be made about education and training, reading, health care or exercise. Capital weighs down on the dominated class and shapes its needs by constricting them. But this is not a 'purely' ideological process: it is a process with a material basis in the conditions of daily life, which must be accepted, in one way or another, since life must go on. and for life to go on, one must accept the unacceptable – however provisionally, though the provisional may last a lifetime; one must be prepared to repress desires, and not allow the arousal of too many needs which are utterly incapable of being met and would only lead to frustration. Does this not give rise,

[15] In his account of his experiences at Citroën, Linhardt has given a very vivid description of this constant obsession with time and with free time: R. Linhardt, *L'établi* (Editions de minuit, 1978).
[16] See J. Fremontier, *La vie en blue. voyage en culture ouvrière* (Paris, Fayard; 1980). This is a stimulating book on account of the questions it tackles, but it deals, in a one-sided way, only with the aspect of resignation and consolation.

especially in relation to cultural practices, to the popular morality of 'keeping in one's place'?

The inertia involved in this process should not be overlooked, though one should not go on to see the workers' needs as the simple products of capitalist manipulation or domination, to see only resignation and acceptance, and finally to despair of the working class, as has not been uncommon since the beginning of the century, particularly among left wing intellectuals bidding 'farewell to the proletariat'.[17] We will come back to this crucial question later.

As for the way in which the state weighs down on needs, much has already been said on this subject in relation to collective consumption, as well as pointing out how the state, through its practices of codifying and formulating needs and its effective, though segregative, restrictive and ·bureaucratic response, could already be found to be present in the civil society, in needs spontaneously felt (though this is not to say that the state itself produces those needs, all by itself!).

Revolutionary political practice and the development of needs

Any practice which aims at the suppression of exploitation and class domination, for an end to subjection, thus assumes the form not only of a struggle for the satisfaction of the needs which are felt but, much more deeply, of a struggle for the expansion, development and transformation of those needs themselves. Breaking up capitalist hegemony entails an explosion of needs which will do away with censorship and self-censorship, and declare their satisfaction possible and necessary. The task of breaking up past frameworks and opening the range of 'objective collective futures' is also a work of producing new needs (for instance, the transformation of a rejection of exploitation and oppression into a desire for control of the production process, and the creation of a new type of political democracy 'which would allow workers to have a decisive influence on the social production of their conditions of existence). This task implies an organised collective political practice: that is to say, political and trade unions revolutionary organisations capable of establishing theoretical and practical bases for a counter-hegemony of the exploited classes. Such political practice cannot remain on a 'purely' ideological level, or it will risk sinking without trace due to the impotence of propaganda. It must produce the material bases for political class consciousness and for more developed needs. The foundations of these material bases are the workers' practices, their solidarity in production,

[17]The title of André Gorz's latest book, *Adieux au proletariat* (Edition Galilée, 1980).

the extent to which their work as well as their daily life provides the creative dynamics to stimulate needs, together with the inexorable violence of exploitation and domination which, whether imperceptibly or brutally, builds up not only resignation, but also discontent and revolt. Political and trade union struggles, strikes, the experience of being part of a collective force standing up against oppression, and the victories gained, however small they may be, as well as the forms of socialisation of consumption established by the unions and left-wing local governments, all extend these material bases.

In order to break the chain of domination, exploitation and deprivation, there must be some material footholds, points of purchase, in autonomous practices and ambitious and coherent collective projects. Without going over the whole debate about the necessity for revolutionary organisations and their theoretical and practical capacity for intervention, let us begin by stressing the indispensable need for some point of purchase outside the relations of domination, something which can open up a space where new needs and new practices can be developed and tested, and where, above all, speech, dignity and democracy can expand and grow: a space where the task we have already mentioned, that of transforming needs and individual, isolated revolt into collective aims and campaigns, expressing those individual needs in issues and policies involving the whole of the social body and even international relations, a space where this work can begin to take shape.

Without this movement of convergence and synthesis and universalisation, involving both the problems and the economic and political structure on a general scale, the (indispensable) multiplication of the most diverse social movements may take place within a corporatist fragmentation and be rendered impotent in terms of any capacity for broader change. This is the main trap of the 'exploded view' of politics, microstruggles against micro-powers, which is so fashionable in some circles at the moment, particularly those influenced by the thinking of Michel Foucault. In Italy, for instance, where the dangers of this sort of corporatist fragmentation are particularly acute, Pietro Ingrao has clearly demonstrated the importance of the process of political 'recombination'. [18] Could this fragmentation, in France, be seen as a backlash to the failure of the Left in the 1978 elections? It is paradoxical that this manifestation of the strength of the capitalist hegemony, [19] subsequently intensified by the

[18] Pietro Ingrao, *Crisi e terza via* (Editori Riuniti, 1978).

[19] This is also a manifestation of the relative weakness of the forces of the Left, who clearly bear their own responsibility for that weakness – the disunity of the Left resulting from the abandonment by the Socialist Party of the principal commitments of the Common Programme, the working-class emphasis and rigidity of the Communist Party's propaganda practices – but that is a different story, and not something which should obscure the primary aspect of the question.

authoritarianism and the more and more overtly antisocial, antidemocratic nature of the policies of the state and its declared support for big capitalist corporations, should have ended in a sort of indifference among many left-wing intellectuals that the victory of the left in 1981 has not entirely dispelled. They have turned away from the awkward question of the state and the centralisation of economic power to concentrate on local problems and local movements, problems which are more specific, more cultural in their nature and which, perhaps, appear to be within the range of individual influence.

It is also worth stressing the significance of the cultural dimension of class organisations, since it is the totality of needs which have to be stimulated, developed and expressed in demands and general programmes. The questions of political and economic power, and of wages, are after all only preliminaries, a key to profound changes, if one is not to fall back into the economism and productivism which sees men as means towards a growth rate, rather than the other way round.

Obviously, working class revolutionary organisations are not the only ones capable of stimulating and expressing needs, as we will see later on. But they do have a crucial responsibility in opening up new directions for society by helping to produce new political needs, by breaking with capitalist hegemony, and by constituting through that action the indispensable springboard towards further development.

The capacity of working-class organisations to carry out their responsibilities efficiently in this regard is, however, neither automatic nor guaranteed.

It is intimately dependent on their political practices, which are themselves linked to their principles of organisation, their theoretical orientations and work, without being reducible to them.

Let us come back to a fundamental point: the truth of needs is that they are being felt. Needs may be codified, censored, channelled in certain directions, but there is no such thing as a false need. No organisation can have a true knowledge of need that would be external, or even superior, to those who experience them.

If a political or trade union organisation seeks to know the workers' needs, and claims to express them, it can only do so insofar as it is itself a locus for their expression and, through that, of their collective development and transformation, their permanent transformation. For this reason, there are two complementarty necessities, for democracy on the one hand, and theoretical organisation and elaboration on the other. The necessity for democracy in this regard goes far beyond a mere respect for the formal rules of representative democracy within the organisation. It is a question of there being an active, productive democracy which impels those who are most cut off everywhere else to find a voice there. It is not simply that the militants must be convinced and convincing propagandists; it is above all, and all the time, a question of their expressing themselves, their expressing their own needs. They should constantly give workers who are not members of the organisation an opportunity to speak, to be questioned, and to be listened to.

The collective mind and democratic centralism: theory and policy

The Communist parties sometimes claim to act as collective intellectuals, producing a scientific analysis of society. For this to be true, at least as a tendency, this sort of constant interplay between speech and listening is at least as important as theory. Theory is the indispensable instrument for the production of knowledge, but it does not fulfil that function in any way that can be termed scientific except insofar as it is continually confronted with practical experience, with the practice of experimentation where the efficacy and coherence of the theory are tested, as are its limitations and weaknesses, trying to see where it falls down.

Whatever its qualities the outset, any theory which aims at a knowledge of the movement of societies will change into a rigid, mystificatory dogma if it is not constantly enriched and tested by 'practical experience'. This applies to Marxism more than any other theory because of its explicitly scientific ambitions. And not just any practical epxerience, dogmatic alibis being legion here too. Political practice 'on the ground', which constantly seeks to stimulate the direct expression of needs by those experiencing them, which is careful to listen to what they have to say, sensitive to change and to the appearance of new problems. . . . A political practice, within the organisation, of confrontation between different points of view, of free expression by all militants, and of a search for progressive syntheses which does not diminish or dilute new aspects, new difficulties, new questions. A political practice which takes account of everything that disturbs the established order – analyses, programmes, demands objectives of struggle – in order to enrich itself and increase its capacity to give political expression to needs.

Communist parties give their organisational principles the title of democratic centralism. Democratic so as to ensure free discussion, centralism to ensure unity and efficiency in the application of the decisions so taken. From the point of view taken here, democracy involves a movement towards centralisation so as to ensure the theoretical and political synthesis of needs and their translation into demands and campaign objectives. One can also see the crucial importance of democracy in the active sense spoken of earlier, within centralism itself, so as to avoid any dilution and dogmatic reduction, any brushing aside of disturbing questions.

The main objective of the activity of a revolutionary party should be to help the deprived and excluded to find a voice and take power. The party, its theory and its programme, should be instruments for the liberation of the exploited classes. There is, however, nothing natural and spontaneous in this work of stimulating the expression of needs, 'reconstituting' and synthesising needs, and translating them into programmes. On the one hand, there is the weight of domination, which has a constant tendency to impose silence on the exploited and the oppressed. On the other hand, there is the tension of political and ideological confrontation, with the need to propagate the ideas and proposals of the working-class movement, setting them against permanent areas of censorship and distortion. This entails arguing convicingly against the prejudices and misconceptions which are constantly refuelled by the adversary's propaganda. Because of this, there is an enormous, and constantly renewed danger of over-valuing the organisation's own pronouncements, tending to see them as a superior truth, a light to be brought to those in darkness.

The main thing is to convince, and anything that does not fit in with the truth as seen by the party is rejected as being the effect of bourgeois ideology and of 'adversary pressure'. Historical examples abound. For instance, in relation to the French Communist Party's attitude to needs, one can recall the position taken in 1955–6, where the Party leaders defended the thesis of the 'absolute pauperisation' of the working class,[20] a thesis which at the theoretical level completely underestimated the development of the working class, of the process of production and the conditions of reproduction of the labour force. At this time, a highly subtle empirical demonstration was attempted, dotted with entirely apposite remarks on the development of needs, modes of consumption and the forms and intensity of the productive consumption of the labour force,[21] but it failed to draw any of the theoretical consequences which would have revealed the absurdity of the thesis of absolute pauperisation, the conclusion at which they had tendentiously aimed from the begin-

[20] See for example the articles by Baby in *Economie et Politique*, No. 10, February 1955, and by Thorez in *Les cahiers du communisme*, No. 3, March 1955, and Nos. 7–8, July–August 1955.
[21] P. Montjoie, 'La paupérisation absolue' in *Economie et Politique*, No. 24, June 1956. The following passages may be quoted by way of illustration: 'The new conditions of the exploitation of labour existing in the large concentrated firms have had as one of their consequences a marked increase in the needs of the working class . . .' (p. 26). 'Moreover, the new needs can be incorporated into the cost of the reproduction of labour-power . . . the more the workers economise on their labour-power outside production the more they can be exploited inside the factory . . . Water in the sink, and the bicycle too are conditions for the deepening and extension of the exploitation of the working class . . .' p. 31).

ning. Let us also recall the more recent development of the Communist Party's view on self-management. As Damette has written: 'the notion has arisen very quickly, after we had struggled against it, which creates a perfectly understandable disturbance, a disturbance which still exists within the Party itself'.[22] In fact, up until the autumn of 1977, the term 'self-management' belonged essentially to the vocabulary and political planning of the Confédération française démocratique du travail and the Parti socialiste unifié, and, more recently, and in a more ambiguous way, to the Socialist Party. For a number of years, the Communists denounced the reformist illusions of self-management, and then, in the autumn of 1977, they suddenly became its champions.[23] Is it not because the term, despite all the ambiguities, deficiencies and confusions it comprises, and which have been rightly criticised, nevertheless denotes a concept, an aspiration, which is positive and important, and which had been relatively underestimated by the Communists? If this had been the case, self-management would not first have been denounced, and then taken up.

The concept of self-management is directly related to the expansion of the needs of active democracy, to which we will return later. It denotes practices which break away from obedience to dogmas or centralised instructions, the diversified expression of needs, and the collective, decentralised exercise of power that questions the centralisation of the state. The fact that the Communist Party took up the concept shows, retrospectively, that the militants who fought against it so rigorously were at least partially in the wrong. But it also shows that they must have been sufficiently receptive to those aspirations for the political switch to have been made. With this example in mind, one is led to look at every position which is either defended or denounced, and ask oneself whether it too might be the subject of a similar volte-face. This is no sterile metaphysical anxiety, but an absolutely indispensable theoretical anxiety if one does not direct it inwards, towards the inside of the party, the central locus directing change, but outwards, to the complex movement of social contradictions which must be followed and then analysed.

There is another theoretical lesson to be drawn from this case; namely, the dogmatism of the wholesale condemnation, and even ignorance of the point of view of other people (people who do not think the same way, who do not belong to the Party or to a union, or perhaps belong to a different one) revealed by these sudden reversals. If from the outset, the critical

---

[22] F. Damette and J. Scheibling, *Pour une stratégie autogestionnaire: entretiens avec Gilbert Wasserman* (Editions sociales, 1979), p. 9.
[23] In a document entitled 'La liberté guide nos pas', published in Autumn 1977 as a contribution to the debate with the unions.

analysis had been more attentive to the possible positive elements in the views of those who were in favour of self-management, theoretical and political progress might have been able to 'intervene' earlier, and might have been able to act as an enriching force and not as a reversal of point of view, only too likely to cause a disturbance. It will be objected that there was political awareness, since a change took place. But does not that put theory in the position of simply being the *a posteriori* expression of political practice? And is that not precisely what condemns theory to stagger from one agonising revision to the next?

There are those who think that this difficulty can be avoided by maintaining a necessary distance between theoretical work and political practice, in order to protect the freedom of the first from the daily demands for certainty of the second. While this is a good solution for activities specifically directed towards research and an understanding of the movement of society, it simply displaces the problem as far as political practice is concerned. From the moment that political practice claims to take into account and express needs in all their diversity, it cannot afford to skimp on being constantly open to the diversity of society and to narrow its capacity to confront continually the contradictory movement of society. And since only revolutionary political practice is capable, in terms of the whole of society, of giving a voice and power to the workers, so that the oppressed may themselves express and transform their needs, in a way that no sociological investigation could ever do, this is a crucial area.

It would be absurd to deny that there is this permanent risk of dogmatic ossification in political theory and discourse. It would also be simplistic to attribute it solely to the 'leadership and the apparatus', postulating a sort of spontaneous clairvoyance at the grass-roots. It would be no less simplistic to lay all the blame on the grass-roots, seeing it as a failure in the work of training of the militants leading to the distortion of a correct theoretical position.

The truth of the organisation, militant ethics and cultural distance

A good deal has already been said and written about the dangers of over-centralisation, of running things '*de haut en bas*', co-opting cadres, and of the links between dogmatism and a tendency towards the confiscation of power by a small group, and so on. We would only like to emphasise that in our opinion it is a central responsibility of the leadership and, more generally, of the cadres of a revolutionary party, to struggle against the dangers described above: and to struggle in practice, because verbal conjurations and the affirmation of right principles can well mask the most dogmatic and authoritarian of practices. One only needs to remember Stalin and his speech about 'man, the most valuable capital'. Besides, 'struggle against' is an inappropriate expression, since what is needed is the permanent invention of a practice which is in no way spontaneous, and which entails a total questioning of the usual relations between knowledge and power. Those who have knowledge and responsibilities (the militants, the cadres, the leaders) should not seek to impose their truth first but should, on the contrary, open themselves up and be prepared to listen, and place themselves at the service of the truth of those who 'do not know', yet without whose knowledge no serious analysis of the totality of social practices and social changes can possibly take place. It is not by any right, or because it is written into its statutes, or because such and such a percentage of its leaders and cadres is drawn from the working class that a political party truly represents the working class and the oppressed. If the organisation and its leadership do not constantly stimulate the process of true expression of the working class through and by the party, the organisation's own truth tends to take over, and to produce a simplified, static, even mythical representation of the working class and of society in general.

All the same, the solution to this problem does not lie solely in the hands of the leadership. The problem is not only the result of the pressure of the dominant ideology and the dominant social relations imposing their logic of domination within the political institution itself. It is also related to political practice in its most individual expectations and consequences. Those who commit themselves politically by the same token invest a great deal of their desires, of their 'existential needs' (and a good deal of their time) in political practice, rather than in their occupation, family or cultural life. This tends to produce the opportunity for a certain austerity in the militant ethic, a channelling of desires into political practice, where the individuals can 'fulfil themselves', with an accompanying relative lack of involvement in the rest of daily life: satisfactions are political, and the blossoming of desires in other fields is something to be looked for tomorrow, afterwards, when the victory has been won and everything is different.

This produces a significant gap between the life of the militant and of the non-militant. Significant not only in time, in distinctive practices, but also in the ideological distance arising from their different images of life. This leads to a risk of non-comprehension of the desires and needs of those who have not committed themselves to politics, but have their being elsewhere. In their investigation of local elected representatives and leaders of associations, Godard and Pendaries have given a good picture of the gap between the pronouncements made by these 'representatives' about the needs, demands, and difficulties facing the 'population', and the almost total absence of any similar pronouncements about their own lives.[24] The present author, in the course of numerous discussions with militants over this question of needs, has frequently noticed the disparity between their support for, and even their political action in relation to, the needs of others and a certain silence with regard to their own needs, the outcome of the political channelling mentioned earlier.[25]

Although the austere militant ethic is a reality, it must not be seen to be the only expression of this disparity. The opposite tendency exists too, and on a very large scale, when political commitment, by lifting the overwhelming burden of resignation, opens the way to the development of a real taste for culture, knowledge and personal fulfillment; then socialisation within a politicised environment provides a stimulus for the development of those tastes and facilitates their satisfaction, both materially (through the opportunities available and the information and network of collective consumption linked to the militant life) and by legitimising them and giving them a value.

From the point of view of its capacity to stimulate the development of needs, this movement, in contrast to the austere ethic, is a positive, perhaps even an indispensable force in the task of cultural transformation which should be an integral part of revolutionary political practice. But it also produces a gap between the militant caught up in it and the social group from which he comes. It is a gap which may not be the reverse of the preceding one, and may even complement it: a certain lack of interest in the personal practices related to the day-to-day culture of the social group may go hand in hand with a commitment to political practice and to other cultural practices validated by it, such as the victorious appropriation of certain elements of the 'cultivated culture' which the dominant class tends to keep to itself. It is not necessarily a negative gap so long as it is recognised, and so long as the needs and practices of those who are not militants,' and who are not caught up in that movement, are recognised for what they are, not only as 'less' in relation to 'cultivated' practices, but as 'more' in terms of being specific cultural practices, in which they can express themselves and which have their own standing. On that condition, the gap between them can be the motive force behind cultural changes contributing to the struggle and the liberation of the oppressed classes. For the transformation of militant workers, through

[24] F. Godard and J.R. Pendaries, *Les modes de vie dans le discours de la représentation, institutions locales et production politique des besoins* (Laboratoire de Sociologie de l'Université de Nice, 1978).
[25] Catherine Claude, in *Voyages et aventures en écologie* (Paris, Editions sociales, 1978) echoes many of the discussions we have touched on here.

politics, into intellectuals, even into professional and permanent intellectuals, is a necessary element in the creation of the working-class counter-hegemony. But it is important not to be 'cut off from the masses'. It is not simply a danger of being too far 'ahead' of them, too far 'above' their level of consciousness. There is also, above all, the danger of being somewhere else, to one side of their real, experienced needs and difficulties.

The necessity for a transformation of political practice along the lines we have indicated is all the greater given the increased pressure of capital and the state bearing down on the daily life of the workers and the exploited classes. The reduction of autonomy and initiative in work as elsewhere, the variety of channels for social control and the pressure for the 'standardisation' of behaviour and views (through education, the mass media) all correspondingly intensify the political need for the achievement of autonomy in the expression of needs.

The ability of revolutionary parties to stimulate the production of these needs and give form to them in demands and political projects for their possible satisfaction depends on a number of factors, starting with the recognition of the importance of these questions. As we have seen, there is nothing automatic about this recognition, and it can not be reduced to a purely subjective movement. It entails a theoretical undertaking involving the mode of organisation, the place allocated to intellectuals, the freedom allowed to internal debate, the ability to synthesise, the weight of centralism and so on. It also entails, to 'feed' this undertaking, that the party should be physically active and present in the places where these questions appear. An organisation which is centred too exclusively on the work place may be badly situated to perceive all the new needs, all the contradictions, appearing in the sphere of consumption. The fact that the French Communist Party has favoured work-place organisation, which is in many respects the source of its strength, is also partly the reason why it lags behind in the general political consciousness of questions of consumption in the widest sense: living conditions, health, the environment and so on.

The 'external' conditions of the struggle have an influence too. Periods in which there is an expansion of influence and alliances, and of the offensive development of the working-class counter-hegemony, work in its favour. Periods of political isolation, of contraction or resistance to a strengthened adversary, work towards a defensive closing-in of the organisation. But it is not enough simply to record this as an inevitable development. Particularly at the present time, when in order to respond to the manifold pressure of the state and of capital, the development and increasing complexity of needs requires not the truth of an organisation promulgated by centralised edict, but an expression of that complexity in ever more direct and democratic forms, in words and in action. It is a period in which the continuous fragmentation, division and disorganisation of the dominated classes by capital and the state demand a converse labour of political unification, based not on an alignment with the supposedly homogeneous needs and demands of a monolithic working class, but on the progressive establishment of the convergence and transformation of the very different needs and demands of the various social groups and fractions of social groups, so as to bring out the interests they have in common while respecting their diversity.

The diversity and contradictions of needs

The considerable extension of wage labour and the extreme concentration of political and economic power have too often led to a belief in the homogenisation of needs, in a growing similarity of living conditions, at work, and in individual and collective consumption; a similarity in expectations, in needs, and thus in political, social and economic demands.

Some sort of similarity is undeniable, and this constitutes the objective base for the possible convergence and alliance between different social classes and social categories: executives, engineers, technicians, teachers, employees, factory workers. But, as we saw in the preceding chapter, particularly with reference to social segregation, there remain sizeable differences between ways of life which remain very different and very unevenly matched (for example in relation to income, consumption, inherited wealth, free time, access to education and 'high culture', among other things).

However, though these differences and inequalities are related to the division constantly being created by the dominant class, they cannot simply be reduced to 'ideological effects' concealing an underlying unity of interests. They are, rather, an integral part of social relations and material practices, visible in the hierarchical relations and division of labour in the work place and, beyond that, in the process of social reproduction which reproduces the places, skills, and relations within the work process and hence, in the specific needs of each social class or social category.

Of course, there is nothing 'natural' in the fact that the processes of social reproduction tend, to a large extent, to reproduce within themselves social classes and categories. For the possibility of 'socio-occupational mobility' which would allow a worker to become a high-grade executive, or vice versa, is strictly limited, whether within one generation or between successive generations.[26] If one is seeking to transform the division of labour and struggle against social inequalities and the elements of the relations of class domination which they transmit, it is important that each individual should benefit from the political and economic change. What some may lose – e.g. executives, in terms of hierarchic power – should be made good to them in the interest, skill and quality of their work, and the reduction in the relative advantages of their way of life should be made through an improvement in the condition of the working class, and not through bringing their living conditions down.

Any quest for an alliance which is a true alliance, based on a true convergence of interests and not on an alignment in relation to the interests of a single group, such as the working class or the middle classes or the intellectuals, must thus ensure and depend upon an expression of the diversity of their needs, and tackle properly the inevitable contradictions which exist objectively over and above their exploitation by the dominant class, so as to find a way of transcending and not merely of stifling them. Whence, for instance, the importance and the difficulty of the discussions already mentioned about the development of the role of the executive or the engineer in relation to self-management in factories, or in relation to the transformation of the division of labour between manual and intellectual labour, between the work of conception and the work of execution. Or, to take another example, the discussions on education and on how to break out of the vicious circle of social inequality, segregation and class domination, and reconcile an improvement in the position of children from the intellectual middle classes with those from the working class, including the children of immigrant workers.

In the 'spontaneous' movement of the expression of needs, whether in relation to political institutions or in terms of the means of mass consumption, it is the most exploited, the most deprived workers whose needs are the most 'spontaneously' censored, brushed aside and silenced. Whence, as we have already emphasised, the crucial importance of their own autonomous political organisation transforming, developing and imposing their needs wherever they are denied: in the place of work, in education, in relation to housing policy, health, culture, the environment and so on.

But this, the main aspect of the political struggle for the expression of the needs of the working class and the most oppressed social categories, cannot be separated from an awareness of the needs of the other social strata. An alliance with these strata is necessary for obvious political

[26] See the excellent work by D. Bertaux, *Destins personnels et structure des classes* (PUF, 1977).

reasons, but also for more deep-seated economic and social reasons: the skill, knowledge and creativity of these workers is, to a large extent, indispensable to the working class in production and consumption alike. To set the development of the productive forces, culture and collective consumption going along different lines, the working class must co-operate with research workers, engineers and technicians, inventors, doctors and teachers, and the rest, quite as much as with the peasants. And this cooperation must be established straight away in the struggle against capitalism and in the offensive upbuilding of a working-class counter-hegemony as the indispensable focus for the convergence of anti-capitalist interests. This implies a recognition of the specificity, indeed the diversity of the economic and cultural qualities and needs of these strata. It also implies a political task of expressing, developing and transforming those needs which, like those of the working class but in a different way, are stamped, in their 'spontaneous' existence, by the pressure of capital and of the state.

It entails the same dialectic of revolutionary political practice which we described earlier: listening as extensively and attentively as possible to what the needs are, and tying this in with the political and theoretical work of transforming those needs. To recognise the social diversity of needs, and the necessity of being prepared to take on board the contradictions which may result, is obviously to recognise the necessity for their political expression. One might think, as certain mechanistically minded commentators have been tempted to do, that the problem can be resolved by political pluralism, with each social category having its own representative organisation. But that is a flatly economistic vision which misleadingly reduces and homogenises the needs of the members of each category. On the contrary, what one can observe is a plurality in the political representation of each class or social category,[27] as well as, incidentally, a variable quality of representation according to the country concerned. For instance, the Democratic Party, which receives the majority of working-class votes in the USA, is in no way a working-class party, and even in the numerous socialist or social democratic parties, the percentage of leaders and cadres of working-class origin is very low. This plurality underlines the extent of the politico-ideological differences and divisions which can exist even within a single class or social category.

Though political pluralism may be necessary as the recognition and expression of this political diversity – a point we will come back to later – this in no way guarantees either the correct political expression of all needs in their social diversity, nor their transformation and convergence in the

[27] See for example M. Dion et al., *La classe ouvrière française et la politique* (Editions sociales, 1980).

manner described earlier. Because of capitalist pressure towards the division and fragmentation of the non-capitalist classes and strata on the one hand, and the repression of the needs of the working class on the other, it is only within the revolutionary working-class movement that one can begin the work of transforming needs and bringing together the needs of other categories of workers and the developed needs of the working class, so as to establish a counter-hegemony capable of abolishing the domination of capital. And the ability of the working-class movement to attend to the diversity of the needs of other categories of workers, to involve and impel the process of their political transformation by detaching them from the capitalist hegemony, cannot simply be resolved by achieving the commitment of a number, even a substantial number, of the members of those strata.

That is a necessary but not a sufficient condition. Their specific needs must be expressed, but without undermining the leading role of the working class (which is what has happened at present with the social democrats) or, on the other hand, aligning themselves totally with it (the 'workerist' tendency). These needs must be taken into account within the movement without falling into either of these traps, by responding to the specific needs and seeing where they converge with those of the working class, and facing up to any contradictions. It is in fact a question of opening up perspectives that make it possible to perceive and so to transcend the inevitable, and to some extent dynamic, contradictions which result from the division of labour. These must be displaced and transformed by a division of labour based on cooperation between the different categories and the contradictions that are directly or indirectly related to the political, economic and ideological relations of class domination.

Paradoxically, the chance of achieving this transcendance depends primarily on the quality and strength of the position and involvement of the working class itself in the systems of social practice in question.

For instance, the necessary alliance with these categories assumes that the revolutionary movement takes account of the needs of doctors, or architects. This was not the case in France during periods which were strongly marked by the tendency to see everything in terms of the 'workers', as for instance in the twenties, when only a few isolated individuals from those professions joined the Communist Party, the majority of both categories being integrated into or closely associated with the dominant class. In other, more recent, periods, such as the fifties or sixties, the influence of the revolutionary movement within these sectors has increased significantly, with the result that the opposite movement took place. Thus the definition of the Communist Party's policies on health and urbanisation was principally carried out by professionals who were members of the Party, because of the political underestimation of these questions and the low level of involvement and mobilisation and of theoretical development within the Party as a whole, that is to say, within its mainly working-class component. This led to a rather narrow and technical approach to problems of health and urbanisation. On the one hand, this reductive approach, underestimating the effect of class contradictions and the weight of state and capitalist orientations bearing down on collective consumption, took only partial account of the needs of the working class and the necessity for a qualitative transformation in this area. On the other hand, this same underestimation led to an almost corporatist vision of the needs of professionals, blurring the necessity for their transformation within the process of a revolutionary alliance and the contradictions that need to be transcended, even those contradictions internal to the professions themselves.

Since the end of the sixties, popular campaigns about housing, living conditions, transport, health and so on, have proceeded and developed in the way we have already described. At the same time, the political vision of the Communist Party has been transformed, extending the analysis of the links between the different areas of collective consumption and class contradictions (the general nature of exploitation, the pressure of monopoly capital, social segregation, state authoritarianism) which has emphasised the necessity for mass struggle in order to impose a broader and more satisfying response to popular needs.[28] Similarly, the Communist Party's capacity for recording, and analysing, and for the revolutionary transformation of the professional social sectors has developed proportionately, bringing out more fully than any simple, hypothetical anti-monopolist convergence the prospects for an alliance. This is not to say that an alliance will take shape automatically, nor that all the internal difficulties of the Communist Party have been settled: the deep crisis of 1977–78, which has taken the PCF back twenty years, is sufficient evidence of that.

It must be added that the diversity of needs not only derives from the diversity of social sectors other than the working class, but is also related to the diversity of the working class itself. Beneath the abstract and general concept of capitalist exploitation of productive labour there is great variety in the concrete forms of this exploitation, a variety multiplied by the variety of conditions of reproduction.

---

[28]On the subjects of urbanisation and health, let us mention among other works P. Juquin, '*Les communistes et le cadre de vie*', Report to the Central Committee of the French Communist Party, June 1976, and Mireille Bertrand et al., *Prendre soin de la santé* (Editions sociales, 1977).

There is diversity of skills, from the manual worker to the electronics engineer. There is diversity of jobs and of the occupational identities and ways of life associated with them: miners, railway-workers, dockers, steel-workers, printers. There is diversity of origins: a worker may be French, Algerian, Portuguese, African, Yugoslav, Turkish, the son of a worker or of a peasant. Workers may be employed in large factories or small workshops. They may live in the old neighbourhoods of the big cities, in traditional working-class areas, in new towns, in remote suburbs, in semi-rural areas. They are men or women. There is diversity too in age and domestic situation: there are young and old, single people and married couples with children. . . .

Socialisation and individuation

This diversity is partly produced by the dominant class, but is also intensified and exploited by that class through fragmentation and division; the politico-ideological movement for class unification responds by demonstrating and expanding these common needs from the immediate needs of survival and consumption to developed political needs: from the need for control over work, the need for control over the economy; from the need to alleviate the daily oppression of labour, the need to construct that political and economic democracy called socialism.

But this diversity is also a fundamental source of wealth: the economic wealth of the diversity of productive forces which stimulates their development, the cultural wealth of the diversity of their ways of life. Nor does that wealth lie only in the diversity of social sectors and social groups. It is also embedded in concrete individuals, in social histories, in social relations, the knowledge, culture and memory inscribed within unique bodies, in the desire of these subjects (in the psychoanalytical meaning of the word) invested in their aptitudes and needs in the widest sense.

Capitalist hegemony is built on the disorganisation and fragmentation of the dominated classes, with the category of the subject (in the philosophical meaning of the word: the isolated individual, master of his actions, the basic material of the social edifice) as its crucial ideological axis. The ideology of free exchange between equal subjects, crystallised in bourgeois law, conceals the social areas determined by relations of production and denies class membership by 'the interpellation of the subject', to quote Althusser.[29] The assertion of this universal essence of Man is embodied in various approaches which aim to establish a universal

---

[29] Louis Althusser, 'Idéologie et appareils idéologiques d'Etat'.

model of human behaviour, as for instance in neoclassical consumer theory, or, even better, in games theory, where a single principle of conceptualisation is supposed to account, step by step, for every social practice.[30] It is simply a negation of social diversity, some aspects of which we have sketched out. And the theory is multiplied in practice: in production as much as in consumption, capital exerts a constant pressure towards homogenisation, towards the standardisation and serialisation of the individual, at the same time as it cuts him off and isolates him the better to dominate him. The domination of the commodity character of labour-power, the organisation of competition in the labour market, are amplified in production. The 'scientific organisation of labour' which made Taylor so famous and, more generally, the whole movement of the transformation of the productive forces by capital, seeks to break up, codify and permanently denature all activity so as to increase the interchangeability of workers. Increases in productivity are sought through the intensification of work simplified into repetitive sequences and their externally imposed articulation within a hierarchical organis- ation and the machine system. This very particular movement of socialisation of production, which depends on the negation of specific abilities, nonetheless constantly reproduces its own limitations, as we show earlier, since in spite of everything it cannot avoid being forced to make use of the concrete use-value of the labour force, and so to depend on its skills.

Quite a different kind of socialisation is both possible and necessary, a socialisation relying on a recognition of aptitudes and differences, and on cooperation collectively organised by the workers themselves on the basis of their specific abilities. There is no contradiction, quite the reverse in fact, between socialisation and individuation, that is to say, between the recognition of individual abilities and the opening up of opportunities for their development, once socialisation has been established and is in the control of collectives of the workers themselves.

Eulogies to difference and the rediscovery of subjectivity are much in vogue today, linked most often to a liquidation of any attempt to analyse the concrete processes of the exploitation of labour, of the accumulation of capital and of class domination. It would be wrong, however, simply to see this as a return to the old idealism and an abandonment of the class war. The revival of bourgeois thought is linked to a profound reaction against capitalist pressure towards uniformity, towards 'normalisation', as well as to the justified criticism of certain structuralist excesses of 'theoretical anti-humanism', with its over-homogeneous vision of the

---

[30]The critical analysis of this theory and of some of its applications are developed in E. Preteceille, *Jeux, modèles et simulations* (Mouton, 1973).

working class, its over-mechanistic conception of determination by relations of production, and to the tragedy of Stalinism and certain debatable tendencies in 'existing socialism'.

Although it is important to resist the great intellectual political purge, of which the *nouveaux philosophes* were the first stage in the publicity campaign, and although it is indispensable to work out a theoretical analysis and political organisation of the convergence and revolutionary transformation of the needs of the working class and of different groups of workers, it would be dangerous both theoretically and politically to abandon to idealism the question of individual diversity, of the subject and his desires.

It is not some notion of humanist morality that makes it right to emphasise the social wealth provided by the individual diversity of needs and abilities, a diversity not drawn from a universal human essence but from the diversity of concrete social relations and of their articulation, as Marx in his *Thesis on Feuerbach* and Althusser's criticisms of Roger Garaudy and John Lewis have made clear.[31] Individual diversity is social diversity.

If one accepts the idea that needs as they are experienced are the investments of desire and that there can be no creativity without mobilising the desire of the subject, then it must be recognised that it is impossible to carry through the concrete analysis of something as 'economic' as productive forces without investigating the production and the mode of existence of those 'supporting agents' of social relations, or without looking into the movement of desire which makes them more or less effective as such, and which must also have something to do with their trajectory within those relations. The subject is the product of a unique social history (which produces him as he stands, including his unconscious, or perhaps starting with his unconscious – an assertion which would make a number of psychoanalysts howl in protest, particularly those following Lacan), and that uniqueness contributes to producing him and his own history.

We will not take these sketchy beginnings of a hypothesis any further here since it is a question which requires much more extensive study, although this area has interested the present writer for some time, Louis Althusser's provocative remarks in this direction not having been without their effect.[32] It must be said that the very definition of the object of investigation is by no means obvious. It falls between two stools: on the

---

[31] See Louis Althusser, 'Marxism and humanism', in *For Marx*, trans. Ben Brewster (London, Allen Lane, the Penguin Press; 1969) and *Essays in Self-Criticism*, trans. Grahame Lock (New Left Books, NLB; 1976).
[32] See 'Freud et Lacan', in *La Nouvelle Critique*, No. 161–2; and 'Idéologie et appareils idéologiques d'Etat', in *Positions* (Editions sociales, 1976).

one hand, it does not quite fall into the domain of political economy or the social sciences, with their concern with the 'macro structures' of social relations; nor, on the other hand, is it really appropriate to psychoanalysis, with its primary aim of understanding and alleviating suffering of the individual. Some sort of theoretical bridge between these two areas has to be built more or less from scratch if one is concerned to establish a rigorous conceptualisation, and not simply to navigate metaphorically on the currents of desire, more or less channelled by the machinery of power.[33]

We would simply like at this point to put forward an idea, which is also the basis for a project: the universe of needs is defined by a double polarity, which is not the opposition of the individual to the social, but the duality of the social itself. On the one hand, there are the individual crystallisations of the social relations making up concrete individuals and determining an irreducible diversity of the movements and investments of the desire of these subjects in needs and practices, while on the other hand there is the organisation of the totality of these social relations governed by the general movement of societies. The movement of needs towards their convergence cannot be separated from the movement towards their diversification. It is also important to note that this 'bipolarisation' – which might almost be described as dialectic, if that word had not been used too often in idealist explanations – has much wider repercussions: for instance, where work is concerned, the bipolarisation between the pole of the interest of the work for the individual performing it, and the pole of the more general social utility of this work and of its products. The tensions and contradictions which result from this, as they may be expressed in the relations between the fulfillment of personal abilities and needs through work and cooperation with the collective or the response to more general social criteria of the usefulness of the products, are at present more or less completely disguised by the dominant logic of the process of capitalist accumulation and its contradictions. But they are none the less present, and they need to be expressed and developed more widely within the logic of a movement towards socialist self-management so as to play a dynamic role in the transformation of productive forces and the division of labour.

If one accepts this theoretical proposition, it will immediately be clear

---

[33] Guattari, Deleuze and the various members of the CERFI had the merit of following Foucault in underlining the importance of looking at capital, labour, power, desire etc., together. But apart from the salutary effect of their challenge, the complete 'shaking-up' of concepts they employ ends up by emptying them of any explicit meaning, and leaves them depending on a series of undemonstrable metaphors. Whereas it seems to us that quite the opposite is needed: an attempt to establish both rigorous conceptualisation (of the economy as of desire) and empirical verification.

that all needs are social, and that the term 'social needs' is redundant. It is not a problem to use the inevitable shorthand of political vocabulary, as may be found even here, to speak of needs or those aspects of popular needs which are most dependant on social policies. But one must be careful not to run the risk of surreptitiously reintroducing the opposition of the individual to the social, and, even more, of according exclusive validity to the 'social', that is to say to the collective, and even to the political at the expense of the individual, in a political ideology which misleadingly identifies social progress and collectivisation, with individuation relegated to the ranks of 'pretty bourgeois deviations'.

Diversity of the forms of the expression of needs: associations

One aspect of the irreducible diversity of needs is that their expression is not restricted to the market or to the sphere of political practice. We have already shown the divisive role played by revolutionary political practice in the development of popular needs and will not go over the same ground again, except to add that on this political practice, and the achievements it makes possible, depend not only the satisfaction of the needs which it expresses and transforms explicitly, but also the satisfaction of a number of other needs expressed in different ways. Most often these are in fact indirectly dependent on general social conditions, themselves determined by economic and political relations on the widest scale. The quest for the solitary delights of angling is clearly outside the field of political practice, and yet it depends not only on rules and laws about ownership but also on river pollution, which is itself dependent on the conditions of industrial activity, on economic policies and attitudes to the protection of the environment.

To a certain extent, the significance of general social conditions (whether economic, political or institutional, or whatever) for the development and satisfaction of all needs makes it possible to say that 'everything is political'. But it would be absurd and dangerous to conclude from this that everything should be expressed in political practice. That would mean subjugating to one particular practice, the practice most related to the pole of convergence and the organisation of the totality of social relations, practices which are more properly related to the pole of the individuation of the social. We are only too familiar with the excesses to which some communist parties have been led by a claim to be able to evaluate works of art in terms of their conformity to propagandist objectives and the way in which they exalted the virtues of the Revolutionary Worker.

The capitalist ideology of commodity consumption and, to some extent, the mode of consumption itself, tend to make needs into a purely 'private' affair: the 'preferences' of the consumer-subject, the isolated management of income by the household. The re-socialisation of practices of consumption and of needs is carried out on the basis of political practice, but constantly transcends it. The transformation and development of needs has to have a base, a starting point, but also has to have an increasing diversity of forms of expression.

As for the diversity of forms of individual expression of needs, it is difficult to do more than specify the conditions which foster it unless one engages in the kind of codification which we are opposed to. Several conditions help to foster that diversity: they relate to the organisation of production and of work (income, management and interest of work, free time); to the general conditions of reproduction (training, culture, access to the means of consumption, the extent of the network of social relations); and to politics (freedom of expression and publication, but also the political conditions for the active use of these freedoms by the exploited and the oppressed, as discussed above).

Two particular aspects of the diversity of collective forms seem to merit close consideration: the development of voluntary associations and the question of pluralism.

Where associations are concerned, one can begin by observing that associations tend to be on the increase in a wide range of spheres, from those which aim to foster a particular common activity, such as leisure ones, to those which through their explicit objectives of realising particular demands bear a close resemblance to trade union organisations.

Obviously this trend is extremely positive in terms of expressing the diversity of needs, and in political terms too. It helps to break down the isolation in which the (capitalist) mode of commodity consumption tends to enclose the individual consumer or the restricted unit of consumption embodied in the household. It is a voluntary movement, not directly dependent on the general conditions of existence which have been imposed (state institutions) or less willingly chosen (the community at work, the family) and for this reason it works towards a fuller expression of individual needs. It encourages a direct takeover and organisation by those involved of the conditions under which they act, and thus counteracts dispossession and state control.

From a more immediate political point of view, this trend is an element in the present proliferation of campaigns and protest movements, of involvement of users in the management of collective facilities, of critical writings, of parallel extra-institutional experiences, all of which clearly bring out the severity of the crisis in the sector of socialised consumption and in the management of living conditions.

Should one conclude from this proliferation of associations for consumer protection, for protection of the environment, for the conservation of buildings, socio-cultural movements, and all the rest, that we are witnessing a spontaneous emergence of the democratic expression of all social needs, the spontaneous democracy of demand, a demand which has only to be stated to lead to social policies?

In fact, this trend is not entirely free of ambiguities, obstacles and diversions.

In the first place, a large number of these forms of campaign, organised as associations and movements, are characterised by having very limited objectives such as housing, the protection of a building or a particular area, a campaign against a specific danger of pollution, and consumer protection. This 'single-issue' character is not in itself an obstacle, or at least no more of an obstacle than in other more established forms of organisation and struggle. But limited objectives are often associated with the treatment of the problem which has given rise to the demand in isolation, highlighting only its immediate aspects, e.g. the apparent responsibility of the 'actors' nearest to hand, such as local elected representatives.

So this limitation, this autonomisation, reproduces in its own way, the rift, real and intensified by the ideology, produced by the dominant relation of capitalist production, between production and consumption and between exploitation and the reproduction of labour-power. The limitation of the aims of campaigns to the most immediate aspects can get in the way of working out real solutions, for these call for an awareness of the deep-seated determination of the problems and thus of the link, in analysis as well as in the objectives and forms of the campaign, between the difficulties encountered in the sphere of consumption and their determinants, which are tied to the sphere of production and to general political and economic processes, the combined forces of monopoly capital and state policy.

This has a variety of consequences which make for ambiguity, reformism (traditionally embedded in the sphere of consumption) and possible cooption by the dominant ideology and the policy of the state. By strictly isolating and particularising the problems of consumption, whether individual or collective, it is possible to imagine that the sphere of production is not involved and there these problems are the price to be paid for the 'progress' of 'industrial society', that all that has to be done is to control and improve and soften their harmful consequences. Thus the 'power of the consumer' tries to put new life into the moribund myth of the bourgeois economy, the myth of the sovereign consumer whose demand was supposed to be the source and end-goal of production. But it only means 'balancing' the powers, not even reversing Galbraith's 'reverse spiral'. The moment that one restricts oneself to correcting distortions, to ameliorating the negative effects, as if one could do so without attacking their structural causes, one is well and truly into reformism and on the way to the possibility of recovery, on a major scale. For some years now the principal governments of the capitalist powers have set up concerted discussions and policies on environmental conservation and consumer protection. The aim is obvious: to channel into a reformist direction, a direction which will at the same time secure monopolist policies, the critical movements and demands which result from those policies through the effects of monopolistic accumulation.

This autonomisation is also often accompanied by a recourse to backward-looking ideologies, whether in relation to conservative – in the true sense of the term – attitudes to the protection of buildings or of urban landscapes, or in relation to regressive and illusory solutions to the problems of energy, transport or ecology, suggesting a return to archaic forms of production, and denouncing technology in general rather than its form and use under capitalism.

The nature of the social groups involved in these associations is an important factor in understanding their limitations and ambiguities. More often than not, they are members of the new middle classes such as teachers, technicians, engineers, middle management or executives in the public or the private sector, or else, more traditionally, shopkeepers, craftsmen and members of the liberal professions. There is a positive aspect to this which is worth emphasising, and that is the extension of the social struggle to strata which had previously been outside it. But there are other political consequences which are less clear in their implications.

On the one hand, the relatively ambiguous, heterogeneous and economically and/or ideologically contradictory position which these strata occupy in relation to the dominant mode of production explain that they can more easily mobilise themselves in the sphere of consumption and living conditions against what for them are the negative effects of the crisis. Their occupational activity is less a field for collective action (though here too things are changing). This can only make the setting up of the necessary link with the economic determinations and struggles within production all the more problematical.

On the other hand, their privileged position with regard to these problems, facilitated by cultural familiarity, and perhaps also by having more free time available to devote to the subject outside working hours, tends to make many of these associations places where the interests and needs of these particular social groups are expressed in a dominant way.

The tendency towards conservatism, touched on previously, may be enhanced by the fact that one of its possible aspect is the defence of earlier privileges which have been progressively eroded by the development of state monopoly capitalism. In this way, an association for the protection of an area may be made up of home-owners who are resisting not only the possible loss of a local beauty spot, but also the building of subsidised government housing which would lower the 'social environment' and damage the market value of their property. Not that sites of particular interest do not need to be protected, but all the social factors concerned must be considered from every angle. A parent–teacher association might well, in the name of progress, defend educational innovations which favour the children of the intellectual middle classes without worrying about the specific problems of children from working-class homes.

Finally, the relative lack of involvement of the working class and, to a lesser extent, of office employees in these questions has a twofold negative effect: firstly, workers who have an experience and tradition of the struggle within production and thus have an ideology which is more fully aware of the determinant nature of capitalist exploitation and of the character of the state, are rarely present to bring that experience and that consciousness to bear in a way that would counteract the autonomisation of the problems of consumption. Secondly, the needs specific to these large sectors of workers, needs which are decisive in our society, are barely expressed within such associations; or if they are, it is all too often in a way that links them or subjugates them to the needs of other social strata.

Because of this, the needs and demands expressed by a number of movements and associations only deal with those of particular social groups. Even attempts by communist-led town councils to revitalise local democratic life by working out housing needs and projects in a democratic way involving the population in consultations and commissions and so on, have often run into the problem of a predominantly middle-class participation and of very limited involvement by the workers.

So although all these various movements, associations and groups can be seen as contributing towards the development of the diversified and democratic expression of needs, the expression of the nees of the whole population, and in particular of the working class, cannot be confined to them alone.

It is not by chance that the development of local associations formed part of the aims attached to the Seventh Plan,[34] nor that such associations

[34]See for instance the Reports from the Preparatory Commissions on the Seventh Plan, '*Aménagement du territoire et cadre de vie*' (p. 33, intensifying local social life; p. 59, the redistribution of power) and '*Inégalités sociales*' (p. 68, support for associations), as well as the report by O. Guichard, *Vivre ensemble*, all published by Documentation Française.

are constantly being pandered to by policies concerning the environment or the 'quality of life', and that even under the Giscard government their capacity for influence was slightly increased by the Galley law for the reform of urbanisation codes. Rather it is because, as we have seen, they comprise favourable terrain for the development of a reformist movement prepared to collaborate to some extent with official policy, or at least to prevent analyses and practices which might bring out the true cause of the lack of satisfaction of needs and express these needs to their full extent for all social classes and sectors in a coherent way, so as to undermine the domination of monopoly capital.

One might add that from the point of view of their internal government, these associations are far from being a paradise of direct democracy, and that sometimes (as the author has seen on occasion, though without being able to quantify the phenomenon) their leaders act in a most autocratic way, imposing their ideas as they see fit.

Without wishing to deny the usefulness of the association movement, it is clear that it cannot replace the revolutionary struggle for the expression of the needs of the exploited classes. This brings us to the question of the relationship between the two and, more concretely, to the relationship of these associations with political and union organisations. In principle there seems to be general agreement about the necessity for the political independence of associations, for public aid to support them, and for the utility of holding a dialogue with them.

In practice, they are the locus for bitter conflicts. The monopoly bourgeoisie has tried to draw them into a federation and get them to collaborate with its policy in particular areas so as to establish common ground with the middle classes and consolidate its hegemony, and even to make use of associations to combat certain working-class local governments. The social democratic movement, which has been traditionally well established in this area, whether in terms of consumer cooperatives (COOP), mutual benefit associations (Mutuelle Générale de l'Education Nationale), or cultural, sports or educational associations (Fédération Leo Lagrange) entertains dreams of a vast 'consumer union' under its control, which will counterbalance the dominant influence of the Communist Party and the CGT on the organisation and struggles of the workers within the work place. In regions where the socialist party has had a longstanding influence in working-class areas, the network of local associations is frequently an extremely important element in its 'local hegemonic apparatus'.[35] In local governments which have become social-

[35] Following the expression used by Lojkine, Delacroix and Mahieux in *Politique urbaine et pouvoir local dans l'agglomération lilloise* (Centre d'Etude des Mouvements Sociaux, 1979).

ist more recently, such a network is even more important – in some cases, particular associations even carry out municipal functions.[36]

It seems, on the other hand, as though the communist influence on the association movement has to some extent lost ground. There are some associations, such as the ARAC (Association d'Anciens Combattants) or the Secours Rouge, where Communists were the primary influence and which played an important role in mobilising working-class areas between the wars. At the present time, however, communist influence and working-class participation (which are not the same thing, though they often go together) are strongest in the Confédération Nationale du Logement (CNL) (tenant associations), or in the principal organisations aimed at the socialisation of consumption on the basis of the place of work, through union action on the works committees, such as Tourisme et Travail or the Fédération Sportive et Gymnique du Travail. As far as relations between communist-led local governments and local associations are concerned, they are usually fairly good when the associations are primarily concerned with the management of facilities or the organisation of particular aspects of collective consumption, but are much worse when associations are more oriented towards demands and protests, a mistrust the local communist representatives explain in terms of the weak working-class representation and the predominant influence of the intellectual middle classes. This mistrust is sometimes justified by the disingenuous political aims of the criticism aimed by certain associations at communist local governments, by the real contradictions which may appear between the needs of different social classes and social strata (the middle-class ecological opposition to the priority given to the construction of council houses or the maintenance of industrial undertakings), and also, in some cases, by the fairly authoritarian ideas and conduct of the local governments, the manifestation of a tendency towards centralism and Statism within the French Communist Party, running counter to the tendency towards greater attention to democratic debate and movements towards self-government.[37]

It seems to us that neither the possible selective membership of the associations, nor the consequent social specificity of the needs they express, nor the political implications, should be underestimated.

---

[36] Such was, for instance, the example of Grenoble before the '83 elections, when the right took over. In a recent study, Dominique Mehl analysed the process of the decentralisation of the municipal government in favour of the associations at Conflans Sainte-Honorine, a town of which Michel Rocard was then the mayor, in *Conflans Sainte-Honorine, le face à face municipalités-associations* (Centre d'Etude des Mouvements Sociaux, 1981).

[37] See my article, 'Left wing local authorities and services policy', *International Journal of Urban and Regional Research*, 5/3, 1981, pp. 411–25.

But these real problems and difficulties form part of the contradictions which, as we have already stated, must be explicitly and openly confronted in order to build up a real convergence of transformed needs. And to this end the point of view of the middle classes must be taken into account, although not to the extent of obliterating the working-class position.

As for the political differences, they lead necessarily to the question of pluralism.

The diversity of needs and political pluralism

We have already emphasised that it is impossible to see the plurality of political organisations (including, in the widest sense, unions, associations and the rest) as a direct expression of the diversity of needs, since it is above all the result of the diversity of social classes and categories defined by their objective situation within relations of production. In fact, in terms of the determination of political opinions, affiliations and behaviour, the ideological process which shapes the imaginary representation of living conditions plays a major role, and this is related not only to the objectivity of the class situation but also to the political and ideological engagements and confrontations which have been experienced materially and subjectively, crystallised within social histories and concrete 'biographies'.

One should not, however, be tempted to go to the other extreme. Although there may not be a strict correspondence, item by item, there are nonetheless special, though not exclusive, relations between the representation of certain social classes or social strata and particular organisations. This has been shown in numerous works of political sociology, whether dealing with electoral behaviour or with the social origin of militants.

For instance, a remarkable piece of research carried out in March 1978 showed, among other results, that out of a sample of 4500 people, 16 per cent of whom were workers, 31 per cent of communist voters were workers. The figure was 20 per cent for socialist voters, 16 per cent for voters on the extreme left, falling to 10 per cent for the RPR (Gaullists) and 7 per cent for the UDF (Giscard supporters), the two main parties on the right. Conversely, the same inquiry showed that 3 per cent of voters belonging to the two right-wing parties were owners of industry or major trading enterprises, or liberal professions (the highest category of the sample) as against only 1 per cent of Communist and Socialist Party voters.[38]

---

[38] J. Capdeville et al., *France de gauche, vote à droite* (Presses de la Fondation Nationale des Sciences Politiques, 1981), Table 20, p. 246.

However, these links should not be confused with the autonomous expression of the needs of each class, which cannot be carried out independently of the economic, ideological and political processes of the class struggle, as it is carried on from day to day.

These processes, as we have already seen, do not simply derive from 'the conflict of ideas', from 'ideological illusions' and 'false consciousness'. They are made up in and reproduced by the social practices which form their 'material base'. The militant revolutionary worker and the worker who votes for the Right and supports the bosses do not lead an identical working-class life, as Denis Poulot has shown in his typology of 'the sublime'.[39] Conversely, it is doubtless not the same life, the same history which has produced the one and the other, nor the breaks which take the individual from one to the other. They have different histories which have different material expressions. In this way, for instance, the survey referred to earlier showed the effect on political choice of owning an estate: at an identical income level, voters favoured the Communist Party or the right wing to a greater or lesser extent depending on their accumulated wealth.[40] And the greater their estate, the greater the workers' confidence in Raymond Barre as Prime Minister.[41]

Needs and political opinions and options are certainly not identical. But we have already underlined the way in which needs, the subjective forms of the objective determinations of the social practices which shape the reproduction of the labour force, were, because of the objectively contradictory character of these practices and the ideological and practical nature of their subjectivisation, determined in their form and their extent by political practice. One could therefore say that needs form part of the imaginary conception of living conditions and of their possible transformation. This to some extent compares with Pierre Bourdieu's notion of 'objective collective futures', with the difference that there is nothing objective about them, because of the contradictory and even conflictual character of the social processes producing them, and also because of the imaginary character of the conceptualisation, where the contradiction is also expressed in the form, among others, of the imaginary work of political ideologies and practices.

It is thus impossible to separate the diversity of needs and the diversity of political ideologies. Favouring the expression of the former means favouring the expression of the latter; transforming the former, means transforming the latter. And vice versa.

From the point of view of the revolutionary working-class movement,

[39] Poulot, *Le Sublime*.
[40] J. Capdeville et al., Table 106, p. 328.
[41] Ibid., Tables 123b and 123c, pp. 348–9.

recognition of the necessity of political pluralism clearly has quite another meaning than from the point of view of the ideology of bourgeois liberalism. It is not a question of recording and guaranteeing the static expression of differences while maintaining the status quo. It is, on the contrary, a question of basing itself on an expansion of political democracy, of which pluralism is only one aspect, in order to bring about the establishment and successful achievement of the revolutionary trans-formation of society. We will not rehearse here the long and involved debate over the question of the dictatorship of the proletariat.[42] It is sufficient to emphasise here that the political aim of the 'peaceful' transition to socialism, and more particularly what is today called Eurocommunism, involves political pluralism not as a concession to democratic traditions which have to be taken into account no matter what one may think of them, but as a necessity, an indispensable means of building up the necessary alliances.

The necessity for pluralism comes first of all from a realisation of the diversity of ideological influences, and from affiliations to and sympathy for different political movements among all categories of workers. From this there follows an analysis of the objective convergence of interests which leads to the idea that an alliance between these different left-wing movements is possible, and that it would provide a shorter route than waiting for the Communist Party alone to grow sufficiently to be able to direct the revolutionary process single-handed and impose itself on all the other movements.

Critical analysis of the historical experiences of 'existing socialisms', particularly analysis of the Soviet Union, leads explicitly or implicitly to this position as well. Even though we lack any really detailed historical analyses[43] – and no doubt they will remain unavailable until the day historians have free access to the archives of the Soviet Communist Party – it seems fairly clear that there are links between the political monopoly of the party, the progressive fusion of party and state, and extreme state centralisation; the repressive, economic, political and ideological effects are all too frequently lumped together and glossed over by the term 'Stalinism'.

It seems more than likely that the rigidity acquired through political

---

[42] See, for instance, the debates held at the Twenty-third Congress of the French Communist Party (*Cahiers du Communisme*), the preparatory discussions published in *l'Humanité* and *France Nouvelle*, as well as the studies of the question which appeared at the time, among them E. Balibar, *Sur la dictature du prolétariat* (Maspero, 1976).

[43] Jean Ellenstein's *L'Histoire de l'URSS* (Editions sociales, 1972) contains interesting descriptions. Equally, *L'URSS et nous*, by A. Adler et al. (Editions sociales, 1978) is very stimulating because of the light it throws on the USSR and the hypotheses put forward.

monopoly by one party, the Communist Party of the Soviet Union, is inseparable from the tendency towards the internal centralisation of that party, and to the establishment of Stalin's power at the end of the twenties through the successive elimination of anyone who might refuse this imposed discipline: an elimination by the administration or the police which led to any creative and contradictory political debate being replaced by the discipline of the application of central decisions, and the violent and systematic excommunication of any divergent points of view. What matters here, much more than this or that 'erroneous' decision for which Stalin was responsible, is the whole body of these political practices of a party, within a party.

Political pluralism alone is no guarantee against this sort of dramatic perversion of the socialist goal. There is no judicial or constitutional system which can singlehandedly guarantee that sort of protection. But pluralism can certainly help towards it, as the necessary condition for a political practice which does not exclude and crush any divergent point of view.

To take this a little further, we believe that pluralism must be seen as a positive, productive and stimulating element, and not simply as a bulwark. The revolutionary struggle must dispense with the Manicheism which sees the Party as right and everyone else wrong on principle. Not only are the political enemies who criticise the party not necessarily in the wrong (consider, for instance, the denunciation of the Gulag in the fifties by members of the right wing or by the first 'dissidents'), but among the analyses, proposals and suggestions made by other parties and organis- ations with whom an alliance is sought there may well be interesting and positive elements which can be 'taken on board' (for instance, the example of self-management we looked at earlier), without that necessarily entailing any concessions on major political problems or glossing over disagreements and conflicts.

It seems to us that the necessity for political pluralism is the political expression of the idea that there can be no true revolution imposed by an active minority on a passive majority. There may be changes in political forms, in the forms of ownership of production and consumption, and the effects will be far from negligeable, but the true transition to socialism, to the government of society by the people itself and not by its 'represen- tative', entails the active, creative, and thus free and contradictory involvement of each individual, whatever their 'political opinions' at the outset.

This is not to underestimate the difficulties. It is worth remembering, however, that the condemnation of social democratic parties and even social democratic workers as 'social-fascists' has not advanced the revolution any further forward. The day revolutionary political forces prevail will only be the beginning of the revolution. After that, the profound change which will return the creative initiative in every area to the workers and the users can only be carried out if the workers and users have been won over and mobilised from the start. All workers, all users, must be able to be actively involved in the processes of building socialist democracy, and not excluded because, on some question or other, their opinions diverge from those of a particular party or a particular 'leader'. The socialist revolution is a complex and contradictory social process, in which new solutions must be forged collectively in open debate. It is not a struggle between revolutionary Truth and its ready-made Principles gradually vanquishing Error.

Reformism or revolution: discourse and practice

Political contradictions and conflicts must be faced for what they are, and not denied in some sort of idyllic vision of a spontaneous popular unity which is only hampered by the jealousies and egoism of the different organisations, or in the corresponding vision of the automatic disqualification of any point of view which does not conform to the official line of the party to which one belongs.

The main aspect of these contradictions is clearly the opposition between political movements seeking to promote an increase in the satisfaction of workers' needs, and the conservative political movements which are concerned to maintain and strengthen the position of the dominant class. The value of pluralism, from the point of view of the former group, seems to us to lie in the undeniable superiority of the open confrontation of ideas upon all forms, whether administrative or police or other, of the exclusion of 'conservative' points of view. It is a superiority which derives from several related elements. In the first place, it is more effective for the working-class movement to win over all those who are undecided in this debate and to mobilise them on its own side, rather than to 'neutralise' them by eliminating them from the debate and holding up the fear of repression. In the second place, all those who, at a given moment, speak up for conservative ideas are not to be consigned definitively to the hell-fire of the bourgeoisie. Finally, the absence of open debate makes the struggle against conservative ideas and forces more difficult, since repression or prohibition does not suppress these ideas but makes them devious and clandestine, and hence all the more difficult to combat.

Another major aspect of these contradictions is the opposition between reformism and revolution. If this opposition is to have any meaning in relation to the question of needs, as we hope to show, it must first of all be separated from all reductionist interpretations.

The most obvious and most current of these is the nominalist reduction: the revolutionary party is the party which declares itself to be so, the party which tradition says to be so, the party which claims to be faithful to the 'heritage' of those who have carried out the Revolution (the Bolsheviks, the CPSU). We do not wish to suggest that such a party (in France, the Communist Party, the PCF) is not, in fact, the true revolutionary party, but that if it is so, it is for other reasons – a point of view which clearly breaks away from communist tradition, in which faithful support of the USSR has long been the touchstone of revolutionary authenticity.

The nominalist reduction is extremely pernicious, as history has shown. The most striking example is the Stalinist practice of the systematic naming and disqualification of 'opponents' to be eliminated. There are other current examples which, though less tragic, are not without their significance.

The most obvious form of this reduction in current political life is the fetishisation of political discourse: if you hold a revolutionary discourse, you are a revolutionary. The proliferation of tiny left-wing splinter groups bears sufficient witness to the fact. But there are more subtle examples: any declaration and, above all, any declaration made by a party which is, as a whole, actually revolutionary (we will return to the definition of this term later) is not automatically revolutionary for that reason alone.

This is because political practice (whether revolutionary or not) is a more complex, more various and more mobile process than the simplistic schema – elaboration of a 'line', application of a 'line' – would suggest. The 'line', where it exists, consists of an explicit body of analyses of the state of the social structure, and of proposals for political action to transform it. Its ideological effectiveness (the knowledge effect, rigourous analysis and the logical deduction of propositions) is only one aspect of its 'truth'. An equally important aspect is the relationship of this 'line' to the totality of the practices of the political organisation: a relationship which may be termed one of representation, in the sense of making visible, and which is carried out through an inevitable ideological shift. This is in part voluntary: statement of the 'line' is made first of all for the benefit of the party which has to be won over and mobilised in this way.

Traces of this can be found in all sorts of means of expression. For instance, in the texts of the Congresses of the French Communist Party, there is a systematic use of the present (the Party represents this, does that, is carrying on such and such a struggle . . .) where one would more readily expect the use of the future or obligatory form (the Party will, the

Party should . . .). That recognition of the difference should be implicit, and that the use of the present tense should assert the immediate identity of the Party with the 'line' which it states is clearly not an innocent act. It is, of course, partly a question of asserting an offensive unity in relation to the 'outside', but it also contributes to the refusal to recognise any such difference in public, a refusal which, for those 'inside', constitutes a 'constriction'. That is to say, the stating of any internal difficulties, divergences, variations, of anything other than more or less intense mobilisation towards the common goal, must remain implicit: errors and shortcomings are recognised in a general way, but never explicitly stated.

This 'constriction', more or less marked according to the times, obviously has negative results: a difficulty in analysing contradictions in the practices of the organisation quietly and openly, a tendency to defend everything totally to outsiders, and difficulties in carrying out internal criticism and self-criticism in a constructive way.[44] It leads to an excessively tight grip on the organisation's own truth, which, as we have shown, is an obstacle to a necessary knowledge of the reality and diversity of needs.

In order to carry out an adequate analysis of the contradiction between revolution and reformism, it is thus necessary to pay attention in the first place not only to what is said and its unifying effect, but also to what is done, in all its diversity and with all its lags and lapses; a consciousness of the disparities between what is said in different situations is totally insufficient. In this way, the term 'double-speak' is currently much in vogue to denote the differences or contradictions hidden behind the official pronouncements of various organisations. Of course, one cannot discount the possibility – even, in some cases, the certainty – of real 'double-speak' on the part of individual political leaders or groups of leaders: an opportunist duplicity in relation to different audiences with different expectations or a duplicity in terms of pronouncements made either in private, within the organisation, or outside. (As for instance the contrast between the Socialist Party's profession of unity at the signing of the Common Programme, and François Mitterrand's telling the Socialist

[44] This question has already been touched on indirectly in the context of the development of the French Communist Party's attitude to self-management. Another more recent example of this sort of 'constriction' is the authoritarian breaking off of debate within the Communist Party on the eve of the elections in April 1978. While everyone knows that there were, and still are, differences and divergences on various aspects of the Common Programme period and on the reasons for the break in 1977, the Party leadership thought that it would be a good idea to declare that the Central Committee was 'unanimous'. The conflict which followed between the Paris Federation and the national leadership is another example of the failure to work out real disagreements. See H. Fizbin, *Les bouches s'ouvrent* (Grasset, 1980), and the various articles on the subject, notably those by P. Laurent, in *l'Humanité*.

International that the aim was to win over some millions of votes from the communists; or some communist leaders who, in 1977, maintained in private that the French Communist Party had not been prepared to compromise for fear of the socialists making headway at the polls, while publicly recommending unity in the face of a breakdown in negotiations about the updating of the Common Programme due to the action of the socialists and the left-wing radicals.)

But to make this kind of 'double-speak' into a major principle of political analysis or explanation is to return to a subjectivist analysis of political practice, by making the consciousness and will of the leaders the final cause in explaining it. It seems to us, rather, that this 'double-speak' is itself a particular manifestation of a much wider problem, the problem of the inevitable gap between what is said and what is done. Inevitable not because of some kind of fate to which one must simply resign, but because ideology is inevitable, for the Communist Party as for any other. It is inevitable because of the combined effects of the ideological and social conditions of the representation of practice (the ideological struggle) and also because one only emerges from ideology through the production of scientific knowledge. Even then it is only a relative way out, a direction. One emerges from ideology only on condition that one constantly reproduces the moment of the break, of challenge and confrontation.

What is involved in 'double-speak' is the totality of differences, gaps and contradictions that occur within the political practice of a single party: a totality held in check and constrained by the ideology of party-subject-strategy, which reigns supreme in political ideology, at least where revolutionary parties are concerned. Other parties, whether social democrat or of the right, are more ready to allow the expression of their diversity, their internal conflicts and power struggles.

This long disquisition on political discourse was meant to clarify the opposition between reformism and revolution, by recognising and situating the trap of political subjectivism. But it should not lead to abandoning a general consideration of left-wing parties and looking at them is an entirely fragmented and unstructured way, through their practice: after all, whatever the differences, gaps and contradictions in the practice of a single party, a resulting whole emerges nonetheless. A refusal to be led into ideological oversimplifications does not, at this level, eliminate the problem: quite the reverse. Let us try and sketch out what is involved, without claiming to deal with the subject in a definitive way.

The opposition between reformism and revolution means, within the heart of the working-class movement, an opposition between two different types of political practice. 'Reformists' are those who seek to improve the situation of the working class within capitalist society through a succession of reforms, each of which is acceptable to the capitalist system. In the ideology of reformism, particularly in its most socialising forms, it is thought that this cumulative series of reforms will gradually transform the nature of society, restraining the power of capital and extending the power of the workers. 'Revolutionaries' on the other hand do not reject reforms, but see them as being, in practice, inadequate, incapable of undermining capitalist domination in any real way, and hence they see the necessity of a practice which will bring out a break, both at the level of relations of production and at that of political power.

To formulate the opposition in this way clearly involves the contribution made by political practice to reproduction on a general scale, or to the general 'destabilisation' of production relations and all its ensuing consequences. This is a point we will come back to.

From the economic point of view, we have already seen that many of the manifestations of reformism occur within the domain of consumption, particularly in relation to the illusions held about the cumulative and anticapitalist character of the development of collective consumption, and underestimate the vulnerability of these facilities, their continual recovery by capital and all the effects of state domination that operate within them. We must also refer again to the most important aspect of all, that of concrete relations of production. Insofar as these are the matrix which shapes all the rifts, inequalities and segregations, there is in fact a radical distinction to be drawn between accepting these relations, essentially as they stand, or struggling effectively to transform them profoundly.

From the political point of view, the opposition between revolution and reformism can similarly be seen as relating to two different views of the power of the state: the first sees the capitalist state as something to be overthrown so as to establish the hegemony of the working class in alliance with intellectual workers, peasants, and so on; the second sees the state as a collection of relatively neutral institutions to be occupied and pointed as far as possible in the right direction.

It could be said that it is only the result that matters, so that it is only after the Revolution that one can judge what has really been revolutionary. But that is to underestimate the nature of the process of revolutionary change, where the moment — decisive though it may be — of breaking with the principal machinery of capitalist economic and political domination is itself the effect of a previous transformation. Thus the revolutionary process can and must be judged at present in terms of its capacity to create the conditions which will bring. about the movement of transformation.

The development and transformation of workers' needs, and their breaking away from the definition and limitation of those needs by capital and the state, is, as we have seen, a decisive element in this. It concerns needs in relation to work – the need for different and more interesting work, the need for a different division and organisation of labour, and of intellectual and collective control over it – as well as needs in every area of consumption and the workers' political need to take their place, as a class, in controlling the processes of social reproduction.

The contradiction between reformism and revolution thus involves here the transformation of needs so as to break with the dominant logic, rather than simply seeking the satisfaction of needs which fit into the system. This is what lies behind present debates on the crisis and the direction to be taken in the division of labour. Should one accept as unavoidable, as the necessary outcome of 'international competition', the running-down of the steel industry, of printing, coalmining, the dockyards and all the rest, and the reorganisation of conditions of work (through automation, the decrease in skilled labour, the intensification of work rates and so on), and seek to respond to all this 'simply' by meeting the needs which fit in with the process: higher unemployment benefits, reclassification of jobs, mobility grants, redundancy pay and the like? Should one seek only the satisfaction of the needs defined by, locked within, a 'recognition of the inevitable'?

An affirmative answer seems to me to define the reformist position. If one accepts that definition, that position is not characterised by a lack of struggles and campaigns, nor yet by 'treachery' pure and simple, but by the limited objectives of those struggles and campaigns.

The absence of a challenge to capitalist control of the production process, to the capitalist division of labour and thus, finally, to capitalist hegemony, does not mean that there is no contradiction between reformist demands and capitalist interests. But it is a limited contradiction and can, particularly in periods of intense expansion of accumulation, be resolved through making compromises. As can be seen from the examples of the union-management agreements in the United States, and the social democratic policies of the United Kingdom or Sweden, these lead to obtaining advantages for workers which, though limited, should not be dismissed, the advantages of the 'state reformism' described by Buci-Glucksman and Therborn.[45] But these compromises do not really hamper the power of capital, particularly since its material bases, primarily within production, remain whole and unaffected. Hence the vulnerability of these compromises and the political powerlessness of the working class to respond under these conditions to any retrenchment of their position in

[45] C. Buci-Glucksmann and G. Therborn, *Le défi social-démocrate* (Maspero, 1981).

periods of crisis. In fact, only the development of working-class needs which attack the very bases of capitalist domination can create the conditions for an offensive reaction which, in the face of any challenge to improvements it has achieved, furthermore sets itself against the development of the capitalist division of labour and of the accumulation which is at one and the same time its cause and its goal.

It must be said that the reformist position as defined here has deep roots in the daily experience of the workers.

In the contradictory determination of needs by the necessities of the reproduction of the concrete mode of production, there is, for the workers, the need to reproduce himself as a marketable commodity appropriate to the needs of capital. And the day-to-day pressure of capital on the needs of the workers is clearly most effectively, most insidiously, felt in the inevitable daily acceptance of the division of labour which it imposes, the acceptance of the exploitation of labour.

In this way, although the daily experience of the workers contains the objective bases for revolt and, over and above that, for revolutionary needs[46], one can quite see why it also fosters the dominant tendency which spontaneously turns towards reformism. Only a practice that is specifically working-class and political (in the widest sense of the term) is capable of developing these revolutionary needs by really opening up other possibilities through experience of the struggle and of its results, and the transformation of conceptions, of the imaginary, which can result from an extension of the struggle by political aims.

The working class is not spontaneously revolutionary. This has of course been said before, but it is a fact which is frequently too soon forgotten by Marxists in a vision of reformism as treachery, as an externally imposed obstacle to unavoidable revolutionary tendencies. If only the complicity between reformism and the system of capitalist domination could be brought to light, then those tendencies would be set free.

Rather, in our view, the basis of revolutionary practice as such lies in the daily work of transforming needs, and transforming, for a start, the needs of the workers. The accuracy of analyses criticising the capitalist system, the coherence of programmes putting forward alternatives, amount to nothing and cannot be effective except through this daily work, where they are indispensable. It is a work which must be unflaggingly and unremittingly carried on, day in, day out. For an organisation to be revolutionary does not mean setting itself up in a

---

[46]Our analysis of the relations between needs and revolution has many common points with the more philosophical work of Agnes Heller on 'radical needs', in *La théorie des besoins chez Marx* (UGE, 1978).

particular state, or acquiring a particular system of ideas; it means a constantly renewed process of rupture, of movement and tension and distance. Nor can it be revolutionary in all places and at all times. It is through the totality of its actions that one can judge whether or not a party is truly revolutionary.

Why and how can one judge? What concerns us here is clearly not the application of labels, but being able to know whether certain groups of political practices are or are not capable of undermining capitalist hegemony, particularly through the transformation and development of needs which break away from the reproduction of the dominant relations of production. Such a break, in order to attack the general structures of economic and political power within a social body, must have behind it an organisation capable of standing up to such a general conflict, through the extent of its political aims and the coordination of particular struggles. It needs only to be emphasised here that the revolutionary nature of practices must thus involve their relations to a political party or political parties. There can be no positive response except through practices which, one way or another, open up this general dimension of the struggle.

Socialism cannot be established in a municipality if capitalism controls the state and the economy right down to the smallest local undertaking. Not only because municipal socialism, restricted to local political institutions and to collective consumption, would be incomplete, but because it would not be socialist at all. The limits of possible demo-cratisation within a municipality are far too narrow; the weight of concrete relations of production on daily life, even outside work, are far too heavy. But within those narrow limits, the democratisation of local political life and of the management of institutions, the orientation of municipal policies towards improving the living conditions of the workers, and the development of collective consumption wherever poss-ible, may well contribute to revolutionary practices if they stimulate the need for more extensive and more radical changes within places of work and within society as a whole.

The same can be said of self-management at work: if it is confined to the isolated self-management of a workshop or an office, it is set within such narrow limits that it can hardly be distinguished from experiments carried out by the bosses to 'restructure' work by appointing teams which themselves manage the distribution of tasks to carry out a given programme. The struggle for true self-management must lead to a profound modification of the division of labour, and must thus seek to influence not only what happens within the workshop, but also within the economy as a whole. It must help to shape the interdependence of different collectives of workers in the work place, the division of labour and cooperation between production units, investment policies, relations with consumers and the search for the definition of products and of ways of producing, and so on.

However it is worth reiterating what we have already said about the relation between needs and the political struggle: the (revolutionary) development of needs does not arise out of a confrontation with ideas. It must have, above all, a material base: it is based on the objective contradictions of the social process of work; it is based on the practice of organisation and on the collective struggle, on the gains, even the provisional gains made through those struggles; it is based on the totality of autonomous democratic social practices which the workers may manage to establish within and around the class struggle. This means, to refer again to the examples cited earlier, that neither the reality of municipal control, nor the concrete relations between workers in the workshop, the office or the laboratory should be overlooked. A political practice which sought to mobilise the workers towards the objective of the total transformation of society without first seeking to engage in a struggle for the local transformation of living conditions and social relations would be revolutionary only in name, and would be destined to fail.

This was one of the main points of self-criticism raised at the twenty-third Congress of the French Communist Party after its failure in 1978. The base, it was said, had been insufficiently mobilised towards the precise objectives of the Common Programme for the left-wing government. The Party as a whole (including the leadership and the press, not only the grass-roots militants!) had not demonstrated sufficiently clearly that victory and the implementation of the programme depended on the workers' struggles within the area of their own particular demands. A wait-and-see, electoralist approach was allowed to develop according to which it was enough for the workers to await the imminent electoral victory of the Left, and then the application by the government of the Common Programme would solve everything. The idea that the Programme involved the workers had, of course, been stated often enough, but it had not been sufficiently applied in struggles on the ground, and a more propagandist approach had prevailed. Even the attempt at 'concrete expression' to which the Communists committed themselves in several areas from 1973 to 1977, was above all directed towards a (useful) demonstration of the quality and effectiveness of the response provided in the Common Programme to the workers' demands and to social and economic problems. It was not sufficiently directed towards a concrete mobilisation aimed at guaranteeing victory and the application of the programme through the struggle, and did not go far enough in preparing the mobilised workers to be themselves the active and inventive creators who would bring this programme into being, as well as guaranteeing, through their action, the real transformation of political and economic relations. It is a matter for regret that this perfectly justified criticism has served, since 1978, to obscure the development of a political practice within the French Communist Party rather different from what one might have expected. The block put on internal debate, a certain withdrawal into sectarianism and a systematic attack on the Socialist Party up to May 1981, as well as a more centralised and propagandist attitude have meant that the Party has, in fact, turned its back on any pluralist, self-managing and diversified development within the social movement. But that attitude is not simply the result of this specific combination of events.

In more general terms, a redefinition is occurring in relation to the nature and domain of the political practices of the dominated classes. This redefinition has two main components. The first is the transcendance of any opposition between politics on the 'small' or the 'large' scale. Because of the increasing complexity of the arrangement of the hegemony, and the diffusion of 'disciplines', to quote Michel Foucault, daily life, the family, sexuality, education, health, the neighbourhood, and so on, are recognised as being systems of practices linked to the dominant social relations and contributing to their reproduction. The movements and struggles and practices leading to rupture, change and innovation which develop within them are thus indispensable as contributions to general social change. Equally, there is within this redefinition an abandonment of the mechanistic reduction of everything to 'production' and to 'politics'. It is recognised that although changes in daily life depend to a large extent on the general social form of production relations and the relations of political power, changes in those relations are not going to have an automatic effect on daily life without specific struggles and specific innovations. The difficulty, and it is no mean problem, is to bring these two positions together without relinquishing either one or the other, and without subordinating one to the other, without seeing struggles with regard to the conditions of daily life simply in terms of an antimonopoly approach, or as an indirect means of increasing support for a party – and without simply looking for local solutions while neglecting the transformation of general conditions.

What one needs here is, in another form, the 'reconstitution' of social movements discussed by Pietro Ingrao, though we do not believe that this reconstitution can or should be carried out through the political centralisation of the state, as Ingrao recommends.[47] It seems to us, rather, that the quest for de-statisation should be a major component in the current

[47] Ingrao, *Crisi e terza via.*

redefinition of political practice. There is a deep-seated convergence between the diversified content of the demands and objectives of the various social movements, and the growing tendency towards self-management. The diversity of needs and of the means for their satisfaction, pluralism, the motive force which should be provided by social conflicts and contradictions being debated and taken over politically – all of this is opposed to political centralisation by the state. Its externality to social practices can only create or simply renew technocratism, reductive normalisation, and the administrative stifling of all political conflict. Present revolutionary demands seem to us in this area to run counter to the history and influence of 'existing socialisms' and the highly centralist organisational concepts inherited from the Third International, as well as to the more or less rigid statism of the social-democratic powers.

Some new mode of political reconstitution of social movements, based on self-management and the extension of direct democracy must be invented. Representative democracy must be made an extension of direct democracy, and not vice versa. It cannot be done in a day, it cannot be done by decree; it means a long labour of transforming the political needs of the masses, the practices or organisations, the forms and practices of institutions. But that crucial objective of revolutionary change is, at one and the same time, the means of bringing it about: the development of social struggles today calls for their self-management, just as the success of left-wing policies depends on the active and creative mobilisation of the workers.

Index